S0-AFJ-149

How To Live With An Imperfect Person

Personal Adjustment: ***The Psychology of Everyday Life***

Personal Adjustment: ***Selected Readings***

Human Sexuality

Exploring Human Sexuality

Psychology: ***Its Study and Uses***

How To Live With An Imperfect Person

by Dr. Louis H. Janda

NAL BOOKS

NEW AMERICAN LIBRARY

NEW YORK AND SCARBOROUGH, ONTARIO

For information address New American Library.

Published simultaneously in Canada by The New American Library of Canada Limited

NAL TRADEMARK REG. U.S. PAT. OFF. AND FOREIGN COUNTRIES
REGISTERED TRADEMARK—MARCA REGISTRADA
HECHO EN CHICAGO, U.S.A.

Library of Congress Cataloging in Publication Data

Janda, Louis H.
How to live with an imperfect person.

1. Marriage. 2. Interpersonal relations
3. Personality. I. Title.
HQ734.J345 1985 646.7′8 84–20669
ISBN 0–453–00488–1

SIGNET, SIGNET CLASSIC, MENTOR, PLUME, MERIDIAN AND NAL BOOKS are published *in the United States* by New American Library, 1633 Broadway, New York, New York 10019
in Canada by The New American Library of Canada Limited, 81 Mack Avenue, Scarborough, Ontario M1L 1M8

Designed by K. E. May

First Printing, March, 1985

1 2 3 4 5 6 7 8 9

PRINTED IN THE UNITED STATES OF AMERICA

To my wife Meredith,
who has had more than her share of practice at
living with an imperfect person

CONTENTS

PROLOGUE

About a year and a half ago, I had an extremely interesting case that served as the inspiration for this book. The case involved an attractive young woman who was trying to develop a career in real estate while continuing to be the perfect wife and mother for two active boys. This woman was becoming increasingly frustrated by her husband's lack of interest in helping to maintain their house and yard the way she wanted them to be kept. It seemed the more she pleaded with him, the more uncooperative he became. And not only was he not helping as much as she would like, but he was becoming a little distant when they were together. This young woman was becoming convinced that her husband did not really care about her.

Although on the surface it was a simple and straightforward case, it proved to be one of the most challenging I have ever had. The husband had stronger needs to have time alone than his wife did, and when she started her career, he found that his days were constantly filled by his work and helping to care for the children. When he did have some free time, he wanted to spend it relaxing, not catching up on the yard work. But he was torn; if he were to take some time to himself, he wouldn't enjoy it because he would feel guilty about not doing something his wife considered to be productive. So he became sullen, and put off doing the household tasks as long as he could, which only made his wife feel angry and unloved.

I was able to give this woman a few ideas about how she could help her husband to change. The most important step was to treat the household tasks as just that—household tasks, whether or not he did them should not be considered as evidence of how much he cared about his family. Secondly, I advised her to ask her husband to be honest with her and tell her which tasks he would be willing to do and which ones he did not want to do, and to hire someone to do the things he would rather not do. And most importantly, she had to make it clear to him that she was more than willing to let him have time to himself as long as he included her as a part of his life.

It took some time—the husband proved to be a slow learner—but by following these few steps, things began to improve between them. Once this woman was able to understand her husband's perspective, she no longer viewed his quirks as evidence of a flawed character that she could no longer tolerate. She was able to approach the situation with a problem-solving perspective, rather than with accusations that stemmed from her hurt feelings.

What made this case so difficult, and so important, was that this woman is my wife.

I have always believed that it is an accumulation of little things that can erode the bonds of a relationship, and my personal experience only reinforces this view. When our partner begins to show characteristics that we do not like, there is a tendency to conclude that these subtle but persistent behaviors must be a sign of a fatally flawed personality. We are willing to treat big issues as problems that deserve an attempt toward resolution, but we sweep the little things under the rug. They are left there to accumulate until they can no longer be ingored, until finally we conclude that we just cannot live with such a person any longer.

I wrote this book for people like my wife—people who have to live with an imperfect person. I hope you find the ideas in this book as helpful as she did.

How To Live With An Imperfect Person

INTRODUCTION

CAN TWO IMPERFECT PEOPLE LIVE HAPPILY EVER AFTER?

I Have to Have at Least *Some* Time to Myself

Cathy and Hal had been married for eighteen months, and both of them had the feeling that it was not going to work.

Hal was surprised to discover that he could feel so bad after marrying someone that he loved so much. He spent almost every evening and weekend in the same three-room apartment with her, yet he felt terribly lonely most of the time. He reluctantly came to the conclusion that, despite their many happy moments, Cathy was too cold and distant for him to spend the rest of his life with.

Hal had envisioned marriage as being a partnership. "You marry someone because you want to be with that person and spend your free time with that person. I want to spend my free time with Cathy, but it seems to me that she isn't interested. If I suggest that the two of us spend an evening walking on the beach, she usually says that she feels tired and wants to go to bed early with a good book. If I want to go to a movie, Cathy is likely to suggest that I go with a friend because the movie doesn't appeal to her. If I had wanted to go places with friends, I never would have gotten married! I consider myself lucky if I can get her to go somewhere with me once a week."

He could not understand why Cathy had married him. She seemed to want to spend all of her free time alone. The straw that broke the camel's back had to do with her reading. She was spending yet another evening reading a book, and he was feeling particularly lonely. When he tried to strike up a conversation, Cathy looked up over her book and said: "Do you mind? I'm trying to read." Hal was not going to stay married to someone who preferred books to his company.

Cathy, on the other hand, felt smothered. She loved Hal, but she had begun to think of him as a needy, overly dependent, and somewhat spoiled child. If she did not spend her every waking moment doing something with him, he accused her of ignoring him. She could not even read a book because Hal would feel snubbed.

Cathy appreciated Hal's many good qualities. She liked his kindness and his quick wit; she had always been on the quiet side, and she enjoyed being around someone who could make her laugh. She appreciated his encouraging her to pursue her career even though his preference was to start a family. But she could not understand why he was so demanding and possessive. "I don't think Hal has realistic expectations about what marriage is like. After we were married I expected that we would settle down as all married couples do. You can't maintain the intensity that you have when you're dating, seeing each other for only a few hours each week. Even if you could, who would want to?

"Hal would be happy if we went out every night. I did what he wanted for a few months, but I knew if our marriage was going to work, I would have to live my life the way I wanted to. I do make a point of going somewhere with him at least once a week even if it is something I'm not particularly interested in. But that's not enough for Hal. He is beginning to disgust me with his inability to ever feel satisfied with his own company. I think I'd be a pretty shallow person if I had to spend my every free moment with other people. I have to have at least *some* time to myself."

Hal and Cathy are like millions of other couples. They have become disillusioned with each other. Perhaps the process began earlier with them than it does for most couples, but in any case, they have begun to view each other in a different light, and that light reveals flaws. Like most people, Hal and Cathy are surprised to find the flaws are so serious. Each may have realized that the other was not perfect before they were married, but they never expected that the little quirks they observed would turn into such serious deficits.

How does this happen? How can people commit themselves to another person for the rest of their lives only to discover characteristics of the other person that make divorce seem essential?

There probably are as many answers to these questions as there are couples, but I believe much of the responsibility lies with the reasons people get married in the first place. Virtually everyone believes that we should marry for love; in fact, surveys have found that a substantial majority of us believe that differences in religion, social background, education, or values can be overcome by love. Of course, in our rational moments we know perfectly well that things do not always work that way, but it's not easy to be so objective when we are in love.

Kacy came from an upper-middle-class family and was an ideal child in her parents' eyes until she announced that she was getting married instead of going on to college. She had fallen in love with a man who was ten years older than she and was working as a laborer. Kacy realized that he would never be anything more than a laborer and that she would never have the kind of life-style that her parents had, but it did not matter; she loved him. When her parents objected to the age difference, as well as a thousand other things, she said that it wasn't a problem because she was bright for her age and he was slow, so actually they were at about the same level. Kacy realized how foolish she had been when she moved back with her parents, pregnant, ten months later.

While few of us have vision as clouded as Kacy's, most of us want to believe that love does conquer all, and although we may see things in a prospective spouse that we don't like, we convince ourselves that they are unimportant and that our love and encouragement will make them disappear.

Hal believed this. "Before we were married I knew that Cathy spent a lot of time alone, but I thought she was shy. She was always kind of quiet when we were around my friends, but I thought that after we were together awhile I could help her to feel more comfortable around other people. I was looking forward to the chance to bring her out of her shell."

God only knows how many people have thought that marriage would be good therapy for their spouse! Like Hal, Cathy was one of them. "I thought that a lot of the things Hal dragged me to while we were dating were just the vestiges of male adolescence. I was sure that once we were married I wouldn't have to see his loudmouthed friends anymore. I really believed that marriage would help him to grow up."

The fact is that marriage does not produce instant changes in people. There is, of course, the honeymoon period, during which people are likely to be more thoughtful, more considerate, and more loving than they will be at any other time in their lives. But that lasts for only a few months, or a year at most. (Just ask my wife.)

On the brighter side, while marriage does not provide an instant cure for anyone's faults, neither does it turn people into ogres. A wedding ceremony has never made a kind, affectionate, and caring man or woman into an immature, cold, and neurotic slob. It just seems that way at times.

What *does* change after living with another person for some time is the way that we understand or explain his or her shortcomings. Early in the relationship, when the bloom is still on the rose, we are tolerant and accepting of the other person's less than perfect qualities. But as time passes, the shortcomings seem to have more and more of an impact on the relationship and are no longer viewed as just shortcomings, but as fatal flaws. So, at one time, Hal could think of Cathy as being somewhat shy and reserved. Two years later, he thinks of her as being cold and aloof, even though, in reality, she has not changed at all.

Sometimes people discover flaws in their spouse that come as a total surprise. People can be fooled, either by their own errors in judgment or by intentional deception. Brad recalls the early years of his marriage and the problems they had with his wife's mother. "One of the things that really impressed me about Ann was her independence from her mother. I had dated several women who seemed to be tied to their mother's apron strings, so when Ann told me that she had moved to a different city to be on her own, I was really impressed. Little did I know that she had moved away because she was incapable of dealing with her mother. After we were married, her mother began to write her letters telling her that she should spend a hundred dollars on herself every month. This was back in the 1960s, when we were living on about two hundred and fifty dollars a month. If her mother told Ann to buy an extravagant gift for some relative, Ann would do it even if we couldn't afford it and she didn't want to. Ann finally cut the strings when her mother started giving her detailed descriptions about all the mistakes we were making in raising our children. It's turned out okay, but you can imagine my surprise when I found out she wasn't independent of her mother at all but actually dominated by her."

Other people discover things about their spouse that were carefully concealed from them. More than one woman has discovered that her husband is gay and married her for social and financial reasons only. Many men and women have discovered after the wedding ceremony that their spouse is deeply in debt as a result of compulsive spending or gambling. Often these deceptions place an unbearable strain on the relationship, and the only course is to end it.

Sometimes the flaws do not become apparent until after the relationship has gone along happily for several years. Sharon did not realize that there was anything about her husband that she did not like until they had their first child. "Val was always a fun-loving person; for the first four years we were married we went out four or five times a week, and we would go off somewhere about every other weekend. It came as a complete shock to me that he resented having to change our ways after our daughter was born. He thought we should still go out every night and leave Linda with my mother on the weekends. First of all, I didn't want to be away from Linda so much, and secondly, since I had had to quit my job, we simply couldn't afford to spend so much on entertainment. For a while I hated him for his selfishness and his immaturity."

Stressful events can bring out qualities in a person that are distressing to a spouse. Losing a job can bring a couple closer together if they both react with strength and dignity, or it can drive a wedge between them if one of them has difficulty in coping. When I was in graduate school, a friend's marriage began to fall apart when his mother moved in with him. Having an elderly parent move in can disrupt a relationship if the couple cannot accept and deal with the flaws in each other that such an event is sure to bring out.

For other couples, the passage of time is enough to change one person's perspective of the other's character traits. Barbara did not begin to question her relationship with her husband until they had been married nearly twenty years. "I married Jim because he was the most decent, kind man I had ever met. He was always concerned with doing what was right, and he seemed to have such good judgment; I thought of him as being very wise. During the first fifteen years of our marriage I thought of myself as being very happy. Now, I think the reason I was so happy was that we were both too busy to spend much time with each other; he was ambitious about his career and had to travel a lot, and I was very busy with the children and trying to finish my education. Now he's a vice-president in his company and doesn't have to travel much, and the kids are in high school, so we have more time together. I'm beginning to realize that he is an arrogant, egocentric person who thinks he is better than everyone else. The only reason he is so concerned with doing the right thing is that he wants to prove how superior he is. I don't think he's changed—I've just begun to see him for what he is."

Barbara is probably right, in part. It is unlikely that her husband has changed all that much. However, her belief that she has just begun to see the real him is not quite accurate.

Barbara was attracted to Jim because he seemed to have all the qualities that her own father did not. He seemed wise and strong, and she had no doubts that he could take care of her. At that time in her life she needed someone like Jim. As she got older, Barbara changed in subtle ways. She had more confidence in herself; she no longer felt that she needed someone to take care of her, because she knew that she could take care of herself. Neither Barbara nor Jim was fully aware of the changes that had taken place within her.

Because she now believed that her judgment was as good as anyone's, she did not look up to Jim for his words of wisdom. She was right in deciding that there always had been an air of superiority to Jim's morality—but he had not changed from an oracle of wisdom to an arrogant, self-righteous egomaniac. She just had stopped needing those qualities in him and had begun to feel annoyed by what she had once valued.

People's needs do change as they grow and develop, and what may have seemed perfect for them at one time may not seem so perfect several years later. Does this mean that we should discard relationships that we have outgrown and look for new, more satisfying ones?

Perhaps this is the best course on occasion, but if you adopt this strategy, it will not take long to accumulate quite a string of divorces. I do not recall hearing of anyone who found the perfect partner on the seventh or eighth attempt and lived happily ever after. All of us, including *our* spouses, are stuck with living with imperfect people. Those who have satisfying long-term relationships are the ones who are able to adjust to this reality.

The Nature of Long-Term Relationships

Two people usually decide to spend their lives together because they are in love. They find that it is painful to be apart, and when they are apart, they spend much of their time thinking about the other person. Their hearts start to pound when they anticipate seeing each other. They cannot bear to think of living their lives without each other.

This is romantic love. This kind of love may be wonderful, but in reality, its life is limited; psychologists believe that on the average, it will last about three years. So what do we do when our three years are up? Do we move on and start over with someone else?

I've known lots of people who do. They cannot live without the excitement of being in love; they believe there is no point in being married if they are not actually "in love." So they go from relationship to relationship, looking for the perfect and everlasting love. But just when they think they have found the right person, they discover that their "perfect love" uses a bitten-off fingernail to clean his teeth, and the thrill begins to fade away—again.

People who adopt this strategy of moving from relationship to relationship are likely to be bitter and disappointed in the end. They are looking for something that probably does not exist. And they will be missing something most people find to be extremely important: a sense of continuity.

Steve, who describes himself as a "love junkie," feels this lack of continuity as he approaches retirement. "I'm sixty-one years old and I'm married for the fourth time. Between marriages I lived with five other women for a few months to a few years. I'm really frightened that I'm going to die alone. When I look back on my life I have mostly regrets. There are lots of high points, and at the time it seemed like I was having a hell of a lot of fun, but I don't seem to have much to show for it. I have seven children from three of the marriages, and four of them won't even talk to me. The other three are polite when I call or when I go see them, but it's obvious that they wouldn't really care if I died tomorrow. Christmas has become a terrible time of the year for me; it's been eight years since I spent Christmas with a relative other than my wife. And I don't think Sarah will stay with me much longer. She's a lot like

I am, but she has more time than I do, so I'm sure she will fall in love with someone new any day now. I don't know what I'll do then."

Psychologists have coined the term "companionate love" to describe the glue that holds long-term relationships together. This is a feeling of liking and respect that people who have been together for some time have for each other, and if given a chance, it grows as our lives become deeply intertwined with another person's.

A basic premise upon which I've based this book is that companionate love is of more value than romantic love over the course of a lifetime. In order to allow romantic love to flower into companionate love, we must learn to live with imperfect people. There is no other choice. It is true that you may be able to find someone who is better suited for you than the one you are currently living with, but that person will not be perfect, either. So if you leave one relationship for another, you are taking your chances. Sometimes the chance is well worth it; there are relationships that can never be more than a guarantee for lifelong misery. But it is possible that with a little understanding, help, and encouragement, the person you live with can change enough so that companionate love with blossom.

One reason that there are so many divorces is that there are so many divorces. Generations ago when a man and woman were unhappy with each other, they were likely to accept that as their fate; divorce was not really considered an option. Now that divorce is commonplace, it has become an option that can be exercised too readily. I've known many couples who use the threat of separation or divorce in even minor disagreements and if a major problem develops, these couples may not even explore solutions other than splitting up. Sadly, it can be easier to change spouses than to change the relationship.

Most couples who have been together for many years can look back to times when they were unhappy with each other. The reality of long-term relationships is that there will be periods that last months, sometimes years, during which there seems to be no point to it all. JoAnn recalls two such times.

"I think there were two major crises in our marriage. The first occurred when our kids started school and I went back to work. Dan was used to my doing everything around the house, and he expected me to continue to do everything even after I started working forty hours a week. I guess I thought it was my responsibility too, because almost a year went by before I said anything about it to him. But during that year I grew to hate him for his selfishness. We finally worked out some compromises after I couldn't hide my misery any longer.

"The second bad time began when our youngest child left for college. I thought I would be the one to be affected, but it was Dan. He was pretty involved with the kids' activities, and I think their growing up left him with a void in his life. He would tell me that he didn't think we had anything in common anymore and that he was thinking of leaving me. That period ended when I discovered he was having an affair. At first I was furious with him, but I did try to understand how he was feeling. It was hard, but I think we just had to learn all over again how to live with each other. Now it seems that our history of good and bad times together has made us that much closer."

We would all like to find someone who could meet our every need, but things do not work that way. If we are to stay in a long-term relationship, we have to learn to live with people who can be thoughtless, selfish, and petty. At times they may do things that seem to us to be stupid, or even self-destructive, on occasion it will seem clear to us that they are trying to drive us away. Whatever their shortcomings, however, we must attempt to understand them and live with them the best we know how.

The world can be a frightening place. All of us have to

deal with uncertainties and self-doubt: Are we competent? Are we lovable? Do other people really care about us? Can we take care of those who depend on us? Can we take care of ourselves? Are we getting the most that we can out of life?

One of the greatest satisfactions of a long-term relationship is that it can help to provide reassuring answers to these questions. Couples that can look back over a lifetime together with contentment and joy are those who helped each other deal with these issues. If we give up on a relationship the first time it becomes difficult, we may be missing an opportunity to help another person find the answers. And if we pass up the opportunity to help another person to grow and to develop, it may say something important about the answers that we have found for ourselves.

Using This Book

As I mentioned earlier, when a relationship is new and our eyes are filled with stars, we are likely to overlook the characteristics of our partner that have the potential to be annoying. Indeed, our partner may not even exhibit such traits when passion is at its peak. But everyone brings some history into a relationship, and it will not take long before that history begins to assert itself.

Our history evolves as we are growing up, and we develop a characteristic way of perceiving and dealing with the world. For those of us who fall in the normal range of functioning, our perceptions and behavior serve to preserve our self-esteem. We interpret the behavior of others and react the way we do because it makes us feel comfortable. And most importantly, we assume that our perceptions and our reactions are the right ones to have.

Psychologists call this relatively stable set of perceptions and reactions a "personality style."

The problem in relationships is that the odds are good that the two people involved will have different personality styles, with each person believing that his or her style is the best way to be. Obviously, at least one, and possibly both, of the partners will be wrong. This book is intended for those of you who believe that your partner's personality style is causing your realtionship problems.

The twelve personality styles described in the following chapters are the ones I have found to be the most troublesome and most common. These styles, which may seem innocent enough upon first glance, can erode relationships over time. In fact, personality styles can be more dangerous to a relationship than more clear-cut problems. If our partner did have an obvious "problem," we would probably feel an obligation to help him or her get past this difficulty. But when there is no one big problem, but rather lots of little things that make up a particular personality style, then we may be tempted to write off our partner as being too different from ourselves, or as having too many quirks for us to live with.

Personality styles are not an "all or nothing" kind of thing. It is likely that any particular person will have characteristics of several of the styles described in the following chapters; if forced to be honest, I can see myself in six of the chapters (however, I'll never admit which six), and my wife in seven of them (with the goal of making my relationship a long-term one, I won't tell which seven). People learn to react to different situations in different ways; in fact, it is quite possible to behave in exactly the opposite ways in different situations. I have known more than one person who would be described best as an Avoider (Chapter 11) when dealing with people at work; such a person is meek and mild around supervisors, and never feels comfortable enough to express his or her thoughts and ideas. Yet the same person can be capable of being a Egotist (Chapter 5) at home, where he or she believes that his or her word deserves to be treated as if it were chiseled in stone. So if you find your partner in one of the earlier chapters, don't stop reading. The chances are excellent that you will see him or her in several of the chapters that follow.

My goal is to do four things in each of the twelve chapters that follow.

First, the quiz at the beginning of each chapter will give you some idea of whether the personality style or problem is relevant to the person you live with. Try to get him or her to take it. If this is not possible, answer the questions the way you think he or she might. Be warned, however, that you could be very wrong in your assumptions. When two people are having problems, almost always they see themselves differently than they are seen by the other person. It might be interesting to compare your partner's answers to your answers for him or her.

The second goal is to give you some understanding of the nature of the personality style. We all have a tendency to impose our own perspective on the behavior of others. Remember Cathy and Hal, whose case opened this chapter? Cathy had decided that Hal was immature and overly dependent, while Hal had decided that Cathy was cold and distant. Neither person's perspective was entirely accurate, but both were understandable, given Cathy's and Hal's individual styles. It is virtually impossible to appreciate another person's problems if you do not have that problem yourself. For instance, I always feel a little annoyed by my wife's refusal to ride the roller coaster with me and the kids. Even though as a psychologist I should know better, it is impossible for me to really understand her fear, since I don't have that particular fear myself. The first step in helping someone to change is to have some appreciation of what the world looks like from that person's vantage point.

The next part of each chapter will give you an idea of how people come to have the problem or personality style being discussed. Many of the styles discussed in the book are such that the people who have them cannot talk about them or do not really understand them themselves. Knowing something about what your partner has probably experienced may help you to feel empathy. And once you have that, you will want to try to help.

The last section of the chapter will discuss examples of how to deal with specific problems. In each chapter I will answer questions from people who have lived with someone with the personality style discussed in the chapter. Some of the questions will reflect issues that, while disturbing to those who live with them, are not too serious. They may be resolved by making a few minor adjustments. At the other extreme, some questions will reflect very difficult situations that may not have a good solution. It is important to know the difference between the two extremes. Some people give up on a relationship when the problems are not that serious, while others will struggle for years trying to resolve a hopeless situation.

Although some psychological terms will be used in describing the various patterns and problems in the chapters that follow, do not assume that the person you live with has a psychological disorder if he or she seems to fit one of the patterns. The people I will describe are not perfect, but neither are they mentally ill. Most of us have a tendency to assume that people who have values, attitudes, and personalities that get on our nerves must be disturbed. Actually, the range of normal functioning is very broad, and it is possible for two people to be within that range and yet think that the other person must be crazy. Hal thinks that Cathy's need to have lots of time to herself is pathological, and Cathy feels the same way about Hal's need always to be with other people, yet they are both well within the normal range; they just have styles that do not go together especially well.

Many of the people who are able to stay in a long-term relationship would make good psychotherapists. They may not have any formal knowledge of psychology, but they do have two very important qualities. First, they are slow to assign blame when things do not go the way they want them to. They do not see differences or conflicts as evidence that one person is right and the other is wrong. They see them for what they are—simply differences and conflicts. And because they tend to view differences this way, these people are willing to compromise. Their self-esteem is not threatened by giving into another person.

The second quality these people have is that they try to understand the perspective of others. They have empathy and can appreciate how others feel. If the person they live with says something hurtful, they do not automatically respond in kind; they assume there is a reason for it. They respond sympathetically, and try to discover what the motive behind such a remark could be. And because they do not bristle and become defensive, the other person is more likely to lower his or her defenses as well. Then together, they may be able to talk in a way that will solve problems rather than generate them.

Of course, no one wants to spend an entire life playing the role of therapist for a spouse, but a relationship will never become long-term if both partners do not have the ability to do so on occasion. The most satisfying relationships are those in which people can take turns being the strong, understanding, and empathic partner. No one can go through life carrying the responsibility of always having to be the strong one, and there is little point in staying in an intimate relationship if one can never be the one who needs the strength and understanding of a partner.

My hope is that the following chapters will help you to develop some of the qualities of a natural therapist. It may not be enough to solve all of the problems that you face, but every relationship is important enough to give it a chance. Remember, everyone who has stayed in a long-term relationship is a testament that two imperfect people *can* live happily ever after.

1

THE COMPULSIVE

The Compulsive Test

1. **If a neighbor came to my house to borrow something, such as a pair of scissors:**
   a. I would make an excuse; I don't like to lend my things out.
   b. I could find it immediately; it would be in the first place I looked.
   c. I could find it within minutes; there are only two or three places it could be.
   d. I would have to stop and try to remember if I owned any.

2. **If I were reprimanded by my boss:**
   a. I would never tell anyone about it, including my spouse.
   b. I would tell only my spouse about it, and then only after much prodding.

c. I would want to discuss it with my spouse and close friends.
d. I would tell anyone who would listen about it.

3. **Telling my children that I love them:**
a. is something I do most every day.
b. is something I enjoy doing, although I would like to remember to tell them more often.
c. is something that I have not done since they were babies.
d. is unnecessary—they should know that I love them.

4. **For dinner next Thursday night:**
a. I have no idea when, what, or where I will eat.
b. I can predict approximately what time I will be eating, but I can't predict what I will eat.
c. I can predict within fifteen minutes what time I will be eating, and I have a pretty good idea of what I will be eating.
d. I can tell you exactly when I will be eating, and as soon as I check the schedule, I can tell you exactly what I will be eating.

5. **I prefer to be addressed by my last name:**
a. by everyone except close friends and family.
b. by my subordinates at work and by tradespeople, such as plumbers and salespeople.
c. only by those who feel more comfortable using it.
d. by no one—I like the informality of being on a first-name basis even with strangers.

6. **Compared to other people:**
a. I can do a job as fast as anyone—although I often have to go back and attend to some details that I overlooked the first time.

b. I can finish a job as fast and as well as most people.
c. it takes me a little longer to do a job than most people, but I make sure it is done right the first time.
d. I would have to be in a class by myself. There are very few people who are as meticulous as I am.

7. **Having good friends and always being with other people:**
a. is the most important thing in the world for me.
b. is something I do value, but I wish I could find more time for it.
c. is probably less important to me than to the average person; while I do have a few close friends, I like to spend time alone.
d. is nice, but is low on my list of priorities.

8. **My family:**
a. frequently accuse me of expecting too much from them.
b. frequently fail to meet my expectations for them.
c. disappoint me on occasion, but pleasantly surprise me just as often.
d. are a pleasure for me.

9. **If I were offered a job that would mean a substantial increase in pay but would require me to move to a different state:**
a. I would arrive at a decision right away, without any qualms.
b. it would be a difficult decision for me but I would be ready with an answer by the time the deadline arrived.
c. I would think about it, but I probably would be no closer to a decision when the deadline arrived than when I first learned of the opportunity.

d. I would put off thinking about it as long as possible.

10. The most important goal in my life:

a. is to reach the top of my profession.
b. is to help my children develop, and to make sure they get off to a good start in life.
c. is to enjoy life on a day-to-day basis.
d. is to experience as many different things as possible.

The Compulsive Test Scoring Key

Each response counts from 0 to 3 points. If none of the responses seems right, choose the one that comes closest. Find the total points scored before reading the interpretations at the end.

1. a. 3 points.
b. 2 points.
c. 1 point.
d. 0 points.

2. a. 3 points.
b. 2 points.
c. 1 point.
d. 0 points.

3. a. 0 points.
b. 1 point.
c. 2 points.
d. 3 points.

4. a. 0 points.
b. 1 point.
c. 2 points.
d. 3 points.

5. a. 3 points.
b. 2 points.
c. 1 point.
d. 0 points.

6. a. 0 points.
b. 1 point.
c. 2 points.
d. 3 points.

7. a. 0 points.
b. 1 point.
c. 2 points.
d. 3 points.

8. a. 3 points.
b. 2 points.
c. 1 point.
d. 0 points.

9. a. 0 points.
b. 1 point.
c. 2 points.
d. 3 points.

10. a. 3 points.
b. 2 points.
c. 1 point.
d. 0 points.

Interpretation of Test Scores

0 to 8 points: You tend to be disorganized and overly concerned with what other people think of you. You could stand a dash of compulsiveness.

9 to 14 points: You are just about right as far as compulsiveness is concerned. Go on to the next chapter.

15 to 23 points: Indicates some compulsive tendencies that may be causing problems. This could be an important chapter.

24 to 30 points: Compulsive tendencies are clearly a problem. This chapter is a must.

You Forget To Crush the Trash!

John is a very neat person. His garage is one of the few in the neighborhood that actually has room for a car. His garden tools are all hung in even rows on pegboard, which covers the three walls. He even has racks for his children's bicycles. If a friend were to ask to borrow some nails, it would take John only a few seconds to find the right size in their clearly labeled bins.

John likes things organized in the house as well. His study looks as if it were in a model home—it has everything one would need, but it seems unused. His books are arranged according to subject, author, and date of publication, and he would never think of leaving his desk with so much as a paperclip out of place. John has ruled the study off limits for his two children, and his wife, Sharon, is on probation after leaving her stationery out while preparing dinner one evening. Unfortunately for her, John happened to walk into the study during that time and saw the "terrible mess."

Sharon does appreciate many aspects of John's neatness. As she says, "I have never once had to pick up after John in sixteen years of marriage." The problem is that John's standards for himself tend to be his standards for the rest of the family. His children sometimes become resentful, and at times angry, over their father's standards for clothing and grooming.

John is fortunate in that his wife forced him into an understanding early in their marriage. He is free to organize the garage and the study, but they must discuss any plans before John does any reorganizing elsewhere in the house. Sharon has had to make many changes in her style as part of their understanding. "My style was to let things slide around the house and then do a thorough cleaning every week to ten days. Because of the way John feels about things, I try to keep things tidy as I go. After sixteen years, it comes naturally to me."

Sharon now laughs about the first few months of their marriage. "At first I believed that it was my obligation as a wife to change to please John. Of course, he encouraged this attitude by implying, however subtly, that I was a bit of a slob for not wanting to be as neat as he was." Sharon remembers clearly the event that prompted her to demand either a compromise or a divorce. "One of John's demands was that boxes and cans be crushed before being thrown in the trash can. He said it was more efficient and economical, since fewer trash bags would have to be used. One morning, when I was running late, I threw a milk carton in the trash can without crushing it. As I was stepping out of the shower, I heard John at the bathroom door shouting: 'You forgot to crush the trash!' "

Compulsives can be a joy to have around—if you have the right relationship with them. Employers love them because they love details, and many jobs will actually be done better by someone who is on the compulsive side. Accountants and computer programmers have to be very detail-oriented. Compulsive secretaries are a real find. You won't find them reading a magazine when things are slow; they will be reorganizing files, checking supplies, even cleaning the office. One woman, during a desperately slow month, actually washed all of her used paperclips!

At home, compulsives can be better than a live-in maid. Although Sharon had to make some adjustments in the way she did things, as a result of marrying a compulsive, she never had to scrub floors, wash windows, or iron shirts; John was not satisfied with the way she did these things, so he did them himself. Bathrooms are a favorite target of compulsives; they do not tolerate mildew in their showers or rings in their bathtubs. Compulsives also make very conscientious shoppers. They love to find bargains, and when a compulsive does the shopping, one never need fear that there will only be one can of tomato paste in the cupboard, instead of the required two, when preparing dinner. Compulsives are also very organized. My wife, for instance, won't let me put the groceries away because I can't group the cans properly; she likes them lined up in our cupboard like soldiers awaiting inspection!

There is, of course, a dark side to this personality style. The compulsive is driven by feelings of anxiety and insecurity, and compulsiveness is a strategy for avoiding anything that might elicit these unpleasant feelings. Neatness can be a refuge in a world that can be very frightening.

Terry, for example, became a real estate agent in the mid-1970s when things were booming. Even though he seemed to be an outgoing, gregarious fellow, it was difficult for him to approach strangers. He felt that once people found out he was a real estate agent, they would rebuff him in some humiliating way. He developed the habit of beginning each day at the office by clipping for-sale ads out of the newspaper and taping them into a spiral notebook. When asked about this activity, he would evasively reply that he was "looking for trends." When his broker's urgings to get out of the office and make some contacts became sufficiently persistent, he would go out with the intention of knocking on some doors, but instead decide that he needed to stop by the courthouse to expand his list of names and addresses.

Things worked out well for Terry for several years. The real estate market was vigorous enough that he was able to make a good living from calls he answered while at the office and referrals from other agents who were too busy to handle all their clients. He was convinced that his success resulted from his thoroughness in learning about the market. But as the 1980s came and the market slowed down, Terry's income dropped sharply. He finally left real estate for a salaried position after going three months without earning a commission check. He blamed his failure on the high interest rates and never did realize that his compulsive newspaper and courthouse rituals had kept him out of what action there was.

One of my colleagues and friends is a good example of a compulsive. He will go through a dozen drafts of a manuscript before submitting it for publication. His final version is always first-rate, but I'm not sure that it is that much better than his second or third draft. I can't help but wonder how much more productive he would be if he did not set such impossible high standards for himself.

Compulsives can be accused of not seeing the forest for the trees. The man who makes an invaluable company controller may not do so well as a vice-president for planning; he thrives on structure and detail but simply cannot deal with the ambiguity of tasks that require a broader perspective. For this reason, people with pronounced tendencies in this direction do not achieve the level of success in their careers that they are capable of. They seek refuge in doing the safe and sure over and over again so as to avoid the possibility of failure at a less well-defined task. They are not capable of the creativity or risk-taking that success in many occupations demands.

Janis is a sad example of this. She was a highly effective history professor. Her compulsiveness made it pleasurable for her to do the painstaking research necessary to write scholarly articles and books. Her course lectures were always enthusiastically received, because she always made a point of finding the obscure details that made historical figures come alive for her students. She was, in short, one of the most respected members of the faculty, and when the chairmanship of the department became open, she was the natural choice.

It was a very difficult two years for her. She learned quickly after assuming her new duties that the job required that she make many decisions that would displease people. She had to allocate travel allowances, distribute funds from the research budget to the members of her department, and mediate conflicts among faculty in the scheduling of classes. And no matter how careful or fairly she made her decisions, someone ended up the loser. Almost always the person who "lost" accepted it well, because everyone was aware that Janis bent over backward to be fair. But Janis herself could not accept her own decisions.

She began to take refuge in statistics for student enrollment. She would spend hours poring over the figures for the past decade. Her rationale was not without merit: "College enrollments were going down, and history departments were hit especially hard. If we couldn't offer courses that appealed to students, we would all be out of a job regardless of what brilliant scholars we were." The other members of her department could not understand how Janis could be spending so much time with her statistics, but given her reputation, they were sure that when she finished, she would present a brilliant master plan for the department. What even Janis was not aware of was that spending time with her stack of computer printouts was a convenient way of putting off decisions that were difficult for her.

An understanding dean convinced her that she should go back to full-time research and teaching when Janis could not bring herself to recommend dismissal for a likable but ineffectual man in her department, and she resigned the chairmanship, a year before her term was up. While she was happy to be back at what she did best, she did feel shaken by her experience as the chair of the department. "I guess it took at least a couple of years before I stopped feeling like such a failure. I finally was able to accept the fact that I didn't have to be a smashing success at everything I did in order to be a worthwhile person. It finally hit me that I didn't expect perfection from other people, so why should I expect it from myself?"

Although compulsive people often give their acquaintances the impression of having busy, full lives, they perform their rituals with little joy. Frank, for instance, could not sit and read or watch television during the evening for more than about twenty minutes. He would begin to feel restless and uncomfortable because he was not "accomplishing something." He would inevitably get up and find something to clean—something that had been cleaned not more than three or four days earlier. And all the time he was cleaning, he would think, with more than a little irritation, that he would love to have more time to himself.

For those who live with a compulsive personality, the most frustrating characteristic of this style is the need to maintain emotional distance from others. These individuals tend to be serious and formal with other people, often including members of their family. Their foremost concern is to protect their self-esteem, and in their minds this requires that they keep their distance from others. They have great difficulty sharing their feelings with spouses, because they have difficulty admitting to certain feelings to themselves. For instance, it took Janis two years to admit to herself, let alone anyone else, that she could not handle the job of department chair. She never could bring herself to admit it to her husband. She told him that she resigned because she missed research so much.

Compulsives are very unlikely to have intimate discussions with husband or wife about self-doubts or hopes for the future. And they are not likely to be understanding if a spouse wants to reveal such things. A discussion of self-doubts is likely to be perceived as a sign of weakness. So spouses of compulsives who do not have these characteristics themselves are likely to feel emotionally isolated and rejected. When their attempts to be intimate are rebuffed, the typical reaction is to wonder: "What's wrong with me?" These perceived rejections, coupled with trying to meet the high standards of the compulsive personality, can have a devastating effect on self-esteem. It is not unusual for a spouse of a compulsive to feel like a failure as a person after a few years of marriage.

Compulsives cannot appreciate these feelings. If their spouse were to complain of feeling unloved, they would probably offer some reassurance such as "Of course I love you. Everything I do is for you and our family." And as far as they are concerned, the words are true. They simply do not know what it means to be emotionally intimate with another person; to be that way would mean exposing one's self. Understanding all this, however, does not necessarily help the spouse to feel loved and needed.

Because compulsives love predictability in their lives, there are some personality types they have a lot of trouble living with. The coquette (Chapter 2) and the ladies' man (Chapter 3) are more than the compulsive can handle. The compulsive would live in fear of never knowing when one of these types would do something outrageous and embarrassing. Strange as it may seem, compulsives are often attracted to these types, and it is not until after the commitment has been made that they learn how difficult it is for them to live with such a person. Most compulsives can tolerate imperfection in their partners as long as it is *predictable* imperfection. So the moper (Chapter 6) and the avoider (Chapter 11) are right up the alley for the compulsive.

Development of the Compulsive

Compulsives begin learning their style at an early age. They are usually bright children who inherited their intelligence from their parents, who are generally well educated. The parents may not have accomplished as much in their lives as they would have liked, and so they seek to fulfill their ambitions through their children. They have high expectations for each child right from the start—they want the child to walk, talk, and read at an earlier age than any of their friends' or relatives' children. Unfortunately, the child is almost certain to fail to meet many of the parents' expectations.

Brad is a thirty-six-year-old dentist who has a thriving practice. Although he could live on half of the money he makes, he is very much concerned because his income has dropped slightly over the past two years. To make up for what he views as the deterioration of his practice, he has begun to offer evening and Saturday appointments while continuing to maintain his regular office hours. He resents his family's complaints that he is never home, saying, "They just don't understand that if I don't keep the practice going, we'll have nothing."

Brad's earliest memories of his childhood go back to age four or five. "I remember my sixth birthday vividly. I had wanted a bicycle more than anything else in the world. I got it, but it was too big for me and I couldn't ride it for two more years. I don't really remember how my parents reacted to my disappointment at not being able to ride my new bike on my birthday, but I do remember feeling ashamed and inadequate."

Receiving gifts that he could not use or was not interested in using became a tradition for Brad. If he got a game, it would be for children several years older than he was. Books were always a little too intellectual or advanced for him. He remembers that the Christmas he was ten he received an electrical science kit that he could not begin to understand. Most of his gifts made him feel a little stupid.

His parents never had the intention of making Brad feel inadequate. They really did love him and they wanted what was best for him; they simply had unrealistic notions of his ability. If they gave him a game that was too advanced for him, it was because they knew he was bright enough to handle it. They believed that the best way to help him develop was to present him with challenges. Indeed, everything they did was motivated by their desire to help Brad.

Brad did very well in schoolwork. "There was never any question in my mind that I would do whatever it took to maintain my nearly straight-A average. The few times I did bring home a B on my report card, my parents would set up a schedule for extra study time so that I could overcome my weak spots. I don't remember receiving any praise for doing so well in school; the entire family simply *expected* my two sisters and I to get A's. After all, how else could you get into a good college?"

Brad describes his childhood as pleasant. He does recall that other children seemed to have more fun than he did, and he remembers wishing that his family did more of the fun things other families seemed to do, but he also feels grateful that his parents prepared him for life so well. It was through their efforts and sacrifices that he was able to get into an Ivy League college and a top dental school; they even lent him the money to start his practice. But in spite of the gratitude he feels, he rarely sees his parents. He does not have the time.

Like Brad, most compulsives learn their style through trying to meet their parents' expectations for them. The expectations are always just far enough above their ability that they grow up with the feeling that failure is just around the corner, and the only way to stave it off is by attending to every little detail and completing every task as perfectly as possible. They are extremely sensitive to signs of failure and will see such signs even where none exist. Many dentists, for instance, may attribute a slight decline in their practice to a poor economy or to increased competition. But Brad was sure that a decline, however slight, was just an early warning of complete disaster.

These people consider any failure to be a reflection of their worth as human beings. Almost everyone fails at something at sometime or another without having his or her self-esteem destroyed. A businessman may develop a product that flops miserably and write it off as a bad idea. Even being fired from a job for incompetence would be a jolt for most anyone, but most people would try to find something they were better at without concluding that they were completely worthless. To the compulsive, however, any failure, however trivial, can be devastating. Their parents failed to provide them with a belief in their basic worth as human beings, and it is extremely difficult for them to acquire that belief on their own as adults.

Living with the Compulsive

As we discussed in the introduction, the styles and patterns covered in this book should not be thought of as being psychological disorders; they may not be the most adaptive way to live, but many people like having some of the characteristics described in this book. This is especially true of the compulsive style. Accountants depend on their compulsive tendencies for their livelihood, and no one could possibly make it as a copy editor without a compulsive streak. And many people like being married to a compulsive person; my wife will never stop trying to convince me that I should be more compulsive. The point is that no one should change, nor expect a spouse to change, simply because he or she has characteristics that seem to fit a fancy psychological term. The only reasonable justification to change is that to do so would make one's life or one's relationships more rewarding.

Here are some specific problems that people have

faced in living with compulsives, and some ideas about how to deal with these problems.

Q: My husband and I have been married for only three months, but I am thinking already that I have made a mistake. He has developed schedules for all aspects of our lives, from what time we get up to what time we eat, and even what days we will have sex. When I try to talk to him about how I would like to have a more relaxed style of life, he just doesn't seem to listen. Is there anything that can be done about this situation? He didn't seem to be this way before we were married.

A: Your husband's need for such strict schedules is motivated by underlying feelings of insecurity and fear. The reason your husband's compulsive tendencies became more pronounced after you were married is probably related to his concerns about whether or not he would make a good husband and father; new situations and uncertainty generally bring out these patterns in the compulsive personality, and most people have insecurities about a new marriage. His way of dealing with these feelings is to try to make his life more structured; it makes him feel safe.

The time to do something about the situation is now, before his strategies for dealing with his insecurity become deeply ingrained habits. The most important thing to remember is that if your husband feels threatened, he will want to impose even more structure on the situation. So when you talk to him, try to do it in a pleasant, matter-of-fact way, although this can be difficult because the demands of the compulsive often make those around him or her angry.

Tell him that you cannot live your life according to a rigid schedule and that you would like to work out some compromises. As you talk about these issues, be sure to offer plenty of assurance of your love for him; tell him how much it means to you that your marriage work. As you indicated, your husband will probably have trouble with such a discussion. He will probably seem to be unaffected by your assurances of love and commitment and may insist that he knows you love him. But he *does* need to hear these things; at some level, he has his doubts.

You must be prepared to make some compromises yourself. During the week, the time that you get up, the time you eat dinner, and the time you go to bed will probably be influenced by your or your husband's work schedule; most people do these things at pretty much the same time every day even if they do not formalize it in a written document. You might agree to follow a weekly schedule that you both can live with, even if you don't like the *idea* of a formal plan. Think of the schedule as something that describes your activities rather than as a document that dictates your life.

If you can do this for him, ask him if he will try to be more flexible about how you spend your time on the weekends. If he is reluctant to agree to try it, tell him that he is free to stick to a schedule for himself but that you plan to get up, eat, and go to bed when you want to on Saturday and Sunday. When we were first married, my wife couldn't understand why I would waste the weekend by sleeping late on Saturday and Sunday. But my stubborn refusal to change has convinced her that I must be allowed this indulgence.

Many newly married couples believe that they have to do everything together after they are married, and they usually end up following the preferences of the person who voices his or her opinions the most forcefully. It may be wise to let your husband know early on that you are prepared to do some things independently if you cannot agree how they should be done. The first few months can set the tone for the entire marriage, and you do not want to lead him to believe that you will always give him his way, regardless of how much you want to please him. I am willing to bet that after he sees you spending a few weekends doing things when and how you want to do them, he will begin to loosen up.

Sex is one area that you are justified in refusing to subject to a schedule. Let your husband know that you want to have sex with him when you both feel like it. Sex and spontaneity belong together; few people would enjoy sex if they knew they were having it only because it was Tuesday night. Again, however, tell him your feelings in a nonhostile and nonthreatening way. As he begins to really feel secure about your love, it should become easier for him to be more flexible. Most compulsives do begin to loosen up once they feel secure, and as long as you press for changes in a loving way, the chances are excellent that you can arrive at a life-style that is satisfying for both of you.

There are, however, some people whose compulsive tendencies are so deeply entrenched that no amount of love, understanding, or gentle prodding will have an effect. If, after a year or so, your husband shows no signs of changing, then you must be prepared to take drastic action. The sad truth is that love is not always enough. And if your husband continues to demand that you toe the mark when it comes to his schedules, your love can turn to resentment and hate.

Your first step would be to suggest that he receive psychotherapy. He will probably refuse, since he honestly believes that your refusal to live the way he would like you to is the *real* problem. Your best chance, then, is to suggest that you both go for marital therapy in order to learn to live together. Again, the chances are that he will refuse. People such as your husband not only believe that their preferences are reasonable and right, they are likely to feel threatened by the prospect of discussing emotionally intimate issues. If your husband is not comfortable discussing his innermost feelings with you, you can be sure that the prospect of discussing them with a stranger will be extremely unpleasant for him.

The only alternative you have left is to consider leaving him. This alternative should never be considered lightly, but there are situations in which it is the only realistic choice. If and when you bring up this possibility with him, try not to do it when you are feeling angry. Remind him that you really want to stay together, but you cannot be happy if you have to meet his expectations for you. There is a chance that your leaving, or just your intention to leave, will be enough to jolt him into making some changes, but you cannot count on it. You have to be prepared to actually leave; if you are not, it would be better not to make the threat as it will only serve to strengthen his defensiveness. If you have reached this point, you have to accept the fact that your husband has deeply entrenched patterns, and the chances of his changing, even with professional help, are not good. It may be that only another compulsive could be happily married to him.

Q: My wife is a compulsive cleaner. Although she doesn't work and has all day to do her housework, she still spends a couple of hours every evening doing something around the house. I would like her to spend her evenings relaxing with me. What can I do to get her to slow down?

A: It is not clear from your question that your wife does have compulsive tendencies. The fact that you spend your evenings relaxing while she cleans suggests that she is not guilty of imposing her standards on you; if she did, you would probably be helping her clean. It could be that she is an active person and needs to be doing something; many people do not enjoy simply relaxing for several hours night after night. When you suggest that the two of you do something that you know she enjoys, does she beg off because of work that she needs to do? Unless she does, I would guess that she is one of those people who likes to be doing things.

Perhaps her "problem" is a narrow range of interests rather than compulsive tendencies. Many women develop the pattern when they have young children of spending most of their waking hours doing nothing but caring for their families and their house. This is especially true if they have a husband who is not inclined to help out. (How do you plead?) When their children become older, they have more free time but no interests with which to fill this time. So it is not so much a case of compulsive cleaning, but rather a case of not knowing how to fill the newly found free time.

Perhaps the best way to help her is to encourage her to develop new interests. This may mean that she would want to spend a few evenings out with friends or going to classes. From the way you phrased your question, I suspect that one of her "problems" may be your possessiveness. It would not be fair to her to expect her to spend her evenings relaxing with you if she is the kind of person who needs to be active. If you can help her to develop new interests and are able to allow her the freedom to pursue them, it will pay off for you; a relationship will be more satisfying in the long run if both individuals are happy with their lives. If she is indeed cleaning because she feels that she has nothing more interesting to do, sooner or later her resentment will begin to build, and her resentment will inevitably affect you.

Q: Sometimes I think my husband believes that he is God. He really seems to think that he has the ultimate wisdom when it comes to what's right and wrong. This wouldn't be so bad except that he cannot seem to enjoy anything. He has to analyze every little suggestion I make before deciding whether he can do it in good conscience.

If I suggest that we take the children to the beach, he will speculate about whether the time could be spent more productively. He will usually end up going, but he won't enjoy it, and his attitude affects the rest of the family. If we go out to dinner he will use it as an opportunity to lecture the children on their manners, or what years were good for Burgundy wines, and afterward he will tell me that he thinks the kids got a lot out of it. The only time he ever expressed his feelings about the restaurant or the time we shared was once when he commented that his dinner wasn't as bad as he had expected.

His attitude has really hurt his relationship with the children. If they were to try to talk to him about a problem—which they would never dream of doing anymore—he would never try to understand how they felt about it, but would instead give one of his long-winded lectures about how one should try to live his life. I haven't had a heart-to-heart talk with him about anything in years. I do want to stay married for practical reasons and because I place a great value on stability, but I am prepared to leave next year, when our youngest child goes to college, if he does not change at least a little. Is there any hope?

A: Some, but it will be difficult for both of you. It sounds as if your husband has an aspect of the compulsive style that I like to call "emotional constipation." Almost everyone would agree that the ability to be emotionally intimate with other people—especially with one's spouse and children—is crucial to a happy and satisfying life, but some people, even though they may agree with this at an intellectual level, seem to have a block that prevents them from achieving this closeness. They want to be close to others, but they are afraid to take any chances in order to get there.

If your husband feels any regret about his distant relationship with the children, then there is some chance that he may be able to change. Some emotionally constipated people believe that there is nothing wrong with the way they relate to others. Also, they may believe that the idea that one should have fun in life is childish. I have heard more than one client say that once one becomes an adult, it is immature to think about having fun; it's all right to be contented, but fun definitely has no place for the emotionally constipated. Well, I am one adult who believes that there is not much point to it all unless you do have some fun.

If your husband does feel that something is missing in his life, then he has some motivation for changing. Because you have developed a distant relationship with him, I doubt that you will be able to help him much in this effort. It would be too threatening for him to talk to you about his doubts, which he perceives to be weaknesses. The most you can do is to make it as easy as possible for him to seek psychotherapy. Talk to him about his relationship with the children; gently point out to him that they have no desire to be close to him, and tell him that you want him to do something about it before it is too late. Concentrate on the theme that you want him to derive more satisfaction from life. At this point you should not bring up your own feelings of dissatisfaction; it would back him into a corner and he might end up doing nothing. Keep in mind, too, that seeing a psychotherapist is an admission of failure for your husband; generally, men have to be suffering considerably before they will try it. So do not expect him to agree to make an appointment the first time you suggest it. Do continue to bring up his apparent absence of joy with life, and when possible, present him with evidence of the distance between him and the children. If your husband does have a sense that something is missing in his life, I think the chances are pretty good that he will eventually go for therapy.

If your husband does enter therapy, the chances of his

changing are good. Most emotionally constipated people are good, decent human beings; in fact, they may be admired and respected by those who do not know them very well. I would guess that your children think of him as a good person, but one who is cold and distant. If he can feel more secure about expressing his feelings, then the chances are excellent that the children will respond. But it is up to your husband to take the first step. Parents set the tone for their relationships with their children.

I also think that your relationship with him will improve and that you may be able to feel closer to him. Because he is basically a good person, you will probably respond to any changes in him; your desire to maintain your marriage is a good sign. You must, however, be prepared to give him a chance. Even though you have no desire to be close to him now, I am sure that you would be happier if you could be emotionally intimate with him. If he does begin therapy, be sensitive to any attempts on his part to open up to you. His attempts will be tentative at first, and if he is to continue to try, he must be rewarded by your responsiveness. If you do give it a chance, I am sure that it will be worth it for you.

Some Final Thoughts

The term "compulsive personality" is used by psychologists to describe a style that has several elements. As we have seen in this chapter, these elements include perfectionistic standards for one's self as well as others, strong needs for orderliness, an inability to develop intimacy with others, difficulty in enjoying life, and a tendency to have conservative political and moral standards. While some people do possess all of these elements, many others exhibit only one or two of them. John, described at the beginning of the chapter, was perfectionistic and had a strong need for orderliness, but he was able to have a close and loving relationship with his wife and children. The husband of the woman we just discussed was not unusually orderly, but he had a great deal of trouble with intimacy.

If someone you know possesses one or two of these characteristics, you should not assume that the others are there and that you will find them if you only look hard enough. For instance, if you have a spouse who tends to be perfectionistic, do not assume that he or she must also be cold and distant. If you start looking for problems, you are sure to find them. And you do not want to find any that you were not aware of previously.

It is also crucial to distinguish between the trivial and the important. Just because your husband's insistence on having his socks rolled up just the right way gets on your nerves is no reason to accuse him of being a compulsive personality. Few people have no compulsive quirks at all; the person you live with is almost bound to have some. Trying to get your spouse to change these harmless quirks will probably only serve to make him or her angry—and rightly so. Save your energies for the patterns that you really cannot live with and that are causing you or your spouse unhappiness. Besides, it probably would be boring to live with someone who was perfect!

2
THE COQUETTE

The Coquette

1. **In high school:**
   a. the boys didn't know that I was alive.
   b. I had two or three boyfriends that I can remember.
   c. I had a different boyfriend every semester.
   d. all the girls hated me because I could have any boy I wanted.

2. **When I was a little girl, my daddy:**
   a. made me call him "sir."
   b. spoiled me a little.
   c. spoiled me a lot.
   d. was putty in my hands.

3. **I learned to use makeup:**

a. in secret when my mother wasn't home.
b. from my mother, after begging her to show me how.
c. from my mother, who was an eager teacher.
d. from my mother, and a variety of charm schoools she sent me to.

4. When I was a teenager, my father's idea of sex education:
a. was to tell me how wonderful it would be when I got married.
b. was to blush whenever sex was mentioned, and to tell me to ask my mother.
c. was to make sure I wasn't exposed to it by censoring the movies and television shows I watched.
d. was to warn me that he thought I was turning out to be "that kind of girl."

5. When I was finishing high school, my plans were to:
a. be more successful than the smartest boy in our class.
b. find a career that I could be happy with.
c. get married and start having babies.
d. find a job or college where I'd be most likely to meet lots of exciting men.

6. If the man I lived with refused to let me buy a new dress:
a. I'd leave him—I wouldn't live with a man who believed it was his right to give or withhold permission for anything I do.
b. I'd use my own money to buy the dress.
c. I'd realize that he knew best.
d. I'd cry until he changed his mind.

7. When I buy new clothes, the first thing I think of is:

a. the image I have to project if I'm going to make it to the top.
b. how much it will cost.
c. what will look good on me, regardless of cost.
d. what will show off my figure to its best advantage.

8. My idea of a typical evening with the man I live with is:

a. going to our respective meetings.
b. watching television or reading.
c. doing something together, like playing Scrabble.
d. curling up in each other's arms in front of the fireplace with a bottle of wine.

9. The best thing about sex is:

a. feeling relaxed and calm afterward.
b. the feelings of closeness and intimacy I have with my partner.
c. being able to please my partner.
d. the excitement that leads up to it.

10. If I reach middle age without a man in my life:

a. I will consider myself lucky.
b. I won't like it but it won't be the end of the world.
c. I will be lonely and unhappy.
d. my life will not be worth living.

The Coquette Test Scoring Key

1. a. 0 points.
b. 1 point.
c. 2 points.
c. 3 points.

2. a. 0 points.
b. 1 point.
c. 2 points.
d. 3 points.

3. a. 0 points.
b. 1 point.
c. 2 points.
d. 3 points.

4. a. 0 points.
b. 1 point.
c. 2 points.
d. 3 points.

5. a. 0 points.
b. 1 point if you finished high school after 1970; 0 points if you finished before that year.
c. 2 points if you finished high school after 1970; 1 point if you finished before then.
d. 3 points.

6. a. 0 points.
b. 1 point.
c. 2 points.
d. 3 points.

7. a. 0 points.
b. 1 point.
c. 2 points
d. 3 points.

8. a. 0 points.
b. 1 point.
c. 2 points.
d. 3 points.

9. a. 0 points.
b. 1 point.
c. 2 points.
d. 3 points.

10. a. 0 points.
b. 1 point.
c. 2 points.
d. 3 points.

Interpretation of Test Scores

0 to 7 points: You probably have had some experiences that have left you feeling bitter toward men, or perhaps you have rebelled a little excessively against stereotypes of women. You do not have to give up your femininity to be strong, competent, and independent.

8 to 15 points: You have achieved a good balance between the different roles that women (or men for that matter) can assume in this world.

16 to 23 points: You may have bought into the notion that women have to be passive and dependent in order to get along in the world. This chapter is an important one for you.

24 to 30 points: Unless you are able to find a man who has low self-esteem and is willing to play the role of father for the rest of his life, you will have chronic problems in your relationships with men. This chapter is a must!

Do You Think This Dress Is Cut Too Low?

Cindi is the kind of woman men remember. And while she is attractive, it is not her appearance that creates such lasting impressions. She is not obviously flirtatious or seductive, but when she is introduced to a man, he is likely to have some wistful fantasies of future possibilities. Something about the way she looks into a man's eyes and offers her hand seems to suggest that she is promising something more than a simple hello and a handshake.

Her husband, George, certainly had this reaction when he first saw her. "I met Cindi when I was a graduate student and she was in a lab course I was teaching. I'll never forget the first time I talked to her. She asked a question and I went over to help her adjust her microscope. When I looked up, her face was only inches away, and she had the warmest, sweetest smile I had ever seen. My heart started to pound, and I couldn't think clearly enough to answer her question. Even though I fell in love with her at that moment, I didn't get up enough nerve to call her until a couple of months after the semester had ended."

Cindi and George were married shortly after he got his master's degree. Cindi did not mind dropping out of college, even though she was only one semester short of graduation. Her husband's career was more important, and besides, she was more than happy to play the role of the young executive's wife. Cindi enjoyed the first year of their marriage, and George thought it was the happiest year of his life. He still could not get over his good fortune—

having Cindi for a wife when she could have had any man she wanted.

Tension began to build between them during the second year of their marriage. As Cindi remembers it: "I was getting bored. George is a good, decent, and stable man, but he's kind of dull. After I had furnished our house and gotten everything in order, there just wasn't enough for me to do. The only thing I enjoyed was our social life, and so, despite George's objections, I saw to it that we were invited to lots of parties. It was the only thing in my life that was any fun. George doesn't feel comfortable around lots of people, and he seemed to resent the fact that I enjoyed myself at parties. He even accused me of being a flirt. Well, I couldn't help it if men liked me. I never did, and never would, do anything to hurt anyone; I just wanted to have a good time."

George's memory of that time in their lives is quite different. "I loved Cindi so much that I would have done anything for her, but it was getting harder and harder to keep up with her. She was a big hit with the men whom I worked with, so we were invited to lots of parties even though I was at the bottom of the totem pole in the company. Because my salary reflected my position, we just couldn't afford a new dress for every party we were invited to, but when Cindi got that sad look in her eyes, I just couldn't say no. The hardest thing to take was the way she would act at the parties. It didn't take me long to find out that her special quality that I found so irresistible appealed to other men as well. I bet she gets two or three dozen offers to freshen up her drink at every party we go to. My stomach would get tied up in knots when I saw men constantly touching her. She claimed it was all very innocent, and I suppose it was. But I would never go up to another man's wife, put my arm around her waist, and ask if I could get her a drink.

"I tried to talk to her about how I felt, but for quite a while she just didn't seem to understand. I'm not the most dynamic and charming guy around, and her behavior really made me feel insecure. She would simply give me a pat on the head and tell me I had nothing to worry about. The turning point came the week of the annual company banquet. It's a formal dinner dance, and most people use it as a good excuse to get sloshed. I had begged her to wear something conservative; she usually wears clothes that I think are kind of cheap-looking, but she claims that I'm being stuffy, and that there is nothing wrong with looking sexy. Anyway, she did tell me that she had bought a new dress, and she promised me I would love it. I thought I had gotten through to her until I saw her come out of the bedroom the night of the party. It looked as if her breasts could pop out of the dress at any moment. But she had a big smile and asked in that little-girl voice of hers, 'Do you think this dress is cut too low?' "

Cindi has a touch of what I like to call the coquette personality. The mannerisms and attitudes of these women are exaggerated to the point of being a caricature of femininity. They make full use of their charms in their interactions with men, and most men respond to them; it is no accident that Cindi, and other women like her, end up being surrounded by a circle of admiring men at parties. Even though these women may not be aware of their motives, they approach these events with a clear sense of purpose. And if they find that they are not awarded their rightful place at the center stage of attention, they will do what they must to achieve it. They may laugh a little louder or maintain eye contact just a little longer, but they will succeed in being noticed.

They tend to be dramatic in most of the things they say and do. For them, it is never merely a nice day, it is "an absolutely beautiful day!" They are never a "little irritated" by a thoughtless comment by a friend; they are "crushed by her bitchiness." Others may be attracted initially by what seems to be her enthusiasm and refreshing honesty, but after a while, it all seems to be part of an act. The coquette is so prone to overstatement and overreaction that it does not take long for those around her to begin to doubt her sincerity and genuineness. And in fact, the coquette does not really experience the strong emotions and reactions she displays. It is part of an act—an act that she herself is unaware of.

Being involved with one of these women can be a mixed blessing. They inspire passion, so the man who believes he has a commitment with such a woman will feel all of the excitement that goes along with passionate love. But because these women have difficulty committing themselves completely to any man, their partner will never feel totally secure in the relationship. Dan, for example, continued to have feelings of romantic love for his wife of twelve years. "I think I am in love with Sara as much today as I was the day we were married. At times it drives me crazy, but I can't wait to see her when I'm on my way home from work. And when we go out for the evening, I'll do everything I can to make it go perfectly. I feel like a fool at times, but I'm still trying to impress her after all these years.

"I've tried to figure out what it is about her that makes me feel the way I do, and the only thing that I can come up with is her unpredictability. I don't think I've ever really been sure that she loves me. Sometimes when I get home from work, she'll be angry at me for some unknown reason and I spend the whole night begging her to forgive me. The next day I'll tell myself what a jerk I am for putting up with her, but then when I get home she'll act as if I'm the most wonderful man in the world, and I'll melt. I've asked myself a thousand times whether

I'm better off with her or without her, but it doesn't really make any difference. I know I could never give her up."

Dan is by no means alone with his mixed feelings about his marriage. While many men decide they cannot or will not put up with a coquette, many others value the enduring intensity of feelings they have for their partners. Stan is one man who would never give up his coquette. "Nancy can be a pain at times, but living with her is never dull. A lot of my friends talk about how bored they are with their marriages, but I can't imagine ever having that problem. I feel hurt at times because I know she doesn't care as much about me as I do about her, but it's worth it. When we're together and she's in a good mood, it's every bit as exciting as it was when we were dating."

In terms of her self-esteem, the coquette has placed all of her eggs in one basket. She evaluates her worth as a human being in terms of her ability to attract men. The chase—or more accurately, getting someone to chase her—is what counts. Sadly, admiration from someone who has been conquered loses its value quickly, and she feels the need to move on to something new.

For some women with a mild case of the coquette personality, innocent flirtations may be enough to provide reassurance of their desirability. Cindi never considered leaving her husband or even having an affair. But it was important for her to know that she could find someone if she wanted to. However, other women may literally move from relationship to relationship, leaving a string of broken-hearted lovers and husbands behind. They are trapped by the endless quest to find the one man who can make them feel good about themselves.

The coquette has taken to heart many of the unflattering stereotypes that exist about women. They do not simply believe them; they live them. For example, the coquette has incorporated as part of her psychological makeup the notion that men want their women to be empty-headed, clinging, and emotional, and it would never occur to her to be any other way.

Donna winces as she recalls what she was like before she realized she had to change the course that her life was taking. "I can't believe how neurotic I was, but I devoted the first thirty-plus years of my life trying to be the kind of woman that I thought men wanted me to be. The only time I felt happy and good about myself was when I had a man pursuing me. Now I feel I wasted a lot of years. I was always very bright in school, but I was never interested in doing anything with it. I wasn't aware of it at the time, but I think I was worried that the boys wouldn't like me if I did too well in school. Men are still an important part of my life, but I have finally learned that there are other things that I can do to make my life seem worthwhile. Besides, I found out that the kind of man that I was interested in got bored with me in short order when I was like something out of *The Stepford Wives*."

In most cases, coquettes are very capable people. They range from above average to superior in intelligence, and they are most likely to grow up in families that offer lots of advantages. They have, however, failed to develop any sense of appreciation for what they could do with their lives if they only tried. So, like Donna, they muddle their way through school when they have the ability to do exceptionally well. If by chance they do not land a man to take care of them before they reach the point where they have to go it alone, they will tend to choose a traditionally "feminine" job; they will end up being nurses, secretaries, or elementary school teachers even though they have the ability to be doctors, business executives, or college professors. To opt for the latter occupations would be unthinkable, not only because coquettes have little confidence in their abilities, but also because they suspect the femininity of women who are in such positions.

Donna's observation that men became bored with her is an important one, because most men do not want to have a long-term relationship with a woman who is empty-headed, clinging, and emotionally unstable, regardless of how attractive and sexy she is. They may be attracted to such women initially, and may think that it would be fun to have a fling with one. But unless they have a few problems with their own self-esteem, they will want more from a committed relationship than a bundle of highly charged feminine charms. Often it is a toss-up as to who will grow weary with the relationship first—the coquette or the man who has to put up with her. I know that the most frequent complaint about women that I've heard from my male friends and clients concerns their dependency, not their appearance.

Being tossed aside by a lover is no fun for anyone, but it is especially devastating for the coquette. Since her self-esteem depends almost entirely upon her ability to attract men, being rejected by one can seem like the end of the world. And if she is rejected, she is not likely to slip quietly into the night. She is likely to raise quite a fuss.

Vic lived with a coquette for nearly two years before he decided that it was not what he wanted. His partner seemed to have a casual view of their relationship while they were together, so he was taken completely by surprise by her reaction when he asked her to move out. "I thought she would feel the same sense of relief that I did when I told her it was over. After all, she was seeing quite a few other men while we were living together. And no matter how innocent it was—she claimed they were just 'friends'—it had to indicate a lack of interest in me. When I first told her, she started crying hysterically. She claimed

I was the most important person in her life and that she couldn't live without me. I wasn't about to change my mind, so she did move out. But she kept calling me at all hours begging me to take her back. She even threatened to kill herself, and once she actually took a handful of sleeping pills and had to have her stomach pumped out. I never would have guessed that that side of her existed."

Vic's partner was an extreme case, but women with just a touch of the coquette personality will be unusually alert for signs of rejection. Even though they may feel they need the excitement of knowing that other men find them interesting, they will be vigilant for any hints that their partner is not completely devoted to them. Cindi, for example, would become angry at her husband, George, when he played golf with his friends. Although she was unable to verbalize why she reacted the way that she did, it was because she felt rejected. If George really loved her, he would want to spend his time with her rather than on the golf course with his buddies.

Second only to being rejected by a man, the biggest crisis in the coquette's life is middle age. No one likes the idea of waking up in the morning to notice a few new wrinkles around the eyes or some more gray hairs, but most people adapt. The coquette cannot. Losing her looks means losing her purpose in life. How can she attract men without her smooth skin and her shapely body? And if she cannot attract men, what good is she?

How the coquette deals with these changes is a crucial turning point. Many develop severe psychological problems, incapacitating depression being the most common. But others develop an awareness that the strategies they have been using for their entire lives simply will not work any longer. They begin to grow psychologically and use some of the abilities that they have ignored up to that point. But this is not likely to happen without the support and encouragement of the people they live with.

As I mentioned in the previous chapter, the one match that rarely turns out well is between a coquette and a compulsive personality. It is, unfortunately, a match that is far from uncommon. The man with compulsive tendencies appears at first glance to make an ideal father figure. So in the eyes of the coquette, he appears to be the kind of man who would make a perfect husband. But the unpredictability of the coquette will be more than he can take.

The course of the relationship between a coquette and a man with other personality characteristics could go either way, depending mostly on the self-esteem of the man. Men who feel secure with themselves are not likely to put up with the siren's immature behavior for long. They will either help her to develop psychologically or, failing that, find a more fulfilling relationship. Men who are not as sure of their self-worth may struggle indefinitely to win the devotion of their flirtatious partner; they will certainly feel frustrated and angry at themselves at times for allowing themselves to be mistreated, but they have to prove to themselves that they can keep such a desirable woman.

Development of the Coquette

Historically, our society has encouraged little girls to grow up to be coquettes. Most parents would be thrilled to have their daughters be prom queens and to know that they are breaking the hearts of all the little boys. And it is usually a given that girls will grow up, get married, and raise a family, so the most important thing is to learn the necessary skills to be able to attract the right man. A man who is not married by a certain age is viewed as something of a playboy, but a woman in the same situation is simply considered an old maid.

Fortunately for women, and the men they live with,

things are slowly changing, and in light of the traditional expectations our society has held for women, it says something for women's resiliency and good sense that there are not more coquettes in the world. There seems to be a growing acceptance of the notion that women can be strong, independent, and competent without sacrificing their femininity and their ability to have a good relationship with a man. Although many would not admit it, men have known this all along. They may like the appearance of a soft, fluffy, empty-headed woman, but they have demanded that the women in their lives be strong and competent partners. They just did not want their women to be too open about it.

The Zeitgeist of our society has not been without its effects. A majority of women do have some conflict about what they would like to be and what is expected of them. Psychological studies have shown that a substantial percentage of women have fears of succeeding in traditional male occupations such as physician or engineer; they cannot believe that a woman can do these jobs as well as a man. Also, many women tend to feel they've failed if they do not have a man in their life regardless of what they have achieved in other areas.

What sets the coquette apart is that she does not have any of these conflicts. She accepts wholeheartedly the idea that a woman cannot be a success and retain her femininity. And that a woman is a failure if she does not have a man in her life is never questioned. To be any other way would suggest that she would be one of those "women's libbers"—in the most pejorative sense of the term.

Along with responding to the general expectations that society holds for women, the coquette receives specialized training in order to end up the way she does. Her mother may take special pains to make sure that her girl is the "perfect little lady." She encourages her little coquette to learn to use makeup at any early age, and pretty, frilly dresses are the norm; jeans, as well as the outdoor play they are intended to be worn for, are discouraged. It is a safe bet that the mother has some of these characteristics as well, and wants her daughter to follow in her footsteps.

The little girl tries to be like her mother, but because she is only a little girl, she is left with a feeling of not being able to measure up. Sharon, a strikingly attractive woman, remembers feeling ugly next to her mother. "My mother would spend hours with me, helping me to get ready to go out. She would make sure that I wore just the right dress, and that I looked just perfect. She would tell me how beautiful I looked, but when I compared myself to her, I would feel scrawny and clumsy. I could never hope to be as glamorous and graceful as she was."

Sharon's early years, like most coquettes', were spent comparing herself to her mother. As she grew older, she began to compare herself to the other women she met. And, of course, the basis for these comparisons was always appearance. Who looked the prettiest? Who could get the most invitations for the senior prom? Who could entice whose date away at the homecoming party?

It is hard to be friends with competitors, and the coquette does not get along very well with other women. Other women tend to view her, not without justification, as superficial and vain. And the coquette has to be ever vigilant; if she were to let down her guard, another woman might steal her man away from her. Any close women friends the coquette might have will be either much older or much less attractive than she; she can feel safe and secure only with someone who is clearly no competition for her.

The coquette is typically created by her father during her childhood years. Such a father encourages his daughter to be coy and flirtatious; although he would be horrified if anyone suggested it to him, there is a seductive quality to the way he treats his daughter. He takes pride in the fact that he is the kind of father who can be wrapped around his daughter's little finger, and wrapping her father around her little finger is one way the coquette can compete successfully with her mother.

The real bind begins when the little coquette reaches puberty. The father has more than his share of conflict about sex, and he is terrified about his little girl's turning into a woman. He begins to distance himself from his daughter. She is no longer allowed to sit on his lap, and he can no longer give her a hug because feeling her body makes it painfully obvious that she is no longer his little girl. Of course, the daughter does not understand what is going on, and she feels hurt and rejected. The only thing she knows is that the most important man in her life no longer loves her.

Such a father cannot stand any sign that his daughter might have an interest in sex. He wants her to remain pure and chaste forever. Laura still winces when she recalls the first time her father became really angry at her. "I had just turned thirteen and I had my first boyfriend. He was walking me home from school, and I was really excited for my mom to meet him. My father happened to be home early that day, and he saw us walking down the street holding hands. He ran out the front door and yelled at my boyfriend—funny, I can't remember his name—to get away from his daughter, and warned him to never show his face again. Then he dragged me into the house and screamed that I was turning out to be a slut. He wouldn't talk to me for three weeks." The lesson was clear for Laura. It is okay to attract boys, but heaven forbid that you do anything about it once you have them!

Laura is an extreme case, but for her, the results were tragic. She was a coquette to the nth degree. She could attract any man that she was interested in, but she did not know what to do with him once she had him. She viewed sex as her rather unpleasant duty, and once she felt confident that a man was in love with her, she made it clear that she did not enjoy sleeping with him. Her one marriage lasted for only eighteen months, and she was divorced before her twentieth birthday. After that, she would let relationships progress until the man asked her either to marry him or to move in with him, at which point she would drop him. She liked the idea that she had devastated so many men. She did not know it, of course, but she was getting even with her father for rejecting her.

Women with a case of the coquette personality as bad as Laura's usually end up in therapy for many years, and sometimes they must be hospitalized for severe depression. It is common for women to have similiar, but less dramatic experiences. Their fathers may not accuse them of becoming sluts, but they disapprove of every new boyfriend. They make it clear that they do not like whatever it is their daughter may be doing once they leave the house. These women are able to form attachments with men, but they try to recreate the father-daughter relationship; the notion that little girls want to grow up and marry a man just like their father is more than a cliché for these women.

As I mentioned earlier, there can be advantages to having a wife with just a touch of the coquette personality. They tend to be lively, energetic, and fun. Because they dismiss anything that is practical or logical as being for men only, they can be frustrating to live with at times, but often they have a flair for things that require imagination and creativity. Recall Donna, who was mentioned earlier in the chapter. She was able to use her flair for the dramatic to her advantage. She started a catering service, and before long, her unusual but appealing way of doing things brought her more business than she could handle. And the demands of her business forced her to gradually become more practical and attentive to the details of life.

The trick is to help the coquette get past her tendencies to self-destruct without her having to give up the qualities that can make her so charming. Let's take a look at some specific strategies for accomplishing this goal.

Living with the Coquette

We do not form relationships with others through some random process; our psychological needs influence the choices we make. So the woman with characteristics of the coquette will try to find a father figure, while the man who is willing to commit himself to her is looking for a daughter. Like George, he is likely to feel unsure of himself around women and wants someone who will make him feel secure and strong; he wants a woman that he can take care of. What he soon discovers, however, is that the woman who made him feel strong and secure initially makes him feel insecure after they have been in the relationship for a while.

It is important to remember that many of the things a coquette does are harmless. They may, in fact, add some spice to relationships that tend to dull with age. Many men who are secure and self-confident can probably tolerate the flirtatiousness of a coquette without any difficulty. But the partners of coquettes are usually in that position because they *do* have some problems with their own self-esteem. While it is always difficult to unravel these things, it may be possible that the man needs to work on changing himself as much as he needs to help his partner change. The first question is a good example of this conflict.

Q: I admit that I'm a jealous person (I have to—my wife has told me often enough), but I think I have reason to be. She must have two men friends for every woman friend she has. The couples we socialize with are mostly people she has met at work, and it's the husband she works with, not the wife. I believe her when she says that they are just friends and that nothing is going on, but it still bothers me. Why can't she be like everyone else? Once you're married, men should have men friends and women should have women friends. Don't you think I have good reason to be upset with her?

A. From your perspective, I suppose you have a good reason to be upset with her, but I think it's your perspective that needs changing and not your wife's choice of friends. The rather silly notion that being married means that you can no longer have friends of the opposite sex is something of a tradition in our society, but your wife is not alone in feeling that it's time that we cast it aside. I agree with her. Both my wife and I value our opposite-sex friends as much as our friends of the same sex.

One thing you might do is to take a look at the kind of men your wife has as friends. I would guess that your wife is attracted to men who are similar to herself—namely, men that seem to be self-assured. Your wife sounds as if she has a lot of self-confidence; not everyone feels secure enough to develop friendships with co-workers of the opposite sex, and usually, couples get together because the women are friends or the men are.

I think the real danger to your relationship is that your wife may grow weary of your insecurity. If she feels that she has to reassure you continually, one day she may decide that she wants someone who will give her some breathing room. Jealous, insecure people have a tendency to smother others. And your wife doesn't sound like the kind of woman who will allow herself to be smothered.

Most men are a little nutty when it comes to women. They don't want the kind of woman nobody else wants—they want a woman that other men find desirable, too. But then they resent it if other men seem to like "their woman" too much. Try to take pride in the fact that you are able to have a relationship with a woman whom other men like. You should also feel good about yourself because you were able to find a wife who has such high self-esteem. Women who don't feel good about themselves will marry anyone who asks them; womn who are comfortable with themselves are much more selective.

Q: I know that I tend to take life too seriously, but my wife doesn't seem willing to take any responsibility at all. Everything was fine until our kids were born, but now I am getting disgusted with her. She wanted to quit her job to take care of the children—she never liked working, anyway—but she does a lousy job of it. The kids look like waifs; they are always dirty and they never have clean clothes. (Neither do I, for that matter.)

She spends most of her time during the day reading romance magazines and watching soap operas. When I try to talk to her about doing a little more around the house she cries and accuses me of not understanding how much work there is to being a housewife. Well, I *do* know; I do most of the work at night. I get mad at myself because when she does start to cry I tell her that it's all right and then do all of her work for her. I do love her, but I don't know how much longer I can go on living like this.

A: Your wife does sound as if she has some of the elements of the coquette personality. Her addiction to romance magazines and soap operas is her way of getting some excitement from life. Of course, everyone wants some excitement, but most people manage to strike some balance between having fun and being responsible.

I think that your wife has gotten herself in a bind that many coquettes find themselves in. On the one hand, she was successful in finding a substitute father for a husband; it sounds as if you're doing an admirable job of filling that role. But once she got that, she found that it wasn't very exciting to be married to a father figure. So she reads the magazines to get a vicarious dose of romance in her life.

The first thing you need to do is stop playing the role of father. When she cries about how hard things are for her, don't pat her on the head and then do her work for her. You wouldn't let your children avoid their responsibilities, so why do you let an adult do it? Try to get her to talk about her situation. If she can admit to feeling unhappy and bored, then you could be on the road to working out a compromise. But whatever you do, don't let her manipulate you with her tears.

Keep in mind that up to now your wife has relied on attention from you to feel good about herself. At this point, she doesn't have the resources to find other avenues of gratification for herself. If you're patient with her, you will be able to help her to develop these other sources of self-fulfillment. Not every woman is cut out to be a supermom, but most can learn to take pleasure in caring for their children and watching them grow. But it is up to you to prime the pump.

People who are trying to change need lots of structure. I think it would be a good idea if the two of you could work out some agreement about your respective responsibilities. For example, if she will agree to keep the children and their clothes clean, you might take on the responsibility of cleaning up the kitchen after dinner. If she agrees to keep the house clean, you might promise to take her out for a romantic evening on the weekend.

Many people find it helpful to have these contracts in writing to make sure that there are no misunderstandings.

If she does not live up to her end of the bargain, don't let her get away with it. Talk to her about it in a calm, reasonable way. If you get angry with her, it will just make her more defensive and all the more unlikely to change. Perhaps you could let her know that if she does not follow through with her end of the deal, you will use your entertainment money to hire a part-time housekeeper. Expect her to have a few relapses, but persist. You don't want to have to spend the rest of your life taking care of children and a wife.

Because the chances are pretty slim that your wife will ever learn to love being a housewife, you might need to help her find other ways in which she can bolster her self-esteem. The best way to do this is for her to find something that she is good at. Nothing breeds self-confidence like successful experiences. The most common way for mothers of young children to do this is with volunteer activities or a part-time job. Don't let her do just anything, but try to steer her into something that will satisfy her psychological needs.

Since she needs attention from adults, it wouldn't do her any good to do volunteer—or paid—work with children. Coquettes often make great salespeople; their vivaciousness and desire to be the center of attention make them naturals for this kind of job. Perhaps she could get involved in real estate, or she could sell advertising for a radio station or local magazine. If she can succeed at something like this, she will probably enjoy the time she does spend with the children more.

Don't expect changes overnight. It just doesn't work that way. But if you can help your wife grow, you will be doing both of you a favor. Being a father figure can be awfully hard work.

Q: I've been living with Anne off and on for the past four years. When she first moved in with me I was the happiest man alive. I wanted to marry her, but she said it would be better if we had a chance to learn how we really felt about each other. Well, after only three months she fell in love with someone else and moved out. But two months later, she came back and begged me to take her back. She said she realized that I was the one she loved.

This has happened six times now. I know that she must have some problems, but do you think that if I keep on taking her back she will realize that I am the right person for her? It drives me crazy every time she moves out, but I love her so much that I'm always happy when she moves back in. But if there's no chance that things will ever work out, I don't want to keep on putting myself through this.

A: I think you realize that you are letting yourself be used. You are Anne's safe harbor; thanks to you, she can go out and have a romantic fling, and when she tires of it or gets dumped, she always has you, so she never has to be alone. You have done a great job of taking on the role of the tireless, self-sacrificing father who will always be there for his spoiled daughter.

No, I don't think that Anne will ever realize—on her own—that you are the one she loves, and be forever after devoted to you. She sounds as if she has a pretty bad case of the coquette personality, and I don't think she will change unless she gets professional help. Most people with self-destructive personality patterns do not want to change; they want other people to accommodate them so that they can continue to live out their conflicts. And I doubt that Anne is any exception.

If you want to live the rest of your life with her, you will have to go through some difficult times. The first step would be not to let her move back in with you the next time a relationship goes sour for her. Tell her that you want to help her and to be her friend, but tell her the truth: Your self-esteem cannot tolerate being rejected by her again. As a condition for your friendship, help her to get started with psychotherapy. Don't think that you can compromise and let her move in with you as long as she begins therapy, though; she has to hurt if she's going to get anything out of therapy, and if you let her move back in, she will be too comfortable. If she is forced to live alone for a while, it may bring out some of her fears, which can help motivate her to stick with the therapy. If she's not hurting, therapy will just become another game for her, and she's good enough to win such games.

If you follow through with this suggestion, be prepared for a pretty intense reaction. The tears and the begging will be the easy part. Women with her personality are prone to sereve depression when they feel rejected, and there is always the possibility of suicidal threats or gestures. Even though it will be hard, you cannot allow yourself to be manipulated by her antics. To give in at this point would mean that you are willing to put up with the status quo. No one can be expected to live his or her life toeing the mark for another person's neurosis.

The only chance you have for a satisfying life with Anne is if her therapy is successful. And even then there are no quarantees. If she can break out of her destructive pattern, she may decide that you are not the kind of man she wants to spend the rest of her life with. But even that would be better than dedicating your life to helping her live out her conflicts.

Q: I don't understand my wife at all. She is one of the sexiest women I have ever known, but she doesn't like sex. I thought women who didn't enjoy sex were the prim and proper type, but she's not like that at all; she dresses sexy, acts sexy, and looks sexy. But she must have the world's worst case of anemia, because she's always "too tired" when we go to bed. When we do make love, it's obvious that she thinks she's doing me a favor. Do you think that maybe she just doesn't love me?

A: Her pattern is one of the classic signs of the coquette personality. She is being faithful to the training that her father gave her: Get the boys to chase you, but whatever you do, don't let them catch you. She has learned that it is okay to present the image of being a sexual woman, but she has also accepted the notion that sex itself is dirty and disgusting. So it's not a matter of love; it is a matter of her overcoming her childhood training.

I think the chances that she will learn to enjoy sex are excellent, but it will be more difficult for her than for the prim and proper type. The prim and proper type generally knows that she is inhibited and is open to the idea that she may be missing out on something. Women such as your wife are usually perfectly happy the way they are; if you were to suggest that she had some conflicts about sex, she could point to a lot of evidence that would—in her mind—prove you wrong. After all, who could dress the way she does, and have had such an active social life before she was married, and yet not like sex? She believes that women are supposed to be the way she is.

In many cases, these women slowly learn to enjoy sex if they have kind, considerate, and persistent lovers. What you have to avoid is accepting her definition of what sex should be like. She probably views it as her obligation to relieve your sexual tensions on occasion, so she would be happy if you got it over with as quickly as possible. Don't let yourself fall into this pattern.

I would guess that your wife likes the trappings of romance, and you can use this to your advantage. Make sex something that starts early in the evening—with a romantic dinner, for example. You have to seduce her, the same way you would if it were your third date. Spend plenty of time caressing her in a loving, affectionate way. Don't skimp on the foreplay. If she urges you to hurry, let her know that you enjoy touching her body and that you are doing it for yourself. If she can relax, she will most likely respond sooner or later. Everyone has the necessary nerve endings, it's a matter of getting past the psychological blocks.

If you do not make any progress after several months, you should try some joint therapy. It is important that you go with her, because if you suggest she go alone she will probably hike up her defenses. Remember, she does not believe she has a problem. A skilled therapist could help her to understand the conflicts about sex that she does have. Once she can talk about her feelings, and with you as a considerate and skilled lover, there will be no stopping her.

Some Final Thoughts

The mark of a well-adjusted person is the ability to play a variety of roles and to select the role that is appropriate for the occasion. Psychologically healthy people can be tender, loving, soft, caring, childlike, and playful, as well as strong, competent, independent, serious, and responsible. They have a sense for when each set of qualities is called for. The problem the coquette has is that she believes these two sets of characteristics are incompatible. In her mind, being strong and responsible would mean that she could not be soft and feminine. And if she were not soft and feminine, no man could ever love her.

The most difficult thing the coquette must learn is that she *can* be strong, competent, and independent without giving up her womanliness. It's so hard for her to learn this because it contradicts the training she received during childhood. But once she gets started, she can turn out to be a fast learner. It can be very gratifying to learn that one can count on one's self, that it is not absolutely necessary to be taken care of and to be the center of attention in order to be happy. She may never become so strong and responsible that she can fill Margaret Thatcher's shoes, but she can learn to be a self-sufficient, self-confident woman. And they are the best kind to have a relationship with.

3
THE LADIES' MAN

The Ladies' Man Test

1. **During high school, girls thought:**
   a. I was the greatest thing around.
   b. I was pretty neat.
   c. I was cute.
   d. I was an alien from outer space.

2. **If I were unattached and I saw an attractive woman sitting alone at a party:**
   a. I would introduce myself.
   b. I would ask her where she has been all my life.
   c. I would find someone to introduce me to her.
   d. I would steal wistful glances at her.

3. **When I was unattached, if I did not have a date come Saturday night:**

a. I would feel depressed and lonely.
b. I would go out and find some new action.
c. I would go out with some friends.
d. I would do what I do almost every Saturday night—stay home and read.

4. Waitresses like me because:
a. they feel like real women when I'm around.
b. I am always pleasant and friendly.
c. I leave big tips.
d. I would never dream of complaining about anything.

5. With regard to women, my friends admire me because:
a. there isn't a woman alive who can resist me.
b. so many women do find me attractive.
c. I can stick with one relationship and be satisfied.
d. I can live so well without them.

6. I've had sex with:
a. at least two dozen women.
b. somewhere between half a dozen and two dozen women.
c. from one to five women.
d. nobody—but I did come close once.

7. Women tend to see me as:
a. a sexy guy you can have a good time with.
b. fun to be around.
c. mature and responsible.
d. blending in with the woodwork.

8. When I meet someone I really care about, the relationship:
a. will be great while it lasts.

b. will be good for both of us.
c. will be forever.
d. will never get off the ground.

9. If I were in a relationship and I met someone new whom I was attracted to:

a. I would think that what my mate doesn't know won't hurt her.
b. I would be very tempted to do something about it.
c. I could never be attracted to someone else when I'm in a relationship.
d. I'll let you know what I would do when I get into a relationship.

10. The relationship I'm in now has lasted:

a. for six months.
b. for several years.
c. throughout my adult life.
d. for my whole life—if you count my mother.

The Ladies' Man Test Scoring Key

1. a. 3 points.
b. 2 points.
c. 1 point.
d. 0 points.

2. a. 2 points.
b. 3 points.
c. 1 point.
d. 0 points.

3. a. 3 points.
b. 2 points.
c. 1 point.
d. 0 points.

4. a. 3 points.
b. 2 points.
c. 1 point.
d. 0 points.

5. a. 3 points.
b. 2 points.
c. 1 point.
d. 0 points.

6. a. 3 points.
b. 2 points.
c. 1 point.
d. 0 points.

7. a. 3 points.
b. 2 points.
c. 1 point.
d. 0 points.

8. a. 3 points if you are past thirty, 2 points otherwise.
b. 2 points.
c. 1 point.
d. 0 points.

9. a. 3 points.
b. 2 points.
c. 1 point.
d. 0 points.

10. a. 3 points.
b. 2 points.
c. 1 point.
d. 0 points.

Interpretation of Test Scores

0 to 6 points: You do not give yourself enough credit. Everyone is capable of being appealing to someone of the opposite sex. You do, however, have to take some chances to find that person.

7 to 15 points: You may wish women found you more appealing, but you may have something that a lot of men want but won't let themselves have—a caring, stable relationship with a woman.

16 to 23 points: Either you are much more appealing to women than the average man, or you have a tendency to view yourself unrealistically. If you tire of relationships quickly and feel a need to move on to something new, the latter is probably the more accurate.

24 to 30 points: Perhaps women really do find you exceptionally attractive, but it is more likely that you are overly concerned with your relationships with women and give yourself more credit than you deserve. No man appeals to all women, and only a handful appeal to most women. You may learn something if you try to look at yourself objectively.

I Never Meant to Hurt Anyone

Frank was a ladies' man—or so he thought. He had been able to attract women ever since he could remember. He recalls that as early as the second or third grade, the cutest girls in the class always wanted to play with him. Second-grade boys would never admit to liking girls, but he did feel a sense of pride that he was the one who was receiving all the attention. He felt that he deserved it; after all, he could run faster, throw a ball farther, and jump higher than any other boy in the school. Being chased by the girls and being envied and admired by the boys made up for the fact that he was not getting much attention at home. He was the third of four boys, and both of his parents had full-time jobs. All the attention he received at school made him feel special. And everyone wants to feel special.

The happiest time in Frank's life was junior high school. "The ninth grade was a high point for me. Girls had always liked me, but I couldn't act as if I cared until about the eighth grade. When I did start to let them know that I liked them back it was great. I had a different girlfriend every week, and my friends would beg me to let me have the old ones. Even my mom and dad and my brothers began to take notice when I would get a couple of phone calls a night from girls. Even though it was all very innocent—I never dreamed of having sex with any of them—I would give anything to have that year over again."

Frank's life took a turn for the worse when he began high school. Instead of being a standout among five hundred students, he was lost in the crowd of nearly three thousand students. He was no longer the star athlete. He could do no better than second string in football and basketball, and while he was the fastest 100-year-dash man on the track team, he lost more races than he won in the citywide track meets. He also became aware that academics was not his long suit. He had done passably well through the ninth grade because he was able to charm his teachers, but high school was a different story. After failing algebra and getting a D in biology his sophomore year, he opted to take business and shop courses instead of the traditional college-prep classes.

His failures in other areas made him try all the harder to charm the girls. By most boys' standards, he was very good at it. He still had lots of girls flirting with him and calling him at night; for the Valentine's Day dance, for which it was traditional for the girls to do the asking, he set a school record with seventeen invitations. But Frank was not satisfied. He could not seem to get the "really classy" girls to go out with him; he wanted to seen with the girls who wore expensive and sophisticated clothes, the ones who were being elected to school offices, the ones who could make or break an ordinary boy's day simply by smiling and saying hello.

These girls, of course, went out with boys who wore expensive and sophisticated clothes, who were being elected to school offices, and who were on the first string of the football and basketball teams. Frank did not quite fit. His parents couldn't afford to buy him expensive clothes, much less his own car to use for his dates. And while the boys he saw himself competing with were planning on attending the prestigious state university or even some elite out-of-state school, the best that Frank could hope for was a small state school or perhaps a community college.

Even though Frank's parents remember being worried

about him during his high school years because he seemed so unhappy, Frank remembers those years with some fondness. "High school was kind of a letdown for me. I realized I wasn't going to win any races in the Olympics and I found out that I just wasn't as smart as most of my friends. But there were lots of good times. I still could attract the women, and late in my junior year I had sex for the first time. My senior year was great—I think I went to bed with a different girl every month. One thing I did learn then was how bitchy some women can be. There were a couple of girls that I really wanted to go out with, but they thought they were too good for me. My favorite fantasy is that I meet them again at our twenty-fifth reunion and they will realize what they passed up. They'll beg me to see them and I won't give them a chance."

Frank was married the year after he graduated from high school. Pat was an attractive, bright girl from the same working-class neighborhood as Frank. She was attracted to Frank's good looks and his charming, flirtatious style. She was also able to sense his feelings of insecurity. His vulnerability made her want to take care of him. Frank loved his wife, and although he would never admit it, he found a great deal of comfort in Pat's strength. The first few years of their marriage were happy for both of them. Since they were both working, they could afford to buy things that Frank's friends, who were attending college, could not. This gave Frank a sense of satisfaction. His friends were gradually but steadily visiting him less and less often, but he felt this was just because they were jealous of him. The only arguments that Frank and Pat ever had revolved around Frank's flirting with other women. Frank claimed that it was harmless, and besides, the women enjoyed it. He could not understand it when Pat claimed that it embarrassed her.

Pat reports that their marriage almost came to an end shortly after the birth of their first child. Frank had always spent one or two nights a week "out with the boys," but these excursions became the rule rather than the exception once Jennifer came on the scene. Pat remembers how devastated she felt. "I thought our life would be perfect once Jennifer was born, but Frank seemed to lose interest in his family. He was going out four or five times a week, and a few months later, one of my friends told me that she had seen Frank in a bar kissing another woman. I was afraid to confront him, because I had quit my job and there was no way that I could take care of Jennifer if he wanted someone else instead of me. I just hoped and prayed that it didn't mean anything to him and that he would stay with us.

"This went on for a couple of years. It became clear to me that he was spending his nights with other women. I think he was careful at first, but he started to get careless. I would find names and telephone numbers and matches from motels in his pockets. I started back to work as soon as I could. I wanted to be able to support Jennifer and myself as soon as possible. When Jennifer was two I told Frank that I knew about the other women and that I wanted him to move out. I was shocked by his reaction. He started to cry and tell me how much he loved me and Jennifer. When I asked him about the other women, all he could say was, 'I never meant to hurt anyone.' "

Men who think of themselves as ladies' men come in all shapes and sizes. Some are like Frank. They are at least reasonably attractive, and they do have some success in attracting women. They are unlikely to be as good at it as they think they are, but they may be pretty good at it nonetheless. Frank, for example, was able to find a woman to spend time with without much difficulty. But he tended to forget about the numerous occasions when he was turned down. In actuality, he met rejection about as often as he met success.

Larry is a good example of a ladies' man who falls at the opposite end of the spectrum. He is a short, overweight, balding man in his late forties, but he continues to believe that young women find him attractive. His confidence in his sex appeal does not seem to have wavered despite his complete lack of success for over twenty-five years and his being told to buzz off (usually in stronger terms) hundreds of times. Larry's favorite target is waitresses. It does not matter that most of them are at least twenty years younger than he is; Larry thinks they're all interested in exchanging sexual repartee with him.

Sheila, Larry's wife, refuses to go out to eat with him anymore. "Larry has always been a flirt, but he seems to have gotten worse over the years. When we were first married, he would make suggestive remarks to other women, but he did it in a gentle, teasing way that most of the girls could accept. It always made me feel uncomfortable, but I knew he was that way when I married him, so I thought I just had to live with it. As he has gotten older, he has become just plain vulgar. What I really can't understand is that it doesn't matter who he's with. He acts the same if we're alone, with our children, or with my parents. He just doesn't seem to realize how disgusted other people are by the way he acts."

Larry, of course, has a completely different perspective. "Sheila claims that I'm vulgar when I do a little innocent flirting, but I think most women like it. It makes them feel appreciated. Who wouldn't feel good when someone lets them know that you think they are sexy? Oh sure, every now and then some uptight chick gets offended, but that's pretty rare. Besides, I'm having fun, and who am I hurting?"

Although they both think of themselves as being ladies' men, Frank and Larry are different in many ways. Frank, while considered a pest by many women, rarely offends anyone. His style is to become friendly first, and then gradually shift the conversation into romantic or sexual directions. He does persist in trying to be friendly to women who are not interested in him, but he does it in a reasonably polite way. Larry, on the other hand, offends most of the women he focuses on. His "innocent flirting" is seen by almost everyone else as a crude form of sexual harassment. A second difference is that while Frank does have sex with many of the women he meets, Larry has not slept with a woman other than his wife in the twenty-six years that they have been married.

They have enough in common, however, to justify placing them in the same category. The most basic similarity is that both of them are motivated by their underlying feelings of insecurity. Although neither Frank nor Larry would admit to or even recognize having such feelings, they have learned that they can make themselves feel better by relating to women in a sexual way. Such men are not searching for sexual variety, but for acceptance and approval—and in some cases, just plain and simple recognition.

These needs for acceptance, approval, or recognition can be satisfied in a variety of ways. Some men, like Frank, feel satisfied only if other women reciprocate their interest. Their goal is to have other women want them—both emotionally and sexually. They will keep on trying until they find a woman who fits the bill. Of course, the satisfaction from finding such a woman is fleeting, and the need to find someone new will surface in short order.

Other men are more like Larry in that they never really expect to have a relationship with the women they flirt with. As long as they are able to elicit some response from women, they are likely to feel satisfied. Interestingly, it does not matter much what the response is. Larry, for example, feels as pleased with himself if a waitress laughs and goes along with his flirtatiousness as he does if she blushes and becomes curt with him. In either case, he takes the woman's reaction as evidence that she is flattered by the attention. He has to be told that his remarks are not appreciated—in very explicit terms—before he will slow down. The satisfaction for these men seems to come from forcing women to acknowledge their existence as sexual creatures.

These men want to be approved of by the women they flirt with, but perhaps just as important is the approval they need from other people. Their feelings of self-worth are bound up in their self-image as ladies' men, and they want other people to see them in the same way. Most boys begin their heterosexual careers partly to win the approval of their friends; the boy who is the first to get up his nerve to approach the pretty new student gets as much pleasure from the envy and admiration of his friends as he does from meeting the girl. Self-proclaimed ladies' men never outgrow this. Their flirting is often intended to impress others as much as to impress the women involved. What they don't realize is that as they grow older their friends are likely to be disgusted by their behavior. I have a couple of "former friends" that I no longer see because I did not want anyone to think that I approved of the way they related to women.

Roger came to realize that he belonged in this category. "I always thought that it was a game to come on to women, and I thought that I was just better at it than my friends were. One day my secretary asked me why I was so much nicer to her when we were alone than I was when other people were around. At first I didn't believe her, but she told me that several of my friends had apologized for me for some of the things I had said to her. I checked with a couple of them and she was right. They thought that I was a jerk around women. All that time I thought they admired me for my way with the ladies."

Because admiration, acceptance, and recognition are so

crucial to these men, their sexual interest in women tends to be superficial. Remember Frank, who would give anything to have his ninth-grade year over again. Most men would rather have his senior year, when Frank was having sex with a number of different girls. But for Frank, being the most sought-after boy in his class was much more important to him than the girls or the sex. Although they would never admit it, men like Larry would gladly give up their capacity to have sex if they could be assured that all women would find them irresistible. The chase is much more important than the conquest. And many of those would not know what to do if a woman took them up on their hints. For these men, the chase is everything; the conquest is terrifying.

Self-proclaimed ladies' men may go from relationship to relationship, but frequently they marry a woman whom they truly care about. They are likely to view her, at an unconscious level, as someone who is unattainable—a woman who is too good for them. They are tied to the relationship because they can never feel completely confident that they have made the "conquest." Such women are likely to be strong individuals who may fall into a maternalistic relationship with their husbands. Like Pat, who married Frank because he seemed vulnerable and needed to be taken care of, these women seem to be attracted to the boyish qualities of their husbands.

Just because these men love their wives and want to maintain the relationship does not mean that they are going to give up other women. On the contrary, aspects of their marriage may strengthen their need to seek acceptance and approval from other women. Frank was one of these men. "Before Jennifer was born, I used to kid around with other women, but I was never unfaithful to Pat. I loved her too much. When Jennifer and Pat came home from the hospital I thought I had it made. But it didn't take long before it was clear to me that Pat loved Jennifer more than she loved me. I was so depressed about it that when a girl I knew asked me if I wanted to come over to her place for a drink I said yes. I felt guilty about it, but I also felt happier than I had for months. I had all those affairs because I felt so bad about what was happening to Pat and me."

Meanwhile, Pat had no idea what was going on with her husband. She loved him as much as she always had—she just did not have as much time to spend with him after the baby came on the scene. She was taken completely by surprise when Frank explained his feelings to her. "I was sure that he'd lost interest in me because of what being pregnant did to my body. I always knew that he appreciated attractive women, and I thought that he was out looking for someone who hadn't lost her figure. I worked hard to get back to my normal weight, but when he still didn't come home I said the hell with him. I'm not one to beg. After I told him I was leaving, I was amazed by his reaction. I expected him to be happy to be rid of me; I never expected him to beg me to stay. At first I was disgusted with him. How can a grown man be jealous of a baby? But I do love him, so we're trying to work things out."

Not all women can work things out. For many, infidelity is the greatest sin imaginable. Once they learn that their husbands have been involved with another woman, they have no interest in preserving the relationship. Many other women, however, have learned to live with it. For many years Marge knew that she could expect her husband to have about one affair a year. "The first time I found out that he had been sleeping with another woman I moved out of the house without even talking to him. He begged me to come back and promised that it would never happen again, so I agreed to give it another chance. Well, it did happen again . . . and again . . . and again. I got to the point where I could accept it pretty well. As Ann

Landers says, 'Are you better off with him or without him?' He was a great father, and in every other way a good husband. I would just tell myself that it was better for him to spend a few hours with another woman now and then than to gamble away all our money or to drink himself to death, or to have some other terrible problem. As far as I know, he hasn't been involved with anyone else for some time now. Maybe he just got too old for that kind of thing, but I think he finally realized that he wasn't going to get rid of me, so he might as well take me seriously."

In order to be able to live with a ladies' man, a woman must be either extremely secure or insecure. A secure woman will see her partner's episodes for what they are—a sign of *his* problems. She may decide she doesn't want to put up with him, but she will not feel that it is impossible for her to live with such a man. She will base her decision on the overall merits of the relationship.

Insecure women will view their partner's wandering as a sign of their own deficiencies. They may think, "If only I could lose a few pounds and get my figure in shape," or "If only I could be more exciting in bed for him, then he would love only me." So they may go on forever trying to win their partner's undivided attention without ever realizing that the problem is his and not theirs.

Living with the self-proclaimed ladies' man can be frustrating and heartbreaking. Few things can be taken as such a clear sign of rejection as a partner's involvement with someone else, or a partner's giving the impression that he would like to be. As difficult as it is, remember that these men do not get involved with, or flirt with, other women because of their feelings of dissatisfaction with their partner. It is a style that they bring with them into marriage or a long-term relationship. Their behavior should not be taken as a sign that the woman is deficient in some way.

Development of the Ladies' Man

As the cases I have discussed above suggest, the core of the ladies' man pattern is self-doubt about one's worth as a human being. These men have grown up with the feeling that perhaps no one really loves them—or even worse, that no one *could* love them. These are not feelings that these men are aware of or would admit to having, but nonetheless, they are there, and they are responsible for their compulsive search for love and approval.

In some instances the reasons for these feelings are obvious. Allen's parents made it perfectly clear to him that he was not loved. He was an only child and an unplanned one. His parents, whom it would be kind to describe as immature, were both interested in their careers and in having a good time. Allen's presence made it inconvenient for them to do so. "They weren't really mean to me. They mostly ignored me. I remember spending most of my childhood with baby-sitters. I do remember a few times when they had weekend trips planned for the two of them and the baby-sitter canceled. I would overhear them talk about how much trouble I was and how much easier things would have been if they had only been more careful."

In other cases it is difficult to understand why children develop these doubts. Frank, for example, could not remember a single incident that would suggest that his parents did not love him. "My mom and dad were both good people. They had four boys and they both had to work to make ends meet, so they couldn't spend a lot of time with any one of us. They weren't the type to show much affection, but they never gave any of us any indication that we weren't wanted. I think I just felt kind of left out. My two older brothers always seemed to have something interesting to talk about, and my little brother was the baby, so he needed more attention. I just wanted them to think that I was someone special, but they never seemed to notice."

In some cases, the doubts about one's lovableness center on the relationship with the mother. Mothers are given more responsibility than they deserve for the problems of their children; fathers, of course, have just as much responsibility for the development of children as do mothers. but in the case of the ladies' man pattern, the mother's role may be somewhat more important than the father's.

Ralph clearly falls into this category. "My mother was a cold, aloof woman who had—and has—lots of problems of her own. My dad tried to make up for it by showering my two sisters and me with lots of affection. I still remember, though, trying to make my mother love me. I don't think she ever has."

Ralph carried his self-doubts into his marriage. He married a woman who had some of the same qualities as his mother. Although his wife was capable of loving, she was somewhat reserved on the surface. Ralph never could feel secure about his wife's feelings about him, and he would periodically seek comfort from other women. Inevitably, after each fling he would be overcome with remorse and would tell his wife about it. What Ralph did not realize was that he was trying to prove to his wife that he was worthy of being loved.

Lots of children grow up feeling a little unsure about how much their parents love them, so these feelings alone will not cause one to become a compulsive skirt-chaser. Most people find other ways of coping with such feelings. They may try to be a big success at their jobs to win the admiration of others. Or they may delve into community activities to prove to others, as well as themselves, what kind of people they are. There are lots of socially acceptable ways of dealing with these feelings.

Ladies' men seek their reassurance from women because they have a knack for it. At some time in their lives, they were quite good at making women like them. Recall Frank, who had girls chasing him the entire time he was in school. Even Larry, who was considered repulsive by the young women he so desperately wanted to impress, had his quota of conquests when he was younger. "I wasn't the best-looking guy in high school, but I could always make girls laugh. I could say things to them that no one else could get away with. I could do it in a way that they would think was funny. Once you can get a girl to laugh, you've won the battle. I haven't lost that ability."

Sadly, Larry is the only one who thinks that he has not lost that ability. His wife, his friends, and especially the girls he tries to make laugh think he is vulgar and boorish. But because he got such good results for a number of years, he cannot see that it no longer works for him. Also, he still believes that his friends admire him for his way with women because his friends of thirty years ago did. Like all imperfect people, he has his blind spot that gets him into trouble without his even knowing it.

When these men tell the women with whom they have a commitment that they never meant to hurt anyone, they really mean it. Even though it may be hard for the women involved to believe it, they do not do the things they do to humiliate, exploit, or in any other way hurt anyone. They are doing it to try to cope with the hurt that is buried deep within themselves.

Living with the Ladies' Man

Living with a ladies' man may be more difficult than living with any other type of imperfect person. Our society still tends to view infidelity as one of the worst sins that a married person can commit. How can a woman be expected to be understanding while she watches her husband flirt with the waitress? How can she face her friends when she knows that her husband has tried to seduce them? It is nearly impossible not to feel very angry at such men. Most women leave such a relationship if they are able to, and if they aren't, their love turns to hate in short order. There are some women, though, who have managed to get past these feelings and have salvaged their relationships. It is very difficult, but it can be done.

Q: I have been living with someone for three years now, but he still sees other women. He says that they don't mean anything to him and until we are married it's okay for him to fool around. He promises to stop as soon as I agree to marry him. I want to believe him, but it's pretty hard. Is there any chance he'll be faithful to me if I do marry him?

A: Not much. It sounds as if he is one of those men whose self-esteem depends on getting lots of attention from women. Lots of men fool around some when they are dating one woman regularly, but most men who feel committed enough to a woman to live with her also feel the need to be monogamous. That's not to say they may not have an affair if they meet someone they are attracted to, but they will at least try to be discreet about it. From the way you present things, your friend seems to take some pride in letting you know about his relationships with other women.

His need for an occasional ego boost from another woman may be especially intense right now. I would guess that he thinks of you as being a little too good for him, and your refusal to marry him is making him feel insecure. His letting you know about the other women may be his way of trying to prove to you how desirable he is. If you did marry him it would do a lot for his self-esteem, and this would help him carry through with his resolutions for a while—but only for a while. Sooner or later he will begin to feel insecure again, this could be anywhere from a few months to a few years after you are married.

Do not fool yourself into believing that you can make him feel so secure that he will never feel the need to find comfort from another woman. Men who fall into this pattern are looking for signs of rejection, and they make sure they find them. It could be something as simple as your talking on the phone too long when he wants you to watch television with him, or your spending a Saturday afternoon shopping with your mother; either could be seen as evidence that you care more about someone else than you do about him. His reactions will not be rational, so do not think that you can help him overcome his feelings of insecurity simply by being especially sensitive to his needs.

I think there is a chance that you could make a marriage work eventually, but since he is so open about his other women now, before you are married, the odds are not in your favor. If you decide to marry him, be prepared to deal with at least a few "other women." It takes time for men to get past this pattern.

Q: Most of my husband's friends are women from the store where he works. He car-pools with them, eats lunch with them, and even talks on the phone with them every now and then. He gets mad when I ask him if there's anything going on, and I guess I believe him. But even if he's not having an affair with any of them, I don't think it's right for him to be such good friends with other women. I should be the only woman he's close to. He says that most of the people he works with are women, so there's nothing unusual about his being friends with them. Should I be concerned about the situation?

A: That depends upon what you expect from him. If you expect your husband never to have a close relationship with another woman, then it sounds as if he has already let you down. But if that is your expectation, it is pretty unrealistic. I know I wouldn't like it if my wife had such expectations of me, and I don't blame your husband for not liking it.

Your husband's explanation for why he has so many women for friends sounds reasonable. The people we work with are a major source of friendships, so if he is around women all day, it is to be expected that he would have them as friends.

The chances are that he does have a close relationship with at least one of them. Most men have difficulty talking about anything too intimate with other men; while women want to share their troubles with other women, men tend to view it as a sign of weakness to discuss anything personal with another man. They do feel comfortable, however, about sharing these aspects of their lives with another woman; when asked, a substantial percentage of men report that their best friend is a woman—not another man. So your husband would be unusual if he were not emotionally intimate with one of his friends.

I think what really worries you is that he will become sexually involved with one of his women friends. While that is always a possibility, he is no more likely to have an affair than a man who has mostly other men for friends. It is possible, contrary to popular stereotypes, for men and women to be emotionally intimate without being sexually intimate.

It could be that your husband is satisfying needs of his own by selecting women for friends. Some men who crave attention from other women are content with emotional intimacy. Perhaps having lunch with another woman now and then does for him what having an affair would do for other men. Even if this is the case, I think you would be wise to let well enough alone. His having a close relationship with another woman does not take away anything from his feelings for you.

Q: My husband thinks that he's God's gift to women. He's been a flirt ever since I've known him, but he's getting worse as he gets older. It wouldn't be so bad except the ones he picks to flirt with are at least thirty years younger than he is. My stomach is tied up in knots every time we're in a restaurant. I pray that the waitress won't ask him what he would like—his favorite opening line. When we were younger, I didn't mind so much, because he was kind of clever about it. But the older he gets, the more vulgar he seems to be.

He's worst at parties. Last month my sister had a big family party for her silver anniversary. He spent the entire evening dancing—if you could call it that—with every twenty-year-old woman there. Some of them were nieces, and some were women married to our nephews. A lot of them came from out of town and he didn't even know them. Most of the women would tell him they didn't want to dance, but he would just grab them and take them off. I have never been so humiliated in my entire life.

When I try to talk to him about it, he just says I'm blowing things out of proportion. He just won't believe that everyone else is as disgusted with him as I am. He actually thinks I'm jealous. Even though we've had a good life together in most ways, I'm finished with being embarrassed by him. Is there any chance I can get him to change, or should I just give up on him?

A: There is some chance you can help him, but you do have to be prepared for some very difficult and uncomfortable moments if you are going to be successful. It sounds as if you want to keep your marriage together, so I think it would be worth the effort. Be warned, however, that it will be a tough battle.

The reason your husband's behavior has gotten worse over the years is that he has had to be more dramatic to get a reaction from the women he wants attention from—the young and attractive ones. As you said, he was clever about it when he was younger. He could afford to be then; when he was flirting with women about his own age, they probably did not mind, since apparently he was good at it. As the difference between his age and theirs increased, they probably felt uncomfortable about his comments, regardless of how clever they were, and chose to ignore them. So his only recourse was to step up the attack. Unfortunately, men with his tendencies do not seem to be able to recognize the difference between a woman who is embarrassed because a stranger says something flattering to her and a woman who is embarrassed because a man is making a fool out of himself. I'm sure that he still thinks that women are flattered by his attention.

The most difficult thing about men like your husband is that they refuse to believe it when they are told that their behavior is disgusting. As I mentioned earlier, I gave up on a few friends because they were offended when I tried to tell them how I thought the women they flirted with were reacting. Anyone who tells them something like that is dismissed as being jealous (as you are), or prudish, a stick in the mud (as I was), and so on. Also, relatively few people are assertive enough to say those kinds of things, so it's easy for such a man to dismiss the few who do have the courage to tell him how obnoxious he is. It is amazing what most people will let others get away with.

The first line of attack should be to encourage as many

people as possible to let him know what they think of him. They are probably holding back, in part, because they do not want to hurt your feelings. Explain to them what the situation is—that he thinks every young woman has as much fun with him as he has with them—and that you would appreciate it if they could let him know how they really feel. Not all of them will do it, but they will be much more likely to with your encouragement.

Second, start apologizing for him in front of him. This will probably make him angry, but it will increase the likelihood that he will get some insight into how others perceive him. One woman who tried this got great results the very first time. When a cocktail waitress asked her husband what he would like (a line that every ladies' man loves), he replied, "A weekend alone with you." The wife apologized to the waitress, explaining that her husband thought he was being clever when he said things like that, whereupon the waitress replied that she was used to rude drunks. Her husband was so surprised that he would be thought of in that way that he never did it again. If you apologize for him, you make it a lot easier for the other woman to make some comment about how she feels.

If these two strategies do not get results, your only option is to give him warning that you are prepared to divorce him if he does not change his ways. Since you sound as if you are ready to take that step now, you do not have anything to lose. He probably does not realize just how uncomfortable his behavior makes you. If you let him know that you are ready to leave him, it will be hard for him to dismiss the issue as trivial.

If it is any consolation to you now, you can expect your husband to slow down in the next few years. Part of the reason he is getting worse as he is getting older may be that he is resisting being placed into the senior-citizen category. He wants to think of himself as a middle-aged man that young women still find attractive. What most fifty-year-old men do not realize is that twenty-year-old women think men in their middle thirties are middle-aged. But in any case, most men do come to accept their status as elderly and realize on their own how absurd their behavior is.

Some Final Thoughts

Most men who get involved with women outside of a committed relationship do not fall in the same category as the men I have described in this chapter—self-proclaimed ladies' men. It is difficult to know these kind of things with any certainty, but surveys suggest that 60 percent of all married men will have an affair by the age of forty. Probably only a fraction of these men are having affairs compulsively to satisfy their underlying feelings of insecurity.

Lots of men—and women—do have affairs to build up their self-esteem, but for most of them it is a highly unusual event. Men who realize they are not going to be president of the company may feel they need the reassurance that a relationship with a different woman can offer. Women who may be depressed by the thought that they are losing their appeal as they move into middle age can be rejuvenated by the attentions of a man other than their husband. With even a modicum of understanding, many people can deal with these relatively rare events and move forward with their relationship.

The kind of man that I have described in this chapter is much more difficult to deal with. He has a compulsive need to receive attention from other women. The satisfaction he receives from any one woman is likely to be short-lived, so he goes through lots of women in relatively little time. One note of optimism is that frequently he does care deeply about his wife, or the woman with whom he has a stable relationship. He regrets hurting the most important woman in his life and is genuinely puzzled about why he continues to do things that do cause so much pain. As long as this caring exists, there is reason to believe that such men can develop into less imperfect people. It requires an extraordinary amount of understanding and patience, but it can be done.

4

THE NICE GUY

The Nice Guy Test

1. **The last time I got really angry:**
   a. was right now. I can't stand such stupid questions!
   b. was the last time I talked to my partner.
   c. was sometime during the past month or two.
   d. was when I was three.

2. **When I get angry with my partner:**
   a. the neighbors close their windows.
   b. I say what's on my mind.
   c. I count to ten before saying anything.
   d. I can't imagine such a thing.

3. **Most people think of me as being:**
   a. a person who says exactly what's on his or her mind.

b. someone who is forthright.
c. a very tactful person.
d. a person who never complains.

4. If I felt I deserved a raise at work, I would:
a. demand that I get it.
b. point out to my supervisor that I was due for a raise.
c. tell my co-workers and hope they would pass it along.
d. hope that my supervisor would remember.

5. As a teenager, I:
a. was a real hell-raiser.
b. got into the usual trouble—nothing too serious.
c. would make my parents mad because I never got home on time.
d. was too scared of my parents to get into any trouble.

6. If somebody said something to me that was insulting, I would:
a. let him or her know I didn't like it.
b. try to think of an equally insulting comment.
c. be mad, but I probably wouldn't say anything.
d. think that he or she didn't really mean it.

7. I think that anger:
a. has to be expressed openly or else it will rot your insides out.
b. should be acted on; you need to solve whatever it is that is causing the anger.
c. has its place, but it can be overdone.
d. is the least productive emotion of all.

8. If my partner asks me to do something that I don't want to do:

a. I make my feelings clear and don't do it.
b. I complain about it, and I may or may not end up doing it.
c. I do it but I grumble plenty while I'm doing it.
d. I promise to do it, but it may take me quite a while to get around to it.

9. If I feel annoyed with my partner:
a. I tell him or her to stay out of my way.
b. I tell him or her about it to try to work something out.
c. I don't say anything to him or her, but I'm a little grumpy.
d. I hardly ever feel that way.

10. My partner asks me if I'm upset about something:
a. never—he or she never has to ask.
b. sometimes—like when I've had a bad day at work and don't want to talk about it.
c. sometimes—I don't like to talk about every little thing that bothers me.
d. all the time—and I wish he or she would stop it.

The Nice Guy Test Scoring Key

1. a. 0 points.
b. 1 point.
c. 2 points.
d. 3 points.

2. a. 0 points.
b. 1 point.
c. 2 points.
d. 3 points.

3. a. 0 points.
b. 1 point.
c. 2 points.
d. 3 points.

4. a. 0 points.
b. 1 point.
c. 2 points.
d. 3 points.

5. a. 0 points.
b. 1 point.
c. 2 points.
d. 3 points.

6. a. 0 points.
b. 1 point.
c. 2 points.
d. 3 points.

7. a. 0 points.
b. 1 point.
c. 2 points.
d. 3 points.

8. a. 0 points.
b. 1 point.
c. 2 points.
d. 3 points.

9. a. 0 points.
b. 1 point.
c. 2 points.
d. 3 points.

10. a. 0 points.
b. 1 point.
c. 2 points.
d. 3 points.

Interpretation of Test Scores

0 to 7 points: You probably do have problems with your relationship, but it is not with being a *super* nice guy. You seem to confuse assertiveness with aggressiveness.

8 to 14 points: You sound as if you are dealing with your aggressive feelings in an appropriate way. Skip on to the next chapter.

15 to 23 points: You don't quite fit the *super* nice guy category, but you could profit from learning to express your feelings of anger more directly. This chapter could be important for you.

24 to 30 points: You clearly have problems expressing and recognizing angry feelings. Don't fool yourself by believing that you can go on like this forever. Read this chapter now!

Honestly, I Just Forgot

Judy is more than happy to tell anyone who will listen that her marriage to Mark is nearly perfect. Mark is the kindest, sweetest man she has ever known. Even though, as Judy is quick to admit, she has something of a temper, Mark never loses patience with her. "Sometimes I do fly off the handle and get a little crazy about little things, but Mark always seems to understand. He can talk to me in that nice calm voice of his and before long, I will be laughing at my outburst. I don't know how I could have been so lucky as to find Mark. I know that I am far from perfect, but Mark has never once, in four years of marriage, complained about something I have done. At times I do feel bad about it, because I don't hesitate to let him know about the things he does that irritate me, but I do feel good that my husband can accept me so completely—faults and all."

Mark feels good about his marriage too. "I love Judy and I think we are right for each other. I admit that there are some things about her that get on my nerves. For example, I really don't understand why she makes such a big deal out of the smallest things. She can get really worked up if when we get home from the store the bread is a little smashed, or an egg or two is cracked. She'll rant and rave about how careless the bag boy is and take the stuff right back to the store and demand to exchange it. She also tends to be a little pushy in planning our lives for us. Sometimes when I'm looking forward to spending the evening with a good book, I'll discover that she has made arrangements for us to go out with friends. I suppose it's good that she is that way, because if it were up to me, we'd probably never go anywhere. So I've learned to accept her for what she is."

The biggest concern in Mark's life is his job. For the past three years, Mark has been working for a large commercial real estate company as a property manager. Everything went extremely well for him for the first few years. Mark's even temper and calm way of dealing with people seemed to make him a natural for handling the day-to-day disputes that occur between property owners, contractors, and tenants. His boss promised Mark often that as soon as he learned that phase of the business, he would receive a big promotion.

About a year ago, Mark received a big disappointment. The manager in the planning and acquisitions department left, and Mark knew that with his education and experience, he was the perfect person for that position. But things didn't work out. As Mark tells it, "I was sure that I would get the job. I knew I had done well in property management. The company had received several letters from both tenants and owners stating how much they appreciated the way I handled things, and in our business, getting a letter with good news in it is very unusual. But at the last minute, the son of the president of the company decided that he would like to try real estate, so he got the job. I couldn't be angry, because I know the president has to put his son before me, but I was really let down. I really wanted that job."

Now, a year later, Mark is in danger of losing his job. After being passed over for the promotion, he decided to work even harder to make sure that he got the next one that came along. But in spite of his intentions, his work has been slipping badly. He has developed a tendency to forget to return phone calls, and he puts off starting to do his reports until he doesn't have enough time to get them done when they are due. Mark doesn't understand what is happening to him. "I'm trying to do a good job, but I just can't seem to do everything that's expected of me. I know I've forgotten to do some things that were pretty important, but hell, nobody's perfect. Why can't they realize how hard I am trying?"

Judy has noticed some changes in Mark as well. While he is the same even-tempered person he has always been, he does not seem to be as quick to smooth things over as he used to be. When she has one of her "little outbursts," as both Judy and Mark refer to them, he becomes sullen and withdrawn rather than trying to make her feel better. "The thing that bothers me the most is that he seems to be losing his memory. On a night that we have plans to go out, he'll forget and work late. Or when I ask him to come home a little early to watch the kids because I'm going shopping with friends, it will completely leave his mind and he'll show up an hour late. He's always very apologetic and I know he's under a lot of pressure at work, but it's really getting on my nerves. Last week was the last straw. We were having my mother over to dinner and I needed a few things from the store. I called him just as he was leaving the office to ask him to pick them up. Well, when he got home, he took one look at me and whined, 'Honestly, I just forgot.' "

Everyone feels angry on occasion. It is not possible to live with other people without experiencing this very basic emotion from time to time. We all have some plans for what we would like our lives to be like—however vague they may be—and other people have a tendency to disrupt them. And when our plans are disrupted, there are very few of us who can adjust without an emotional reaction of some kind.

Most of us will feel some irritation or anger, depending on the magnitude of the disruption, but there are many people like Mark who simply cannot admit that they have these feelings. For them, anger is extremely frightening. They cannot recognize it in themselves, and when they see it in other people, they panic because they do not know how to deal with it. Their immediate impulse is to do something to smooth things over as quickly as possible, since anger is viewed as a bad thing that must be deflected rather than dealt with directly. So Mark is quick to try to humor Judy whenever she expresses the least amount of irritation. In his role as property manager, he will do anything for his clients, no matter how unreasonable, to keep them from getting angry. As a result of using this style, people like Mark are able to think of themselves as nice guys, and they are able to avoid dealing with their own underlying conflicts.

But the feelings are there, and they demand expression. They may never be expressed directly, but they will be expressed. Mark's nice guy routine causes him to "forget." He admits that he does not like it when his wife makes plans for the two of them without consulting him, but he cannot admit, even to himself, that it makes him mad. He even uses a convoluted line of reasoning to conclude that it's all for the best; as he says, if his wife did not make plans for them, they might never go anywhere. But not even Mark can go on forever repressing his own feelings so as to be able to avoid any friction. So he has to work late to complete a report, or he has to see a tenant whose problem absolutely cannot wait until the morning. Or he simply forgets. He is always properly repentant; he promises not to let it happen again, and he is so sincere that Judy forgives him and really does believe that he will do better. But he does worse and is destined to do worse as long as he feels compelled to hang on to his nice guy routine.

Nice guys vary in terms of how much awareness they

have of their own behavior. Mark, for instance, hasn't the foggiest idea what is going on. He really thinks of himself as even-tempered, and if it was pointed out to him that he has conflicts about expressing anger, he would deny it. He would say that he viewed anger as an unproductive emotion and simply does not experience it. Mark could never admit that he felt angry when the boss's son received the promotion that he knew he deserved; if asked, he would say that there was nothing he could do about it, so what would be the point of getting angry? He knows that he tenses up anytime his wife or someone he works with expresses any anger, but he explains this by saying to himself that anger simply gets in the way of solving problems.

He sees no connection between his feelings and his forgetting; he believes that he just tends to be absent-minded, and if it seems to be getting any worse in recent months, it is because he is under so much pressure at work. He feels genuinely bad about his lapses, and he promises himself, as well as others, that he will do better in the future.

Other nice guys have a pretty clear idea of what they are doing. Marsha, for instance, takes pleasure in frustrating her husband with her lapses. "Gary has a hot temper, and you just can't deal with him by getting angry back. So when I'm mad at him, I'll do something that I know will get to him. I'll forget to pick up his dry cleaning during the day so he'll have to go out for it himself. Or I might forget and put starch on his shirts. He always gets mad about it, but when he sees how devastated I am, he always ends up apologizing." What Marsha does not recognize is that her husband's temper is merely an excuse for not expressing her own feeling of anger. She does not get mad at anyone else, either, but she is not around these people as much as her husband, so it is easy for her not to acknowledge her inhibitions.

Other people fall somewhere between these two extremes. Jerry does not like his brother-in-law, but he would never dream of telling his wife no when she asks if it is okay if he and his family come to visit for a week. He feels an obligation to be nice to them, because, after all, his wife is nice to *his* relatives. He deals with this conflict between being a nice guy and acting on his feelings by looking for things to do the week of the visit. A trip to the beach has to be passed because a meeting at work comes up that he cannot afford to miss. An out-of-town client is visiting, so he has to miss dinner because no one else in the office can deal with this person as well as he can.

Jerry does not do these things intentionally. "At the time, I don't think there's anything unusual about the things that seem to come up while he's visiting, but afterward, I realize that it's not just a coincidence. I miss important meetings when my parents come to visit, and I know that there are half a dozen other salesmen in the office who could take the out-of-town client to dinner. And I don't fool my wife. She tells me all the time that I just don't like her brother. What I don't understand about myself is why I just can't admit it. I have never told her how I feel about him, and I'm not sure why I don't like him. He seems like a nice enough guy.

"I must admit to doing other similar things. I confess to being torn between feeling an obligation to do house-maintenance kinds of things and hating to do that kind of work. I'm very good at promising my wife to do anything as long as it's two weeks down the road. Two weeks later, of course, I've completely forgotten whatever it was I promised to do. This isn't a pattern I engage in deliberately—I'm completely sincere when I promise to repair the fence or paint the trim on the house. But the evidence is too strong for even me to deny that my excuses for not getting around to it ring rather hollow."

Being a nice guy is one of those styles that can prove to be adaptive for a while, but turn out to be fatal to one's psychological well-being in the long run. For instance, children who never express their anger toward parents or teachers are treasured by both. When *super* nice guys first begin their careers, their bosses love them for their even-tempered, agreeable ways. In intimate relationships, these people are initially seen as being exceptionally kind, considerate, and thoughtful. Remember how Judy liked the way that Mark seemed so accepting of all of her faults? Nice guys often make it to adulthood with other people thinking of them as being paragons of mental health.

Their repressed feelings start to catch up with them after they have been in relationships for a while and their careers begin to progress. After being with Judy four years, Mark is beginning to show subtle signs that he resents her taking control of the relationship. Of course, he feels helpless to express these feeling directly, so he begins to withdraw. While he used to try to humor his wife out of her bad moods, he has taken to walking away from her and giving her the "silent treatment." His silence might be tolerable, except even then, he will not admit that anything is bothering him.

The only alternative for people like Mark is to withdraw psychologically and emotionally. First, he tries to humor his wife out of her fits of anger. The next step is to use the silent treatment; and finally, he just stops caring what she does altogether. His reward is being able to tell himself what a nice guy he is and what an impossible woman his wife is; he can tell himself that no one could get along with someone like her. Of course, he does not really know this, because he has never really tried. His primary motive is to avoid confrontation at all costs even if it means losing an important relationship.

On the job, they may make great supervisees, but they usually make poor supervisors. After graduating from college, Marsha got a job in a large department store in a management-training track. Her willingness to do anything asked of her without complaint made her a favorite for the first two years of her job. But when she did receive her first important promotion and was responsible for the floor workers in a large department, she was in real trouble. If she saw employees standing around talking rather than doing their jobs, she usually turned the other way and pretended not to see them. If she needed to have someone do some extra work, she was so fearful of the possibility that the person would be mad at her that she would ask in an almost apologetic way. It did not take long before her employees learned that she could not confront anyone, and they took advantage of her. When she reached the point where she could no longer contain her anger at one of her people, she would recommend to the personnel department that the employee be let go; that way, she never would have to confront the person. Nine months after she took over, morale and efficiency in her department were way down.

At the core of the nice guy syndrome is the inability to distinguish between shades of irritation, hostility, and anger. These people place politely asking a waiter to take back a steak that was not prepared as ordered and screaming at the paper boy for not getting the paper on the porch in the same category. They are both viewed as acts of aggression. The most inappropriate act of hostility and the most reasonable assertion of one's rights and wishes are seen as one and the same. So Mark would have as much trouble asking his wife to stop making plans without consulting him as he would giving his boss a piece of his mind for treating him so shabbily.

Nice guys can be frustrating to live with, because they have trouble distinguishing these emotions in others as well. They are likely to accuse the people they live with of being angry anytime they express dissatisfaction about anything, regardless of how tactfully it is done. Most people who know Judy, for example, do not think of her as an angry woman. They admire and respect her because she does let people know what she thinks about things, and she is not afraid to stand up for herself. After watching Judy and Mark together, it does not take long to realize that anytime Judy so much as changes the tone of her voice, Mark accuses her of being angry. It is ironic that while the manager of the grocery store where Judy and Mark shop appreciates Judy's letting him know when something is wrong, Mark views her returning things as a sign of her bitchiness. But the manager is smart enough to know that if he takes care of Judy's complaints, which are always reasonable, she will keep coming back. Mark's inclination is simply to try another store.

Like Judy, the people who live with nice guys often end up feeling that they must be inadequate in some way. If their partner never complains about anything and becomes increasingly distant, there is only one reasonable conclusion. They really *do* need to learn to control their "bad temper." They may think that if only they could learn to be nicer, like their partner, then everything would be okay. They believe that the deteriorating relationship is their fault, that they must have driven their partner away with their anger and their demanding ways. Unfortunately, to be "nice" enough to satisfy the nice guy would require them to completely suppress any expression of their own needs, wants, and desires. They have not driven their partner away; rather, the nice guy has retreated to avoid facing his or her own conflicts.

If a nice guy happens to get together with someone who also tends to avoid conflicts—such as the compulsive personality or the avoider—everything may work out reasonably well. These people often go through life keeping their feelings to themselves and may be as happy as they are capable of being. There will always be some distance between partners when both of them are trying to avoid conflicts, but they usually get what they want—peace and quiet. It is at the cost of intimacy, but for these people this is a small price to pay.

Nice guys will not do so well if they are paired up with someone who resolves inner conflicts in a more aggressive way. Ladies' men, coquettes, and egotists are examples of personality types that would stretch to the breaking point the nice guy's ability to overlook. The nice guy's anger would build past the point of no return if he had to cope with such patterns of behavior.

Development of the Nice Guy

A crucial part of the socialization process of any child is teaching him or her to control feelings of anger. We all come into the world with no ability to think of anyone but ourselves, and during those first few months of life, when we do not get what we want, we are quick to let others know about it; when we are hungry, we scream until someone feeds us. It does not take long, however, before most of us begin to learn that we have to inhibit our own selfish wants and defer to others. For instance, as toddlers, we learn that we cannot have a toy that another child is playing with simply because we want it. We learn that it is important to share, and that having a temper tantrum will not always help us get what we want; in fact, it may get us a trip to our room or a spanking instead.

During these early experiences, parents begin to differ in the kind of training they provide for their children. Some are quite indulgent in giving their children what they want. They do not want to see their children unhappy, so they allow themselves to be controlled by their child's temper. As everyone knows, indulgent parents are likely to have spoiled, demanding children.

Other parents are quick to teach their children that temper tantrums will get them nowhere. Mark is now able to realize the kind of lessons that he has provided his children. "When our first child was still quite young, we used to spend a lot of time with some friends who had a boy eighteen months older than Timmy. It used to really upset me that they wouldn't seem to notice when their kid was being a little brat. I would never let Timmy take anything away from their boy, and when their kid wanted something that Timmy had, I would encourage him to share. I think now that I overdid it. Timmy never got to play with anything that the older boy was interested in."

Mark's conflicts about anything that might even hint of being aggressive were so strong that he could not help his son stand up for his rights. Mark was teaching his son that it was better to give in to others, no matter what the cost, than to allow any signs of anger or hostility; even allowing his own son to continue playing with a toy that he already had was somehow seen to be an act of aggression. It is no surprise that Timmy is beginning to show signs of the nice guy syndrome.

Children learn from their parents that there are limits to how much anger they can express. Few parents while expressing anger to their misbehaving child would allow the child to express anger back to them. But parents do differ in the extent to which they allow their children to express their feelings. I have seen clients whose parents had listened at the door after sending them to their room as children, and if the parents heard even one angry epithet, they would come into the room and administer another dose of punishment. As adults, these people find it nearly impossible to express any negative feelings. They make great nice guys.

Other parents are so concerned about letting children express themselves that they will allow their child to hit them. And after the child is worn out from the physical assault on the parents, he or she will be comforted because he or she is "so upset." Children who receive this kind of training may not turn out to be nice guys, but they will have more than their share of problems as adults.

Carl Rogers, a psychologist who has written a great deal about the importance of being in touch with one's feelings—both positive and negative—has used an example that helps to clarify this issue. Consider the scenario in which a four-year-old boy is suddenly faced with a brand-new baby sister. There are bound to be times when he does not like this state of affairs, because it means that he no longer has the exclusive attention of his parents. By the time baby sister is able to crawl around the floor, she will undoubtedly do something like knock over big brother's blocks. Big brother knows from experience that Mom and Dad are not going to administer justice, so he takes matters into his own hands and gives baby sister a pinch while telling her how much he hates her.

Mom and Dad, if they are like most moms and dads, will rush to the scene and tell big brother, among other things, "You don't hate your little sister, you love her. We all love her." So now big brother is in a bind; if he insists that he really hates his little sister, he risks losing the love of his Mom and Dad. Depending on the rigor of Mom's and Dad's training, big brother may begin to articulate, to himself as well as to Mom and Dad, that he does indeed love baby sister. But the gut feelings are still there; deep inside, he knows there are times that he really does hate baby sister. So the boy learns that if he is to be loved and accepted by others, he cannot have feelings of anger.

Rogers's advice to parents who are faced with this dilemma is to allow the child to acknowledge his feelings while at the same time teaching him that there are limits on his behavior. The thing for Mom and Dad to say would be: "We know that you feel very angry at baby sister at times, but we will not allow you to hurt her." The child who grows up hearing this message does not develop the notion that any feelings of anger or hostility will result in his being rejected by others.

The crux of the training that nice guys have received is that the feelings, wishes, and desires of other people are more important than their own. It is somehow not only selfish, but an act of aggression to express one's own feelings and wishes. Marsha, the department store supervisor we mentioned earlier, recalls receiving this message loud and clear while she was growing up. "My mother has lived her entire life trying to please other people. If that isn't bad enough, she has to do just the right thing so that others won't think she isn't a nice person. The best example of this that comes to mind, even though it's such a silly little incident, took place while we were on a family vacation. I was only about eight years old, and it was the first big trip I had ever been on, so I was excited about everything we did. One morning while we were eating breakfast, I was very impressed by the can of warm syrup that came with our pancakes. I thought it was the best smell I had ever experienced. When I asked my Mom if she wanted to smell it, she said no. She didn't want the other people to think she was being fussy." As sad as it is, there are lots of people who will deny themselves the simple pleasure of smelling warm syrup because of what other people might think.

Many nice guys never change, because they never admit to having a problem. Like Mark, they cling to the idea that they just do not experience anger. At times they may recognize that other people are taking advantage of them, but they comfort themselves with the thought that they are somehow more civilized than these other people are.

Marsha finally entered therapy because of her deteriorating job situation, and she was able to make considerable progress in learning to recognize and express her feelings. She became very enthusiastic about her new style and decided to help her mother get over her nice guy routine, but her mother was not willing to give it up. "My mother has a 'friend' who is always making snide little remarks to her. One day when my mother was complaining to me about this friend, I told her that she should tell her that the comments bother her, and that she would appreciate it if she would stop making them. My mother agreed that that would be a good thing to say, and we even practiced how she would say it. The next time I saw Mom I asked her how it went and she told me she had decided not to say anything. She thought her friend has had such a hard life that it would be mean to say anything that would hurt her feelings."

There are many nice guys like Marsha's mother who never will give up their routine. They cannot be convinced that their style is actually hurting them and their relationships. Marsha's mother felt close to very few people, including her husband, because there were so many things she felt that she could not say to them. Others, like Marsha, will not stop to take a look at themselves until something big in their lives starts to go wrong. But once nice guys recognize that they might be better off by changing, they often make rapid progress.

Living with the Nice Guy

For those of you who live with a nice guy, be warned that the cure can be worse than the disease. Once they come to the realization that they cannot go on living their lives trying to please others, they can overreact in ways that are pretty dramatic. They may decide that rather than letting an endless list of self-generated obligations to others dominate their lives, they are going to do exactly what they want to do, and the hell with anyone else. This can be quite a shock to the person whose partner has always been unfailingly kind, considerate, and unselfish.

These dramatic turnarounds are the exception and not the rule, but they do happen. In most cases, the nice guy is apt to change much more gradually and probably will never turn out to be the kind of person who seems insensitive to the feelings of others. But in either case, some adjustment on the part of the partner of the nice guy will be necessary. Anytime one person in a relationship changes, it is likely to upset the equilibrium, and changes in nice guy routines have more potential for upsetting equilibria than most personality patterns, as you'll see in the last question.

Q: The first time I got really mad at my husband, he stopped talking and walked away from me. At the time, I didn't know what he was doing; I thought he was sick or something, because why else would he just stop talking all of a sudden? Well, I've since learned that that's how he deals with any kind of problem—he just clams up.

When I try to talk to him about something that bothers me, he only tells me that he's sorry and that he'll try to do better, but he never tells me how *he* feels about the situation. I know he must get mad at me sometimes, but he denies it. We've been together for three years, and we seem to have a solid relationship, but I'm worried about what might happen to us if he never opens up. It just doesn't seem natural.

A: You have good reason to be concerned about the situation, and I think you should try to do something about it now rather than waiting until your relationship begins to crumble. And the odds are that it will begin to crumble sooner or later. Nice guys cannot keep their own wishes under wraps forever, and unless your partner can learn to express his wishes more directly, the chances are that he will leave the relationship—psychologically if not physically.

You are right when you say that his never admitting to feelings of anger is not natural, but you must keep in mind that it is natural to him. Most nice guys had at least one parent with the same style, so for them, it is perfectly normal to avoid, rather than face, conflict. He probably feels a little superior because he is able to view himself as being so even-tempered and so logical about problems. In other words, he has no reason to want to change and lots of reasons for wanting to stay the way he is.

The most important, and most difficult, step in helping him to change is convincing him that it is the best thing for him to do. Start by telling him how important it is to you for the two of you to talk about your problems. Let him know that you don't believe him when he claims to have no complaints about you. Remind him that the number-one reason relationships don't make it over the long haul is the failure of couples to communicate openly and honestly with each other. And whatever you do, don't let him off the hook the next time you do have an argument. Keep after him until he starts to talk back to you.

If you do manage to get him started, you must be prepared to hear some things that you don't like. The chances are good that your partner has accumulated quite a backlog of angry feelings, and they will be exaggerated because they have been festering for some time. Second, you will probably be shocked by what he has to say, because it will seem so completely uncharacteristic of him. If you are used to a calm, logical, even-tempered, self-sacrificing angel, it may take some time to get used to an ordinary man who respects his own feelings as much as he respects yours and expresses them openly.

When he does begin to express himself, do not discourage him by either wilting or grinding him into the ground. His attempts to express himself will be tentative at first, and if you send him the message that you really cannot tolerate hearing about his feelings, he will be convinced that he was right in the first place and resume his nice guy routine. Remind him often that you appreciate his being more open with you. Treat him with kid gloves for a while; he needs time to gain confidence in his new way of relating to you. And most important of all, always respect his feelings. You may not think he is justified in feeling the way that he does, but even if you are right, they are his feelings, and at least he's expressed them.

Keeping feelings under cover slowly eats away at a relationship. The longer nothing is done about it, the more damage will be done. It is always possible to repair the damage, no matter how severe, so long as both partners are willing, but the earlier couples start to work on the problem, the easier the job will be. Since you still feel that you have a good relationship, I would guess that there has been very little damage up to now. Signs that the damage is severe would include your feeling shut out, lonely, and unhappy, and your partner's feeling depressed without knowing why. If you get to work now, I think there is every reason to believe that you can help your partner learn to be an excellent communicator. And if you can do this for him, you will have done much to help him have a happier and more satisfying life in general.

Q: My wife is always forgetting things that are important to me. In just the past month she forgot to take my suits to the cleaners for three days in a row, forgot to buy my secretary a birthday present for five days in a row, and forgot that we were going out to dinner with an out-of-town client of mine.

I remember reading about passive-aggressive personalities in my college psychology course, and I remember that one of the symptoms is that they express their anger by forgetting to do things for other people. I am beginning to think that my wife has that problem, although in many ways it is impossible to believe, because she *can* express her anger just fine at times. Do you think there is any psychological significance to her forgetting these things? Or could she be, as she claims, absentminded? She says that taking care of two young kids takes up all of her mental energy and she just has trouble remembering everything she needs to do.

A: Your memory is correct in that forgetting can be a sign of the passive-aggressive personality—the technical name for what I prefer to call the nice guy syndrome. It is true that most nice guys will tend to "forget" things, whether it is to pick up the clothes at the cleaners or buy a gift for Valentine's Day. But forgetting in itself is not a sign that an individual is a nice guy. Some people really are absentminded, and it would be a mistake to place much significance on their forgetfulness.

To decide whether your wife's forgetfulness has any significance, you need to look for patterns, and from the incidents you provide, I would say that the pattern is obvious: All of the examples you gave involve things that are important to your job. Mentally review the things that she forgets. Does she forget to make reservations when just the two of you are going out to dinner? Does she forget to send her best friend a birthday card? Does she forget to buy baby food for the kids? Or is her forgetting limited to things that are related to your job? If her forgetting follows the pattern that your examples suggest, then I would say the answer to your question is yes; her forgetting *does* have psychological significance.

It is not unusual for a person to "forget" for psychological reasons and still be a pro at expressing her anger on other occasions. Behavioral patterns are not an all-or-nothing phenomenon; they come in degrees. So it is quite possible for your wife to express her feelings openly about some issues and still have conflicts about others. Lots of people have no difficulty expressing themselves about most aspects of their lives, but do have one or two areas that are impossible for them to face head on.

It sounds to me as if your wife is in the same bind as millions of women: She wants to have a career *and* to be a perfect mother. Unfortunately, these two goals do not seem to go together very well. My guess is that your wife "forgets" things that are related to your job because she has some resentment that you, rather than she, need to have your clothes cleaned for work, and take out-of-town clients to dinner. She would probably deny having these feelings; keep in mind that she is probably denying them to herself as well, because she feels guilty for having them. She knows that she has made the choice to stay home with the children (I hope it was her choice and not yours), and that it would be unfair to blame you for her feelings of dissatisfaction. She cannot express her feelings about running job-related errands for you because she believes that she "should" be happy to do these things for you. Because she cannot admit her resentment to herself or to you, she "forgets."

The kindest thing you can do for her, and for yourself in the long run, is to help her face her conflicts about motherhood versus a career. She may very well want to be home with the children until they get older more than she wants a career, but it is important for her to talk about it. Help her to admit to herself that there may be times when she resents staying home with the children all the time, that at times she feels trapped. Paradoxically, the more one denies feeling trapped, or angry, or resentful, the more intense these feelings are likely to become.

If staying home with the children is indeed her number-one priority, that's fine, but try to help her to feel she's a part of your career. Share office gossip with her the same way you would with your other friends. Ask her advice about difficult situations you face. Whatever you do, don't make her feel like your girl Friday whose only value is in taking care of the trivial details so that you can concentrate on the important stuff. This means that you should start taking your clothes to the cleaners and buying your secretary's gifts yourself.

The other possibility is that your wife would like to resume or start her career but feels guilty about leaving the children. If this is the case, you must help her to realize that she doesn't have to be home all day long to be a good parent. Lots of families in which both the husband and wife work have children who are happy and well adjusted. It's harder, and it takes more effort, especially on your part, but it is well worth it if it means your wife will feel fulfilled. If you are able to help your wife resolve her conflicts between motherhood and a career in a thoughtful, loving way, it will pay dividends for you in the future. Two people who can help each other grow and develop are bound to find more satisfaction within the relationship.

Q: I think the woman I'm living with has some hang-ups about expressing her feelings openly. Whenever we have a disagreement, she tells me what's on her mind in a very calm and controlled way. I'm a screamer, and I think it's much healthier to get all that emotional energy out of your system. I've tried to encourage her to be more expressive, but she says she's not that kind of person and doesn't want to be that kind of person. I don't think I want to have a long-term relationship with someone who can't communicate more openly. What do you think our chances are?

A: You don't have to scream to communicate; lots of people are completely open with the people they live with and never raise their voices. In fact, the more open one is with others, the less likely it is that he or she will feel the urge to scream.

If your partner does indeed express her feelings when the two of you have a disagreement, I don't see anything wrong with her doing it in a calm, controlled way. It is true that many people who never raise their voices do have some inhibitions about expressing their feelings, but there are lots of people in the world like your partner—people who are open and honest with others but are simply not screamers.

You might want to ask yourself why *you* yell when you have a disagreement. Yelling and screaming can be just as good a way to avoid expressing feelings as the silent treatment. Make sure that you are yelling something worthwhile when you have a fight, and not just yelling to put up a smokescreen.

Q: My husband went into therapy because he was depressed. The therapy has helped him a lot, but I've about had it with his new personality. Before he started, he was a mild-mannered, sweet man. Now, he's constantly giving me "feedback"—God, how I hate that word!—about how I am trying to manipulate him. I only *wish* that I could manipulate him; now that he's being "true to himself," nothing ever gets done around the house because he's out with his friends. When he does stay at home, he's too busy working on his self-development to give me any help. Is this just a stage he's going through, or is this what I have to look forward to for the rest of my life?

A: It is not unusual for people to overreact to the suggestions they receive in therapy. If your husband was the type of man who meekly did what was asked of him while never expressing his own wishes, I'm sure that the message he received in therapy was that he had to start paying attention to how he wanted to spend his life. If he really has become as self-centered as you say, I would guess that it is just a stage he is passing through. Sooner or later he will realize that being "true to oneself" does not mean never having to do anything that you don't want to do. When we live with other people we have to make compromises and agreements; after all, who *really* wants to wash dishes or clean bathrooms? We all have to do things that we're not wild about no matter how true to ourselves we are.

Even when he does eventually tone down his self-development work, you will have to prepare yourself to make some adjustments. It sounds to me as if you liked having someone at your beck and call who never complained about fulfilling your work orders. I would guess that those days are over. Once people experience freedom from self-generated feelings of obligation, it is rare for them to opt for the old chains and bonds. The freedom feels too good.

Your situation can be a very uncomfortable one. Your husband gave you the power over the relationship, and now he is taking it back. Lots of people like yourself cannot adjust and eventually leave the relationship; they cannot cope with being an equal rather than the boss. I urge you to try to adjust. While it can be nice to have a partner who is willing to carry out your orders, it can also be very lonely. I believe that if you stick with your husband and learn to be his partner rather than his supervisor, you will be much happier in the long run.

Some Final Thoughts

While I do believe it is crucial for people to be able to express both their good and bad feelings if their relationships are to thrive, I am by no means advocating a "let it all hang out" type of style. A few years ago, some writers were suggesting that couples should be as vicious as possible with each other when fighting. They even recommended that couples buy foam bats so that they could express their anger physically without doing any permanent damage.

This uninhibited expression of anger misses the point. As I said earlier, expressing anger is no guarantee that there is any communication going on. Besides, the free expression of anger only serves to promote more vigorous and more dangerous expression of anger. Contrary to popular stereotypes, it is not the Casper Milquetoasts of the world that go berserk one day and physically abuse their families; it is the people who have few inhibitions about getting angry that are likely to be physically abusive. It's not that big a step from throwing dishes at a wall to throwing dishes at another person.

The trick is to express feelings in such a way that the partner has a chance to respond. Calling one's partner a string of obscenities will not accomplish anything. The person who is able to say "I'm really angry with you because . . ." is allowing his partner to respond regardless of whether it is said in a quiet or a loud voice. And once partners begin responding to each other, they are halfway home.

5
THE EGOTIST

The Egotist Test

1. **When I think about myself:**
   a. I never cease to be amazed at how wonderful I am.
   b. I am pretty pleased with the way I turned out.
   c. I am glad about my good points, but I have more than my share of weak spots.
   d. I get very depressed.

2. **When I am at a party:**
   a. I like to have a group of people around me so that I can tell them what I've been doing.
   b. I like to try to talk to as many different people as I can.
   c. I like to find a few people that I can really talk to.

d. I try to blend in with the wallpaper.

3. **If I liked to do something but I wasn't very good at it:**
   a. I can't imagine such a situation.
   b. I wouldn't do it—I don't enjoy doing things I'm not good at.
   c. I would do it anyway.
   d. I'd do it—I have to do things I'm not good at, since that's the only choice I have.

4. **When I was a child, I:**
   a. was much more mature than the others kids my age.
   b. was a leader—I could get other kids to do what I wanted.
   c. had several good friends.
   d. was lonely much of the time.

5. **If my partner got sick on a day when I had a busy schedule:**
   a. I wouldn't change my plans—I can't disrupt my day just because my partner gets sick.
   b. I would be mad at my partner for getting sick on such a busy day.
   c. I'd try to find some help so I could follow through with my schedule.
   d. I would gladly stay home and take care of my partner.

6. **When I think about the failures of my life:**
   a. I don't have any to think about.
   b. I know who's responsible and I'll get even with them.
   c. it makes me want to make sure I don't make the same mistakes again.

d. I realize what a loser I am.

7. **The person I live with would have to be:**
   a. appreciative.
   b. a real winner.
   c. a kind, loving person.
   d. desperate.

8. **If I gave an opinion about something—about politics for example—and someone disagreed with me:**
   a. I would think that the other person didn't know what he or she was talking about.
   b. I would feel irritated.
   c. I would enjoy the discussion.
   d. I would admit that I was wrong.

9. **If I hadn't heard from a friend for a while:**
   a. I would be too busy to notice.
   b. I would be mad at him or her for not keeping in touch.
   c. I would give the person a call.
   d. I would know that he or she had finally gotten tired of me.

10. **I think that people who live much differently than I do:**
   a. must be weird.
   b. are missing out on a lot.
   c. simply have different preferences.
   d. are luckier than I am.

The Egotist Test Scoring Key

1. a. 3 points.
b. 2 points.
c. 1 point.
d. 0 points.

2. a. 3 points.
b. 2 points.
c. 1 point.
d. 0 points.

3. a. 3 points.
b. 2 points.
c. 1 point.
d. 0 points.

4. a. 3 points.
b. 2 points.
c. 1 point.
d. 0 points.

5. a. 3 points.
b. 2 points.
c. 1 point.
d. 0 points.

6. a. 3 points.
b. 2 points.
c. 1 point.
d. 0 points.

7. a. 3 points.
b. 2 points.
c. 1 point.
d. 0 points.

8. a. 3 points.
b. 2 points.
c. 1 point.
d. 0 points.

9. a. 3 points.
b. 2 points.
c. 1 point.
d. 0 points.

10. a. 3 points.
b. 2 points.
c. 1 point.
d. 0 points.

Interpretation of Test Scores

0 to 8 points: You have some serious problems with your self-esteem; it is not necessary to go through life feeling so bad about yourself. On the bright side, there is no danger that you will ever become an egotistical personality.

9 to 16 points: You probably have a pretty healthy self-image. This chapter doesn't apply to you.

17 to 23 points: Either you have an unusually good self-image or you are trying to hide something. I think you might do well to take a close look at yourself to determine which it is.

24 to 30 points: Your high opinion of yourself is most likely causing you some problems in your relationships. This chapter could be very important to you.

You Just Don't Understand Me

Phil is a very self-confident person. He has, from his point of view, every reason to be. He is bright and handsome, has lots of friends, and has a successful medical practice specializing in dermatology. Everything has always gone his way. The only thing Phil cannot understand is why his wife has begun to talk about leaving him. Why would she ever give up such a good thing?

His wife, Kelly, can rattle off a long list of reasons. "Phil is the most selfish, most self-centered man I have ever known. It's bad enough that he expects me to be his slave, but he is selfish when it comes to sharing our lives too. He will come home (never when he says he will) and spend an hour and a half telling me about the clever way he treated a patient, or how he outsmarted a colleague, and never once ask me how my day was. In fact, if I wait until he's finished telling me how great he is and start to tell him something that's on my mind, he usually tells me that he wants to read the paper or watch something on television. He's so insensitive that he doesn't even realize what he is doing."

If Phil were able to look at his life a little more objectively, he might notice that there are a few cracks in it. Although he has six other physicians who are associates in his practice, he has never had one stay with him for longer than three years. And although he has a lot of people whom he considers to be friends, these people seem to pass through his life the same way his associates in the practice do. Not that Phil would ever consider doing so, but there is not one person in the world to whom he feels close enough to share his problems with Kelly. Like his wife, other people are initially attracted to Phil, but they soon grow weary of his preoccupation with himself.

Realizing what Phil is like has been a painful process for Kelly. "I can't help myself, I still love him. He is interesting, fun, and full of life, and he is gentle with me and the children, even though he is basically indifferent to anyone but himself. Nothing would make me happier than if he felt toward me just a fraction of what I feel for him. But I just can't go on living with myself if I continue to live with him. Something happened the other night that makes this crystal-clear. I had made plans to go out to dinner and a movie with a friend whom I haven't seen in a long time. Phil came home and announced that on the spur of the moment, he had made arrangements to play racketball that night, so *I* would have to either find a baby-sitter or cancel my plans. When I told him how unfair I thought that was, he started telling me how hard he works, how much pressure he is under, and how much he needs any recreation he can get. The real killer was that when I wouldn't back down, he said, 'You just don't understand me.' "

Phil is a classic case of the egotist. He has no self-doubts whatsoever; in fact, he is incapable of entertaining any self-doubts. It really is a complete mystery to him how his wife could even think about leaving him. He knows he is attractive—after all, women are constantly flirting with him. He makes a lot of money, so he can give Kelly anything she wants. Kelly makes no secret of the fact that she finds him to be an exciting lover, so that couldn't be it. The only conclusion that Phil could come to was that Kelly must be having some psychological problems. After all, he knows that there are dozens of women who would love to be married to him.

People who are well adjusted are pretty pleased with the way they are, but they can recognize and admit to their shortcomings. Egotistical personalities believe that they do not have any. They may tell people that they are not perfect, but deep down they don't really believe it. Phil, for instance, would admit that he's "a little insensitive to others and maybe a touch conceited," but he thinks that it's part of his charm that he can be open about these traits. What he actually believes is that someone as successful as he does not have time to listen to the trivia that other people waste their time on, or to worry about what kind of impression he makes on other people. So if he seems insensitive or conceited to others, that's *their* problem—not his.

These people vary in the degree to which they feel comfortable with their assumed superiority. Extreme cases, like Phil, have no doubts whatsoever, and hence they do not react very much when something happens that might bring their superiority into question. For instance, Phil never wondered if the fact that his associates kept leaving him might be caused by something he was doing wrong. Even after hearing the same complaints several times, Phil's only thought was that these people could not live up to the high standards he had set for them; he never felt the need to defend himself. When his wife told him that she was not happy with their relationship, he could not even entertain the possibility that he could be contributing to her feelings. He assumed that Kelly was having "a case of the housewife syndrome."

In other instances, the egotistical person's sense of superiority is more tenuous. These individuals are likely to be very threatened when they are confronted with evidence that suggests their fallibility. And threatened people are likely to be angry and hostile. Carla is a college professor who has dedicated her life to knowing more about mathematics than anyone else in the world. (She doesn't, of course, but she likes to think she does.) She prides herself on the high standards she maintains for the students in her classes. The only problem is that she confuses high standards with giving inadequate explanations of the material she covers. She assumes that if the students were really trying, they would be able to untangle her confusing lectures.

When her students rebel, as they do every semester, Carla cannot tolerate any criticism regardless of how tactfully it is presented. Her sense of superiority is only a thin veneer that covers underlying doubts about her competence. So when a student proposes the possibility that the grades in the class are so low because she is not presenting the material very clearly, she becomes angry and accuses the students of being lazy and stupid. Carla does the same thing in other relationships as well. Her husband has learned not to make suggestions about how she might handle problems with the children differently, because "Carla does not take constructive criticism well."

People like Carla usually have some awareness of their conflicts. They know that they have trouble dealing with criticism, but they find it hard to talk about these kinds of issues in a calm, nondefensive way. Carla wants to be different, but she just cannot seem to pull it off. "Every semester I vow that things will be different. But as soon as I grade the first test and find that the grades aren't as good as I had hoped, I find myself getting angry. By the time I pass back the tests in class, my heart is beating fast and I'm just waiting for someone to say something. I don't know why, but I seem to approach every situation as a contest and I've got to be the winner." While Carla knows that something is going on with her, she is not aware that deep down, she fears that she is not as bright and capable as she would like to be. She needs to be number one, but part of her knows that she is not. And for her, that is an unacceptable notion.

One of the most frustrating things about egotistical personalities is their inability to have any appreciation for the feelings of others. They are so preoccupied with themselves that it simply does not occur to them to wonder how other people are feeling, or even to care. Phil's pattern of regaling his wife with stories of how wonderful he has been during the day and then turning to the newspaper when she begins to talk about herself is not at all unusual. It did not enter his mind that he was being thoughtless; he just did not care about anything Kelly might have to say. If the partner of an egotistical personality got sick, he or she would probably be annoyed at the disruption the illness would cause; the fact that the partner was not feeling well would be beyond the egotist's comprehension.

At times, their self-centeredness can seem almost bizarre. Boyd was in group therapy that I was conducting for "midlife crisis." At one meeting a woman began the session, in tears, by telling the group that her husband had been in a serious automobile accident, and because he was self-employed, he had no insurance to pay the hospital bills, or any source of income to tide the family over until he could start working again. Boyd listened patiently for a few minutes, and then as soon as there was a brief silence, he began to tell the group about how he did not find his work to be as challenging as it used to be. When the group became angry at him for showing no sympathy and talking about problems that were trivial compared to the woman's, Boyd responded, with complete sincerity, "My problems are as important to me as hers are to her."

Because of this inability to have any empathy with or even interest in other people, egotistical personalities do not have relationships in the usual sense of the word. They have people whom they like to have around because they satisfy certain needs. They do not enter into a relationship because they want to care for or share their life with another person. They are incapable of sharing. This is not to say that relationships—or at least the appearance of having relationships—are not important to them. They can be very important, but for different reasons from those the rest of us have.

Phil, for instance, believed that he loved his wife, so once she managed to convince him that she was serious about leaving him, he became very depressed. His reasons for wanting her to stay, while perfectly reasonable to him, would seem more than a little superficial to anyone else. Phil believed that Kelly was the perfect wife for him. She was very attractive, she was a good mother, and she got along well with his colleagues. She did a good job of running *his* house, she was willing to do all the volunteer and charity work that the wife of such a prominent person as he was expected to do, and she did not place too many demands on his time. It is not difficult to get the idea that any one of a thousand women could take Kelly's place and Phil would not even notice. In fact, Phil has even joked—with more than a tinge of seriousness—that he would love to have a Stepford wife: a robot who would do all of the things he wanted doing without any complaints and who would give him the unqualified adoration he needed.

Some egotistical personalities can go through life without any problems. It is possible for them to find a partner who not only tolerates but admires their style. People who have problems with poor self-esteem see the complete self-confidence of the egotist as an enviable quality. Because they are so unsure of themselves, they are happy with much less than most people; if their egotistical partner does not seem very interested in them, they may not even notice, and they are likely to be happy with whatever they can get from the relationship. It is very hard for someone with no self-confidence to believe that it is possible to have too much of it. So if an egotistical personality does find one of these people, they could live together happily ever after. The tragedy is that in this case, the egotistical personality would never learn how much it is possible to get from a relationship.

It is more likely that the egotist's ways will catch up with him or her sooner or later. Even if the egotist does manage to find someone who is initially attracted to his or her style, it is usually only a matter of time before it grows tiresome. Kelly, for instance, fell in love with Phil because he seemed so self-confident and had such a clear idea of what he wanted to do with his life—qualities that Kelly lacked. But as Kelly got a little older and a little more sure of herself, she was able to make the distinction between self-confidence and self-centeredness.

Phil never would have considered the possibility that he might be happier if he could change if he had not been scared to death at the thought of losing Kelly. Faced with the choice of losing her or taking a crash course in self-examination, he opted for the latter—with more than a little reluctance. Happily, the results were gratifying for Phil. He learned to listen to his wife, and he learned things about her that he never knew; he came to value her opinions, and they spent more time doing things together that they both enjoyed. Phil never became a doting husband, or the kind of person that would be anyone's closest friend, but he did learn to make contact with other people. It is an irony of this particular style that while egotists are often surrounded by people, they are usually psychologically isolated.

Often it does not take much change for these individuals to be very special people. As part of this personality style, these people have a sense of infallibility that allows them to take risks, to search for adventures, to try to get the most that they can from life. If they can be helped to care about other people, then they are able to share some of the sense of excitement they are capable of having about life. A relationship with a person such as this would have the potential to be both rewarding and exciting.

Development of the Egotist

To state it very simply, but accurately, spoiled, indulged children grow up to be spoiled adults who expect to be indulged. Egotistical personalities are likely to have had parents who considered them to be God's gift to the world. They viewed their child as something special and communicated that idea at every opportunity. If children hear over and over again that they are special and better than everyone else, they begin to believe it.

There is another side to the coin of being spoiled that plays an important role in the development of the egotistical personality. Parents who gratify their child's every desire and treat their child's every wish as if it were a command do more than spoil their child; they are teaching the child that other people are weak and subservient. By example, they show the child that other people can be manipulated with very little effort. And saddest of all, because they are willing to sacrifice their all for the child, they create the expectation that everyone will do the same for the child.

There are any number of reasons why parents spoil their children. Some do it out of guilt; they may not have as much time as they would like to spend with their child, so they try to compensate by satisfying every whim when they are together. Sheila, for example, was an only child, and both of her parents worked. Her mother hated to leave Sheila during the day, but the family finances left her with no alternative. To try to make up for what she believed to be dereliction of her motherly duties, she let Sheila do pretty much as she pleased when she was with her. Sheila could stay up as late as she wanted to at night; after all, that was the only time they had together. If Sheila wanted an ice cream cone before dinner, she got it. Her mother simply could not bring herself to say no to Sheila.

Sheila expected the same treatment from the adults at the day-care center as well, but they were less willing to give it to her. When the director spoke to Sheila's mother about "some potential behavior problems," she refused to believe that Sheila would be capable of causing such problems. Any problems that Sheila might be having were a result of her having to leave her mother at such an early age, and what Sheila needed was someone who was more understanding to take care of her. After Sheila's mother went through all the local child-care centers, she tried live-in baby-sitters. She went through several of these before she found one who was "understanding enough"; unfortunately for Sheila, the baby-sitter who was "understanding" did not especially care what Sheila did. She was content to watch television while Sheila went her own way; as long as Sheila didn't kill herself or break anything too expensive, everyone was happy. Sheila, of course, learned a very important lesson: If you are persistent enough, you will always end up getting your own way.

Other parents may perceive some special quality in their child (regardless of whether it is there) and rationalize their indulgence as their trying to nurture that special quality along. Phil, for instance, was a cute, precocious child. His father wanted him to be the great surgeon that he could not be because he himself could not afford to go to medical school. He was not so indulgent that he let Phil do anything he wanted to, but he did tell Phil almost daily that he was a very bright child—much brighter than any of his classmates—and that he would accomplish much more than anyone else would, and if Phil received less than an A from a teacher, it certainly was not Phil's fault; his teacher was just incapable of understanding his creative mind. Phil believed his dad. By the time he was in elementary school, he did not question the idea that he was smarter than anyone else in his class. By the time he was in high school, he did not question the idea that he was smarter than any of his teachers.

With this basic belief in their superiority as a foundation, egotistical personalities have a knack for arranging things to provide confirming evidence. Simply saying things with complete confidence can go a long way; most of us have a tendency to believe that if people say something forcefully, they must know what they are talking about, and if we do not have any special expertise in that area, we would probably choose not to risk letting our ignorance show. So egotists get the impression that other people agree with them when they are actually just too unsure of themselves to speak up. Besides, even if they were challenged, it would not have much of an effect; people with this style can rationalize away a challenge, regardless of how logical or factual it may be, as easily as the rest of us can fall off a log. Besides, egotistical personalities are not likely to spend much time with those who do not agree with and admire them.

They do have some sense of their limits, which allows them to avoid situations that might lead to failure. For instance, a high school student who has no conscious doubts about his intellectual superiority may know deep down that he cannot come out on top if he takes all the college preparatory courses. So rather than risk being just one of the crowd in physics and chemistry classes, he may elect to take business math instead. It is easy enough to rationalize that business math is more relevant to the real world than physics could ever be.

The degree of confidence that egotists have in their superiority does seem to be related to their actual superiority—if indeed they are superior. Phil, for instance, learned from his parents that he was better than anyone else, and the message he received from his teachers and peers wasn't all that different. Phil was a bright, attractive, charming child. He was the teacher's favorite from first grade on; he was clever enough to know what the limits were, so he was able to get special treatment without crossing over the line into obnoxiousness. The other children admired him as well; he was always a little aloof, but again he knew how to "act" modest, and he did it often enough to avoid getting a reputation of being stuck-up. The result was that Phil felt comfortable with his superiority. He did not feel a need to respond to challenges because in his mind, there could be no serious challenges.

Carla, on the other hand, got the same message from her parents that Phil did, but the rest of the world did not treat her quite as well. Unlike Phil, she did not make any effort to keep her opinion of herself a secret. She was bright, but not exceptional, and her teachers used somewhat higher standards in grading her work to try to put a dent in her arrogance. She made no attempt to hide the fact that she thought that she had better things to do than play childish games, so she was unpopular with kids her own age. It was a real struggle for her to maintain her sense of superiority; she required frequent pep talks from her parents as she was growing up. And as an adult, Carla feels that she has to be ready to counterattack whenever her position as number one is challenged.

People like Carla receive two sets of contradictory messages: one set from their parents that they are number one, and another from the rest of the world that they are nothing special. These people learn that they have to watch out for those who will try to deflate their self-esteem. And because their high self-esteem is only a veneer that covers their self-doubts, they cannot tolerate any such challenges—the truth hits too close to home. So their defenses are always mobilized which can cause them to become hostile and angry at any hint of criticism. People like Phil, on the other hand, have no need to be defensive; they are so confident of their superiority that they have trouble recognizing a critical remark when they hear it.

Living with the Egotist

Living with an egotist can be a tough job. Their inability to recognize their flaws extends to their egotism. Your pointing out that they could be more caring and interested in others is not likely to impress them; their need to maintain a facade of infallibility will make it easy for them to turn things around and put you into the category of being a chronic complainer. Helping an egotistical personality to change can be done, but it is not a job for the fainthearted. If this is what you face, be prepared for a battle, but also be assured that the battle can be well worth it if you succeed.

Q: I've been living with Kurt for nearly four years now, and I'm beginning to wonder how much more time I should give this relationship. When I met him, he was working as a waiter to support himself while he developed himself as an artist. I fell in love with him, and because I thought he was so talented, I agreed to continue working to support us both so he could devote himself completely to his painting. I still love him, but we're no closer to the kind of life I want than we were four years ago. He is still developing his technique while I'm still working *and* doing all of the housework. All he does is paint and drink wine with his artsy friends, who love to tell each other how talented they are. He sells a painting to one of his friends every now and then for a little money, but he has made no effort to sell to the public. When I try to push him a little, he says he's not quite ready. I believe he loves me, because every time I talk about leaving he begs me to stay, but then I think if he really loved me, he would take what I want out of life a little more seriously. Do you think there is any chance that we have a future together?

A: I'm not surprised that he begs you to stay when you talk about moving out. Who wouldn't be upset at losing a full-time maid, cook, and lover who, on top of that, pays all the expenses? The fact is that you are allowing yourself to be used, and as long as you continue to do so, there is no chance that you will have a future together that is satisfying to you.

Lots of people make sacrifices for their partners; that's one of the joys of having a partner. However, when they make sacrifices, there should be, and usually is, an element of mutuality. In your situation, for instance, you might have agreed that you would support him for a period of time—say two years—while he tried to make it as an artist. During that time it would be fair to expect him to take on the major responsibilities for the housework. Then, at the end of two years, it would be your turn to try something you wanted to do; perhaps you might want to go back to school while he pays the bills. I don't mean to suggest that every sacrifice has to be returned by the partner exactly, but the only thing you seem to be getting out of your deal is the pleasure of watching Kurt paint. I would imagine that the excitement of doing that wears off pretty fast.

People like Kurt take it for granted that other people exist to satisfy their desires. I doubt that it has even occurred to him that he is exploiting you; as far as he is concerned, your arrangement is perfectly natural, and in fact, he probably thinks you are lucky to have such a talented man for a partner. The first step in trying to make your relationship work for you as well as for him is to recognize that you have the tendency to allow others to exploit you. This won't be as easy as it sounds. It would be hard for anyone to recognize that they have allowed themselves to be used for four years; time is a precious commodity, and it is very difficult to admit that you've used up such a chunk of it with so little return. Try to face your feelings squarely. Keep in mind that it is all too easy to be deceitful with ourselves. Obviously, you are beginning to have some doubts or you wouldn't be questioning your future together.

Once you can recognize what you have allowed yourself to get into, resolve to put a stop to it. Tell yourself that no matter how you feel about Kurt, you will not allow yourself to be used. If you were to continue as you are, sooner or later you would end up hating either Kurt or yourself, and neither of these alternatives is acceptable. The first thing you can try to do is to sit down with Kurt and tell him as openly as you can how you feel about your relationship. Ask him what he thinks he could do to make things equitable. For the reasons I mentioned earlier, I would be surprised if he came up with anything; he probably does not see anything wrong with things as they are.

The next step would be to act on your feelings. Decide what you think it would be fair to expect him to do, and then tell him so, emphasizing that if he doesn't do as you say, then you are prepared to leave him. If he believes you are serious, he may agree to give your way a try, but it is almost certain that he will drag his feet; after all, he is giving up a pleasant situation. So give him a little time, but don't let him procrastinate forever. Set a time limit in your own mind, and if he hasn't followed through by then, you have to make good on your threat to leave.

In the meantime, there might be something you can do to help his career as an artist along. I think it is a safe bet that he doesn't try harder to sell his paintings because at some level, he is afraid that he is not as good as he likes to think he is. Most of us would want to know if we are headed down a dead-end street, but people like Kurt would rather maintain an illusion than risk discovering an unpleasant truth. Why don't you take some of the risks for him? Show some of his paintings to people who know about such things. Try the art professors at a local university, or people who work in galleries; often the owners of art supply stores or shops that do framing are able to give an informed opinion and possibly give a talented artist a shove in the right direction. If you get nothing but negative reviews, you may decide to let Kurt maintain his illusions (he probably would dismiss such comments anyway), but if you hear anything encouraging, it might be the boost that Kurt needs to get him started.

If your deadline arrives and Kurt has made no changes, then you must leave. If there is any possibility of a future for the two of you, this will shake him up enough to get him moving. People who are as comfortable with their style as Kurt is need something dramatic to happen before they can be motivated to take a look at themselves. You must prepare yourself for the possibility that he will let you go without much of a protest. Kurt has made it this far by finding people who allow themselves to be exploited, so he may not have too much trouble finding a replacement for you. The only comfort, if indeed there is any, is that you are better off knowing now what the situation is than coming to grips with it five or ten years down the road. It is much harder to live without your self-respect than it is to lose someone you love. Good luck and be strong!

Q: My wife is never wrong. We can't ever even have a discussion because if I disagree with her, she gets angry and accuses me of trying to put her down. Just last week she read an editorial about the federal deficits, and remarked that rich people should pay more taxes in order to bring them down. Being a good Republican, I tried to explain to her that taxing the rich would remove the incentive to make money and hence would hurt the economy. She got mad, said, "Well, what do I know?" and stomped out of the room.

It's even worse if we disagree about something that concerns us directly. One silly argument we have over and over concerns our children's eating habits. She believes that we should force them to eat everything on their plates, but I think if they say they are full, there is no reason not to believe them. I've tried to make compromises; for example, if they don't eat their vegetables, then they can't have dessert. But she won't budge; she always gets mad and tells me that her opinion doesn't count for anything. I'm getting really sick of it. How can I get her to be more reasonable?

A: The first thing I would wonder about is your role in all of this. When you say that you try to "explain" your economic theories, it hints of a paternalistic and condescending attitude. Do you really discuss issues with her or do you try to educate her? If it is the latter, I don't blame her for being irritated when you disagree with her. I do think your compromise about your children's eating habits is a reasonable one, so I'll assume that your description of the situation is reasonably objective. But take a look at yourself, too. No one likes to talk to people who are condescending, so be sure that you show respect for her opinions while expressing your own.

As you describe her, your wife does sound like one of those people who believe that their self-worth is dependent on always being right—one possible characteristic of the egotistical personality. In her mind, when you disagree with her, you are telling her that you think she is stupid or poorly informed. So the crux of the solution is to convince her that such is not the case. (I know—easier said than done.)

First of all, tell her your perspective in a calm, reasonable way. When one person is being unreasonable, it is hard for the partner not to get a little stubborn as well, but you do have to fight the temptation. Tell her explicitly that when you disagree with her, that's all you are doing; you do not mean to suggest that your opinion is worth any more than hers is. Let her know that you would enjoy having such discussions with her, but that she makes it very hard to do so. Even if she does agree with you at this stage, she probably won't believe you; people don't change as a result of one comment regardless of how insightful it is. So you will have to move on to step two.

Step two is to try a little humor. After you have told her how you feel about your disagreements, preface all of your remarks with an exaggerated sense of humility. For instance, you might say, "I think what you said was a brilliant analysis of the situation, but I have another thought, humble as it may be." Be careful; there is a thin line between kidding like this and sarcasm, and if she thinks you are being sarcastic, she will merely reinforce her defenses. But a majority of people do respond to humor, and if you can get her to see how silly her defensiveness is, she may feel less of a need to be that way.

Humor doesn't work for everyone, and if you don't see any change in her attitude after a few weeks, the only alternative is to stop responding to her when she expresses an opinion. Sooner or later she will notice that you aren't talking back, and so when she asks about it, tell her the truth: That expressing your opinion only leads to an argument, so you will share your opinion with only those people who want to hear it. This should have an impact on her if she values your relationship at all. Again, don't expect miracles; she isn't likely to have a sudden flash of insight the first time this happens, but if you persist, she should get the message sooner or later.

As for the more personal issues, such as the children, again, try humor first. If that doesn't work, you can't afford just to let her have her way, because children are too important. Try to bargain with her; for instance, let her decide when they do their homework if you decide how much they have to eat at meals. You did not give any indication that she has poor judgment, so keep in mind that even if you don't like her way of handling things, it will work out okay in the long run. If you can get her to divide up the areas that each of you will be responsible for, then there is a chance that she will not have such a strong need to view every issue as a must-win situation. If the compromising helps the two of you to get along better, that may be rewarding enough to encourage her to try more of it.

I hope you will be able to help her change. The need to always be right makes it impossible to have a relationship in the meaningful sense of the term; relationships mean sharing, and you can't share with someone who won't ever give in. Remember too that if your wife is like this with you, she is doing the same thing with other people. So you would be doing her a big favor if you can help her to see herself a little more clearly.

Q: My husband is very selfish with his time. He spends almost all of his free time on his hobbies or Boy Scout activities with our two sons. We hardly ever get to take a family vacation because every year he uses one of his vacation weeks going to summer camp. I hate to admit that I'm jealous of fish (his hobby is fishing) and Boy Scouts, but I feel left out. Don't you think he has a problem in that he never thinks to include me on any of the family activities?

A: Perhaps he is a little insensitive, but I don't see any indication that he has a "problem." As a former Boy Scout and current part-time Scout leader, I can assure you that any adult who takes on the responsibility of entertaining a large group of boys—who are by their very nature energetic, and who have their own ideas about what is entertaining—is not selfish. It can be very rewarding to take on such a responsibility, but I don't think there is an adult in the world who could not find something else that he or she would have more fun doing. So if your husband does spend a considerable portion of his free time with Scout activities, I would guess that he is a very unselfish person.

The question I would ask is: How did you get to be the family wallflower? When all of the children in a family are of the same sex, it is common for the parent of the opposite sex to feel left out, but it is certainly not inevitable. I know lots of examples of both men and women who are extremely involved with and close to their children of the opposite sex. You may not be able to go on Scout camping trips with your sons and your husband, but there are a number of other activities you could participate in if you wanted to. The point is that if you do not enjoy the activities that the rest of your family does, then it is up to you to do something about it.

It could be, too, that you and your husband have different ideas about what a marriage should be like. Some people believe that husbands and wives should have lots of common interests and should spend much of their free time together. At the other end of the continuum are those who would rather have more separate lives; having someone there as a constant in their lives to share the joys and sorrows is enough for them. One style isn't any better than the other, but it does make for problems if the man and the woman do not have the same expectations.

If you think that this might apply to your relationship, you need to do some hard thinking. My experience is that it is very difficult to get people who like having a life relatively separate from that of their partner to change into people who value lots of common interests. It would be much easier for you to develop interests that bring you pleasure than it would be to get your husband to give up fishing and Scouting and start spending his free time with you. So you have to decide how important it is to you that he change. If you are happy with your relationship in other respects, then you have too much to consider giving up. If you feel miserable because of this difference and you do not believe that any compromise would work out, then you have to think about what kind of relationship would make you happy. I'm inclined to bet that your husband will be willing to make some compromises if you talk to him about it. Don't, however, expect him to give up activities that bring him pleasure.

Some Final Thoughts

As I was writing this chapter, I couldn't help but think of Abraham Maslow's work. Maslow is one of the fathers of humanistic psychology, and he spent a great deal of time studying people whom he considered to be unusually well-adjusted; he coined the term "self-actualized" to describe these people.

The primary characteristic of these people, according to Maslow, was an inner strength and inner comfort that allowed them to live life to the fullest. They typically had very few close friends, and spent much of their time alone pursuing their own interests. Maslow said there were occasions when they could appear to be cold and uncaring; one of his subjects suddenly divorced her husband of twenty-five years because she felt she no longer loved him, and another abruptly cut his ties with a lifelong friend because he discovered that his friend had been dishonest.

I could give more examples, but I think the point is already clear: There is a fine line between Maslow's self-actualized people and egotistical personalities. There are, however, important differences. Egotists care only about themselves. Self-actualized people have a commitment to themselves, but they also care about humanity in general; sometimes they do seem to lose sight of the individual, but they are capable of having close personal relationships as well. The point I want to make is that we should not be too quick to label someone who does appear to be arrogant and self-serving—which self-actualized individuals can appear to be—as having a psychological problem. They may very well have a different perspective on life and different goals for themselves. It is always important to make the distinction between helping someone who does have a problem to change, and trying to change someone simply because we don't like the way he or she is.

6
THE MOPER

The Moper Test

1. **As a child, when I said goodnight to my parents:**
   a. they smothered me with hugs and kisses.
   b. they gave me a goodnight kiss.
   c. they said goodnight back.
   d. they shook my hand and told they would see me in the morning.

2. **When I was little, if I got upset about something:**
   a. my mom or dad would hold me and comfort me.
   b. my mom or dad would ask me what was bothering me and try to make it better.
   c. my mom or dad would sit down with me and try to analyze the problem.
   d. I would go to my room so I could be by myself.

3. **When I have a problem, I like to:**
   a. talk it over with anyone who will listen.
   b. talk it over with someone I can trust.
   c. think it through on my own.
   d. try to put it out of my mind.

4. **When I feel sad:**
   a. everyone knows about it.
   b. only my closest friends and family know about it.
   c. I keep it to myself.
   d. I don't allow myself to feel sad.

5. **When I am really down about something:**
   a. I can't function very well.
   b. I tend to be very quiet.
   c. only those closest to me can see a difference in my mood.
   d. I can carry on so that no one realizes that I'm feeling bad.

6. **Some really big problems in life:**
   a. have no solution.
   b. are nearly impossible to overcome.
   c. can be overcome if you put your mind to it.
   d. are no match for anyone who tries to overcome them.

7. **As I get older, I find that:**
   a. relationships are more important to me than ever.
   b. I value my family and friends more than when I was younger.
   c. I have time for only a few close relationships.
   d. I want more time alone than I used to.

8. **I believe that:**
   a. I am in complete control of my life.
   b. I am responsible for how I feel, although there are a few things that are beyond my control.
   c. I can influence what happens to me, but there are a lot of things that are beyond my control.
   d. I have no control over my life; I am a victim of fate.

9. **My mood is:**
   a. usually up; I feel full of enthusiasm most of the time.
   b. up and down; I have lots of good moments but they are offset by the bad moments.
   c. more down than up; the bad times outweigh the good.
   d. pretty even; I don't seem to have ups and downs.

10. **Most days:**
   a. are filled with interesting things for me to do.
   b. are good ones, but there are some bad ones mixed in.
   c. aren't worth getting out of bed for.
   d. are completely routine.

The Moper Test Scoring Key

1. a. 0 points.
b. 1 point.
c. 2 points.
d. 3 points.

2. a. 0 points.
b. 1 point.
c. 2 points.
d. 3 points.

3. a. 0 points.
b. 1 point.
c. 2 points.
d. 3 points.

4. a. 0 points.
b. 1 point.
c. 2 points.
d. 3 points.

5. a. 0 points.
b. 1 point.
c. 2 points.
d. 3 points.

6. a. 3 points.
b. 2 points.
c. 1 point.
d. 0 points.

7. a. 0 points.
b. 1 point.
c. 2 points.
d. 3 points.

8. a. 0 points.
b. 1 point.
c. 2 points.
d. 3 points.

9. a. 0 points.
b. 1 point.
c. 2 points.
d. 3 points.

10. a. 0 points.
b. 1 point.
c. 2 points.
d. 3 points.

Interpretation of Test Scores

0 to 7 points: Whatever your problems are, depression or moping are not among them. The chances are that your enthusiasm for life and your ability to be close to others prevent you from having many problems that you can't handle.

8 to 14 points: This describes the way most people get along. You may have some situations in which you have trouble sharing your feelings with others, but you seem to be in pretty good shape.

15 to 22 points: You probably have some problems with your outlook on life; you could be happier than you are. This could be an important chapter for you.

23 to 30 points: This chapter is a must for you. It is not necessary for you to feel so alone in the world or to derive so little joy from life.

I'm Fine, Just Leave Me Alone

It was a typical weekday morning for Sarah. The kids had left for school an hour ago and she was sitting next to a stack of dirty dishes reading the morning paper. She didn't fully comprehend the words that her eyes were passing over, but reading the morning paper until lunch was a ritual that she had been following for the past two years. After having lunch, Sarah would settle down and watch her favorite soap operas for a couple of hours, and then she would furiously clean for twenty minutes so the house would look presentable for when the kids, Josh and Kerry, got home from school. When they did, Sarah would automatically ask them how their day was. And while they described it in animated detail she would nod, with a faint smile on her face, for fifteen minutes or so, without hearing a word they were saying.

Sarah's next major struggle was to prepare something for dinner. There had been a time when she enjoyed cooking, but in recent months her family ate a lot of hamburgers. They could be fixed in a few minutes and did not require any advance planning beyond remembering to take the meat out of the freezer. When her husband, Jack, walked in the door about five-thirty, Sarah would give him a perfunctory kiss on the cheek before getting everyone to sit down for dinner. After dinner Sarah would lie down and rest while Jack cleaned up the kitchen. After her rest, Sarah would be able to face the ordeal of getting lunches made for the next day, getting the kids to do their homework, and best of all, getting the kids into bed. Then Sarah could sink back into her favorite chair with a good spy novel and have a few hours of peace before she had to face Jack's advances. It had been about a week since they last had sex, so she thought she had better go along with it tonight if she wanted to avoid a scene.

Jack's feelings toward his wife were a mixture of concern and anger. He was concerned because Sarah had changed so much in the past two years; while she had never been the type of woman who seemed to get too excited about anything, she used to be a kind and caring wife and mother, and now she seemed unable to find any joy in life. He was angry because she no longer seemed to be interested in him—or anyone else, for that matter. He tried hard to do things to make her happy and to make her life easier, but all he got in return was that vacant look and that little smile that seemed to make the corner of her mouth tremble. He wanted his old wife back, but his attempts to find her only met with frustration.

Sarah was only dimly aware that she had changed. She knew that she was not particularly happy with the way her life was going, and she knew that she was unusually close to tears most of the time, but she did not accept Jack's charge that she was like a different person. The only thing she needed was some time to herself. Her life was little more than a never-ending series of obligations to other people, and there was nothing she could do about it. Every few weeks or so she would resolve to develop some new interests, but nothing ever came of her good intentions. If she could have one wish, it would be that Jack would get off her back. When he asked, as he did almost every day, what was bothering her, she wanted to scream: "I'm fine, just leave me alone."

Depression has been called the common cold of mental health. It has been estimated that 20 percent of Americans, or nearly fifty million, suffer from some of the symptoms of depression. Depression can be one of the most serious of all psychological problems because there is the possibility of suicide, but a majority of these fifty million people are like Sarah; they are not happy with their lives and they feel incapable of doing anything about it, but they are not so depressed as to be unable to carry on with their day-to-day responsibilities. They are what I like to call mopers.

The ability to carry on is what separates the clinically depressed person from people like Sarah, a good example of a moper. Clinically depressed people have trouble just making it through the day. They often cannot get up in the morning and fix breakfast. If they manage to get to work, they will not be able to concentrate; it is not unusual for their careers to take a nose dive or for them to lose their jobs. It is painfully obvious to both family and friends that the clinically depressed person is suffering. They may spend hours and sometimes days lying in bed and staring at the ceiling; they are more than willing to talk about what failures they are or how worthless their lives have been. But even though it can be frightening to have a friend or spouse who is clinically depressed, in some ways it is easier than living with the moper. It is obvious that the clinically depressed person needs help. It is usually not at all obvious what the moper needs.

Mopers are different, too, from those people who have periodic spells of depression. All people have times when they feel really down, times when they wonder how they are going to make it through the day. These people are different from the mopers in that they do not mind admitting that they have these feelings. They want and appreciate support and attention from their family and friends. Mopers are chronically sad. They do have periods when they feel okay, but they are likely to spend more of their lives feeling down than feeling up.

Another thing that distinguishes mopers from other types of depressed people is their need to maintain distance from others when they are feeling down. While most depressed people want to talk to others about their troubles, mopers feel compelled to keep their problems to themselves. Once they start to slip into their blue mood, they put up a wall to keep others out. They are unable to derive any comfort from the support and encouragement of the people in their lives. The response "I'm fine, just leave me alone" typifies the moper.

Jack did not learn that Sarah's problem was depression until they entered marital therapy nearly two and a half years after she began to slip into it. He imagined all sorts of reasons why he seemed to be losing his wife, and most of his reasons centered on his own failures as a husband. "I never considered the possibility that Sarah was simply depressed. I just didn't see the signs. After all, she never complained of feeling that way. She never seemed happy, but she was always pleasant. I thought that she just didn't want to be married to me anymore. At times I was sure that she was having an affair. Her distant attitude toward me and the fact that she seemed to lose interest in sex seemed to point to it. So I'd try harder and harder to be the perfect husband. I did a lot of the housework so she wouldn't be so tired, and I tried to think of fun things we could do together. But nothing seemed to make any difference. She finally started to talk about her feelings after I told her I couldn't stand being so rejected by her and that I was moving out."

It was Sarah's fear of losing Jack that helped her face her situation. Until that time, she did not label herself as feeling depressed, either, so when she told Jack that nothing was wrong, she meant it. From her point of view she was telling the truth.

At some level, however, Sarah did know that something was wrong, but she was unable to understand just what it was herself, much less articulate it to Jack. She knew that she had nothing to look forward to. She knew that she felt overwhelmed by her responsibilities to her family even though she managed to meet them in a reasonably efficient way. And she knew that she felt empty and lonely much of the time. But she explained all those feelings away by telling herself that she was going through a difficult time in her life; she was sure that sooner or later things would get better. What Sarah could not see was that unless she did something about her situation, things would never get better.

The moper is sometimes called the smiling depressive. Like Sarah, these people suffer from many of the signs of depression, but they present a facade that prevents other people in their lives from knowing what is going on with them. It is not that they are intentionally trying to fool people; their laughing-on-the-outside-crying-on-the-inside manner is a style that they have adopted to achieve some semblance of balance among their conflicts. In truth, they are fooling themselves every bit as much as they are fooling other people.

The basic struggle that mopers face is between the desire to be strong, competent people and the fear that they are not that way at all. Their desire and their need to be strong and competent makes it impossible to admit to others—much less to themselves—that they have a problem they cannot cope with. To mopers, to have problems implies weakness, and it is intolerable for them to admit such weakness in themselves.

On the other side of the coin are self-doubts that prevent them from trying to make the changes that would make their lives more satisfying. At some level, they know there are things they could do that would improve their lot in life, but to try them out is to risk failure. And failure would be more evidence that they are indeed as incompetent as they secretly fear.

So rather than recognize all this, they retreat into a state of psychological numbness. They blame the situation.

They blame a cruel and capricious fate. They blame anyone and anything but themselves, because deep down, they know that they have only themselves to blame. Randy was one man who has made it through this conflict. Blessed with the clear vision that hindsight so often provides, he was able to describe his struggle. "I always knew that I had a lot of ability—in fact, I prided myself on it—but I was always afraid of failing. So I made a habit of selecting a course in which the chances of failure were pretty slim. After I graduated from college, I started to teach math in high school. I liked it for a few years, but then I started to get bored by it all. I wanted to try to make it as a stockbroker, but by then we had two kids and the risk of failure just seemed too high. I felt trapped. I started to withdraw from my family and friends more and more.

"At the time, I really believed that there was nothing I could do about it. After all, I had a wife and kids to support. How could I do something that might jeopardize them? I learned that it was my own insecurities that were standing in the way after my wife took away all my excuses. She went out and got a job and told me that I had two years to try to make it as a stockbroker. When I objected that we couldn't live on the money she made, she said we would sell the house and move into an apartment if we ran out of money before the two years were up. She told me that if I didn't try it she would leave me, because she was sick and tired of living with someone who was never happy. Within eight months I was making more money than I had teaching, and I was infinitely happier."

During the course of marital therapy, Sarah learned that she had basically the same conflict. She had promised herself that she would resume her career as a medical technician once her children were in school, but when the time came, her self-doubts began to surface. Could she really go back to school and compete with kids that were ten to fifteen years younger than she was? And even if she did make it through school, could she stand the pressure of a demanding profession where a mistake could mean the difference between life and death? Because Sarah liked to think of herself as a take-charge woman, she allowed herself to be only dimly aware of these doubts. She found other, "more logical" reasons why she couldn't go back to school quite yet. After all, her children were still young and it was important to them for her to be there when they got home from school. And her husband was at a crucial phase in his career; he didn't need the added burden of trying to juggle schedules to accommodate her.

Sarah was right; these were more logical reasons for her not to go back to school, and they were accurate. Her kids did like her there when they got home from school, and her husband's life was much easier with Sarah as a full-time mother and housewife. But people do not always operate according to strict rules of logic. Her logic did not make her conflicts go away, so she slipped into a moper personality.

Jack's reaction to Sarah was typical for partners of the moper—he felt he was being rejected. All that Jack could see was a woman who no longer seemed to care if he was there or not. While there had been a time when they laughed together freely, the only thing he could get from her now was an uncomfortable smile. While Sarah had been an enthusiastic sex partner, she now seemed to act as if it was her rather unpleasant duty. While before they could enjoy doing virtually anything, so long as they did it together, now Sarah did not seem to enjoy anything they did. In short, the signs of the moper are virtually the same as the signs that one has grown weary of the relationship.

The one important difference is that the moper's inability to experience joy and pleasure permeates most, if not all, areas of his or her life. Sarah, for instance, was quiet and withdrawn not only around Jack, but around her friends as well. She could be friendly and polite if she was around them, but it just seemed to be too much of an effort to make the arrangements to see them. Similarly, Randy's passion was his Saturday-morning doubles at the tennis court before he became a moper. After a while, it began to seem like torture to go out and run around in the hot sun for a couple of hours, but out of habit and a vague sense of obligation, he would drag himself to the tennis court every Saturday morning anyway. These people increase their distance from *everyone* in their lives, not just their partners.

Probably the only type of person who can live with the moper and not be affected by the apparent rejection is the egotist. The egotist is so wrapped up in himself or herself that the moper's lack of response is not much noticed. As long as the moper continues to function—take care of the kids or bring home the paycheck—many egotists won't mind all that much. (I am always a little taken aback when an egotist comes to therapy after a family problem has developed to the point where one of the family members has done something pretty dramatic, and claims never to have noticed that anything was wrong. But it does happen.) Anyone except an egotist would probably feel either guilty or angry, depending on their style, about the behavior of the moper.

If you are living with someone who seems to be chronically unhappy, difficult as it may be, you have to step back and look at your partner's whole life. While mopers' behavior does seem to be terribly distant, you must keep in mind that it is not you that they are rejecting but their own self-doubts, and that the easiest way for them to do this is to place a little psychological distance between themselves and the rest of the world. Their need to protect themselves can make it painfully frustrating to cut through all this, but it can be done.

Development of the Moper

Mopers learn two important things as they are growing up. First, they learn that they are not as bright or competent as their parents expect them to be. They get the message that nothing they do quite measures up, although they tend to be above average in ability and do see evidence that they are capable people. Their parents' disappointment that they do not accomplish even more, however, takes its toll on their self-esteem. In this way, they have much in common with people who have compulsive characteristics; no matter how much they achieve, they have the vague feeling that they should accomplish more.

The difference between the training that the moper and the compulsive personality receive is a matter of degree. The parents of the budding compulsive are likely to make up detailed plans for overcoming the perceived deficiency; the parents of the incipient moper are more likely to voice their disapproval of their child's shortcomings and let it go at that. Todd remembers how his father almost seemed to enjoy telling everyone about his inability to do anything practical. "One of my most vivid childhood memories is my father going on and on in front of all our relatives at Thanksgiving dinner about how I would have to go to college because I couldn't do anything with my hands. He seemed to be particularly impressed by how little I knew about cars. Along with feeling completely humiliated, I felt angry because he never took five minutes to try to teach me anything about them; I wondered how he thought I was supposed to learn. Every time I tried to do something he would take over and tell me that I would ruin his tools and just make whatever I was working on worse. The one thing I did learn was not to ask my father for any help."

The second lesson that mopers learn is not to let anyone

know if they are feeling bad. Todd learned this lesson well, too. "When I was upset about something—going back to when I was only five or six—my father's favorite phrase was 'Don't be such a baby.' I guess he thought boys shouldn't cry, because I knew that if he was around I'd better look happy or I'd get sent to my room 'until I could cheer up.' I don't remember ever talking to my parents about a problem I had. In fact, I didn't know anyone did that until I went to college and I met people who would tell me about the advice they got from their fathers. The only advice I ever got was to 'grow up.' "

The tragedy of Todd's childhood is that his father loved him very much. Todd was his only son and he wanted Todd to be all of the things that he was not; he believed he was doing what was best for Todd, that he was toughening him up for the real world. Unfortunately, his father's actual feelings for Todd are not nearly as important as Todd's perceptions of how his father felt about him. Todd believed his father saw him as a weak, ineffectual crybaby, so he had to struggle to prove that he was competent and strong.

What Todd and people like him learn is that when you are feeling bad, you are better off by yourself. Most of us learn that other people can be a source of encouragement and support. As we are growing up, we find that our parents' love can be a sanctuary from the disappointments of the world. And although we inevitably learn that our parents cannot solve all of our problems, we do find out that the warmth of other people can provide a respite from the pains of growing up. Todd simply did not learn that other people could do this for him; even as an adult, he had the feeling that other people, including his wife, would think that he was being a "baby" if he admitted that he was anything but happy.

Sprinkled in with these two messages is a dose of family formality. Mopers usually grow up in families where there is little, if any, outward display of love and affection. Sarah, for instance, does not remember ever being hugged or hearing her parents tell her that they loved her. "The only thing I remember is that one of my parents would tell me that the other said something nice about me. So sometimes my dad would tell me that I made my mother very proud or my mother would tell me that my father said that I looked very pretty when I was all dressed up. But neither of them ever said anything like that to me directly." So once again the lesson learned is to keep your distance from others.

Living with the Moper

Mopers often make it to middle adulthood before their style begins to cause them serious problems. They almost certainly have periods of feeling down earlier in their lives, but because things change so fast during early adulthood, their self-defeating style does not have a chance to take root. In their late teens, they may feel depressed about a relationship that goes sour, but it probably will not be long before someone new comes along. They may be unhappy about their college career, but they will either finish or drop out to make that problem go away. In other words, when they are young and everything in their lives is in transition, they are able to fall back on their resources and arrive at some kind of solution to the problems they face.

It is when they reach their thirties and forties, when they have achieved some stability in their lives, that they are likely to encounter trouble. Sarah's conflict about returning to school, or Randy's conflict about changing careers, will not go away in a few months. These conflicts will remain until they are dealt with. It is during these times that mopers are likely to learn about the difficulties they have being intimate with others. They may not be able to label their problem clearly, but they do begin to recognize the feeling of being all alone in the world. This tends to make them withdraw from others even more, so that a self-defeating vicious cycle is firmly established. Here are some specific cases.

Q: I'm really worried about my husband. He has had his own business for the past twenty years, but the last few years have been tough on him. I know that things aren't going well, because we've had to cut back on a lot of things, but he won't tell me what's going on. When I ask him, he'll only say that things are a little slow but there's nothing to worry about. Well, I know that he's plenty worried. He stays up until three or four in the morning, and he won't talk to me or the kids unless we ask him a direct question, and then you can tell he's only being polite; he just wants to be left alone. Losing him hurts more than losing any of the material things we have. How can I get him to let me help him?

A: It's going to be tough, because I would guess that your husband has a lifetime of experience being the strong man that others can depend on. In fact, I wouldn't be surprised if this is one of the qualities that you found attractive to begin with; it is not unusual for someone to be drawn to people like your husband because they seem to strong and then to encourage them, either subtly or openly, to be that way. This makes it hard, many years later, to reverse fields and share the burden with a partner. All his life, he has heard the message that he has to be the one to shoulder the load.

I'm certainly not saying that it is your fault that he is the way he is. But people do not form relationships randomly, and his strength may have been something you needed, and hence promoted, at one time in your life. The problem is that neither people nor relationships remain static. It seems that you have changed, since after twenty years you want to know the details of the business. (Many spouses would prefer not to know; they want to be spared any of the unpleasant details.) So now that your needs, as well as your husband's, have changed, you are finding it difficult to reach a new equilibrium that proves to be satisfying for you both.

The most important thing that you have to do is to strike a balance between letting him know that you are there and are willing to share his problems, and putting too much pressure on him to open up to you. The best way of letting him know that you are there is to tell him precisely how you feel. Tell him that you know that everything is not all right; let him know that his insomnia and his change in mood are obvious to you. And then tell him that you feel left out, that you want to help but you don't even know what is going on.

Not putting too much pressure on him is crucial. If he has the feeling, justified or not, that he is being nagged about his problems, he will probably withdraw all the more. He needs to perceive you as a strong, capable person who can indeed carry part of the burden he finds so heavy. If he detects any desperation on your part, he will probably conclude that you would only be more upset if he shared his problems with you.

So while you need to tell him how you feel, don't tell him too often. Make sure he gets the message, and then give him subtle prompts when he seems to be particularly concerned. For example, on one of the nights he can't sleep, you might get up and ask him if he would like to talk about what's on his mind. If he says no, leave it at that, and go back to bed and wait for the next opportunity. If you are persistent without appearing to be pushy—I know how tough that can be—I think he will let you in on his thoughts sooner or later.

It is important for you not to take on the responsibility for your husband's problems. Don't feel that you must be a failure somehow just because your husband won't let you help him, and don't let yourself feel personally rejected by his uncommunicativeness. If he doesn't change eventually, you may decide that you don't want to live with it, but do not assume that is is your fault.

If you can maintain this posture of being concerned about him, but perfectly willing to go on with your own life in any case, it will increase the chances that he will begin to talk to you. It is a paradox with mopers, but the harder people try to get into their world, the harder they try to keep them out.

When he does begin to show a few chinks in his armor, don't expect it all to come out at once. There is probably a lot that he is not admitting to himself, so it will take a while before he learns that he can trust himself, as well as you, to open up. When he does start to talk, try to maintain the same concerned, supportive, but calm attitude. If you respond too strongly, even if it is with love, it might scare him off again. You need to give your husband a chance to get used to the changes in himself and in his relationship with you.

What you have going for you is that your husband probably does want to be close to you; most chronically sad people have stable relationships, and they like things that way. Your husband's problem is that he doesn't know how to be intimate when a problem comes up; as you indicated, everything is fine when there is smooth sailing. The moper needs to learn how to rely on others when the waters get rough. I would think that your caring and loving attitude, as evidenced by the way you asked your question, will win out in the end, and that you will be successful in helping your husband get past his problem.

Q: I'm getting more and more frustrated with my wife. She promised that as soon as our youngest child started junior high school, she would go back to work. Well, it's been over a year now and she still hasn't got a job. What really makes me angry is that I don't think she's trying. Even though she knows we could really use the money, I don't think she goes on more than one or two interviews a month. The worst part of it is that she seems to be losing interest in her family as well. All she does anymore is read novels. When I ask her what the problem is she just says that things are tight out there. I would think that anyone with a college education could find a job within a month if he or she really wanted to. How can I get her moving?

A: Because men rarely have to face the kinds of situations that women face all the time, it is virtually impossible for them to imagine what it is like, and you sound as if you fall into this category of not understanding. Imagine for a minute that you had not held a paying job for ten or fifteen years and were suddenly forced back into the job market. And imagine that the person closest to you had been developing a career during those years and had achieved some measure of success, but because of your absence of an employment history, the only things open to you are menial jobs that are far below your education and intelligence, and jobs in which the majority of your co-workers are nearly a generation younger than you. On top of this, suppose that all of your life you had been told that your most important role was taking care of your children and your family; getting a job would of course, represent some degree of dereliction of duty. So unless you were really desperate for money, I would bet that you would be reluctant to jump in with both feet, too.

What I am saying is that this is not an easy time for your wife. The fact that she spends much of her time reading may suggest that she has fallen into being a moper; she is having trouble dealing with the situation, so she is attempting to escape from it all through her novels. But if the only thing you are doing for her is reminding her how much you could use the extra money, I'm not surprised that she is reacting the way she is.

The first thing you need to do is to let her know that you understand how hard this is for her. Even if you don't really believe it, tell her; if you show some understanding, perhaps she will begin to share some of her concerns with you, and then you may be able to genuinely understand.

Next, you need to give her help in the nitty-gritty details of finding a job. Since you have been out in the working world all these years, there are a lot of things you take for granted but she simply does not know about. Help her prepare her résumé; sit down with her when she writes letters. Even going through the ads with her could give her a big boost. Many very capable and intelligent women do not realize that they do indeed have marketable skills even though they have not worked for some time. You might see ads for jobs for which you know she is qualified but which she doesn't have enough confidence to apply for. You need to build up her confidence. Take every opportunity to tell her how well she would do in various situations.

Many organizations have workshops for women who are in your wife's situation. You might contact local women's organizations, universities, or even employment agencies to see if they do have groups for women who are returning to the work force. Such a group could help your wife learn the skills that are necessary to find a job and give her the confidence to go out and do it. Also, being able to talk to other women who are in the same situation would be a big help to her; she may feel—and it sounds to me as if she could be right—that you don't understand, and it's always nice to be able to talk to others who are in the same boat.

Finally, be prepared for your life to change once she does get a job. The tradition in our society seems to be that when women return to work, they do not give up any of their household duties. Since your wife seems to be the type of person who will not complain about it, she may fall into this pattern, but it will not be long before she resents it. If you wait for this to happen, your relationship will be in real trouble. You must be willing to take on half of the housework. When one of the kids is sick, you need to share the responsibility of making the necessary arrangements. Do not assume that just because you make more money your job is more important; your job and your wife's job are equally important, and you should be equally willing to take time off, if necessary, for emergencies.

Remember that your wife's situation is not her problem alone. Together you made decisions about how you would structure your family. True, most decisions like this are made passively, since tradition seems to dictate that the woman will be the one to stay with the kids, but it is a mutual decision nonetheless. So getting your wife back to work should be a mutual project as well. If you can help her in this endeavor in a supportive and caring way, it will pay dividends in the future of your relationship.

Q: My husband never tells me what is going on at work. It's almost embarrassing, because my friends are always telling stories about what's going on at their husbands' offices. I don't think my husband is having any problems, but I wonder if he could be holding it all inside. Do I have reason to be worried?

A: I don't think so. Since you do not mention any other problems in your relationship and you haven't noticed any signs that he is unhappy, I would chalk up his not talking about the details of work to a temperamental difference.

Some people like to share every endless detail of their day with their partners while others find such details too tedious to talk about. Your husband may be the kind of person who prefers to forget about work when he is at home.

I would be concerned if he never mentions anything about his job. Everyone is bound to have some disappointments as well as some victories when it comes to a career. If he does not share these major events with you, then you need to start encouraging him to open up a little. But if his style is to let you know about the big things that happen but to ignore the usual office gossip, then I would let well enough alone.

Q: Recently my husband received a major promotion that will mean a big boost to his career. After getting it, he told me that he had been depressed about his job for two years; he had thought he was at a dead end and had not expected to get this last promotion. I felt devastated by this; I didn't even know that anything was bothering him. What kind of a relationship do we have if he can be depressed for so long without my even knowing it?

A: You have a typical relationship with a moper. Your husband's unwillingness to confide in you reflects his personality structure. However, even though it is understandable that you would feel shocked and let down by your husband's confession, it would be silly to conclude that your relationship has been a failure if you have been happy up to now. That's not to say that you can't work on your relationship to make it even better, however.

Your husband's admission that he was depressed, and your surprise at his confession, reflects a common difference between men and women. Women are generally taught to be emotional specialists; they are taught to value their feelings and to express them freely. Men, on the other hand, tend to learn that real men keep things to themselves. To them emotions are a sign of weakness; after all, boys are not supposed to cry.

This difference in training results in some startling differences in mental health statistics. It has been estimated that four to six times as many women as men receive a diagnosis involving depression. But in my experience, the people I call mopers are much more likely to be men than women. Women believe they have a right to be depressed; men don't, and feel they must keep it to themselves. So your husband was doing a good job of playing what he considered to be an appropriate male role by keeping his feelings of depression to himself.

If you want to change things, I think you will have plenty of opportunities during the next few months. Any big promotion involves a lot of stress, so I would guess that your husband will have plenty on his mind that he could talk about. Let him know that you were hurt by his keeping his feelings of depression to himself, and that you would like him to feel that he can discuss his concerns with you in the future. Follow the suggestions discussed earlier. Be persistent in reminding him that you are available, but allow him to have a little distance as well. He may be a tough nut to crack if he completely fooled you for two years, but keep trying. Remember, he has probably never even considered the possibility of sharing his troubles with you, and it will take him a while to get used to the idea.

Some Final Thoughts

How much should a person share with a partner? It is not a simple question to answer. There are some psychologists who advocate that if a relationship is to be meaningful, couples must feel free to tell each other every thought that they have. I think that this position does not take personality differences into account. The type of person that I am most concerned with is the individual who does not share bad feelings because they are viewed as a sign of weakness; these are the people who may have difficulty recognizing their own feelings and whose relationships are likely to deteriorate over time. But those individuals who can recognize their feelings and who tend to keep things to themselves as a matter of preference do not necessarily have a problem. The message is, don't look for problems that are not there. There are bound to be enough there already without finding any extras.

7

THE MONEY-SICK

The Money-Sick Test

1. When my clothes begin to look a little worn:

a. I try to patch them up.
b. I start looking for sales.
c. I buy some new clothes.
d. I never keep anything long enough for it to look worn.

2. I think it is important to have enough money in the bank to:

a. cover the last check I wrote.
b. deal with emergencies that might come up.
c. take care of my family for a year.
d. provide financial independence.

3. **Going shopping is:**
   a. my favorite pastime.
   b. something I like to do.
   c. something I don't mind doing.
   d. worse than a trip to the dentist.

4. **If I suddenly came into $25,000, I would:**
   a. live it up for as long as it lasted.
   b. pay off my bills and blow the rest.
   c. treat my family to a nice vacation and save the rest.
   d. add it to my nest egg.

5. **I think I could be happy if:**
   a. I could make $10,000 more a year.
   b. I were financially independent.
   c. I did not have to worry about bills.
   d. my family and I stay healthy; money is secondary.

6. **The presents I get from family and friends:**
   a. are never as nice as what I give them.
   b. always show their thoughtfulness.
   c. are usually nicer than what I get for them.
   d. are few and far between.

7. **I think about money:**
   a. several times every day.
   b. more than most people I know.
   c. only when it comes up—like when I'm paying bills.
   d. hardly ever—life is too short to worry about money.

8. **It is important to me that my family and friends:**
   a. think I have more money than I really do.
   b. have a realistic idea of how much money I have.

c. believe I have less money than I actually have.
d. not be concerned about my financial situation.

9. When I'm around people who have a lot more money than I do:

a. I feel uncomfortable.
b. I feel angry that I don't have more.
c. I find myself looking up to them.
d. I don't think about their money.

10. If a friend offered to sell me a Persian rug for much less than it was worth:

a. I would snap it up in a minute and thank my lucky stars there are so many fools in the world.
b. I would buy it, but I would feel a little guilty about it.
c. I would insist on paying more for it—not what it was really worth, but more.
d. I would insist on paying as much as the rug was worth.

The Money-Sick Test Scoring Key

1. a. 3 points.
b. 1 point.
c. 0 points.
d. 2 points.

2. a. 3 points.
b. 0 points.
c. 1 point.
d. 2 points.

3. a. 2 points.
b. 0 points.
c. 0 points.
d. 3 points.

4. a. 3 points.
b. 2 points.
c. 0 points.
d. 1 point.

5. a. 2 points.
b. 3 points.
c. 1 point.
d. 0 points.

6. a. 2 points.
b. 0 points.
c. 1 point.
d. 3 points.

7. a. 3 points.
b. 2 points .
c. 0 points.
d. 1 point.

8. a. 3 points.
b. 1 point.
c. 2 points.
d. 0 points.

9. a. 2 points.
b. 3 points.
c. 1 point.
d. 0 points.

10. a. 3 points.
b. 2 points.
c. 1 point.
d. 0 points.

Interpretation of Test Scores

0 to 8 points: You have a healthy attitude toward money. You are able to use it to make your life more enjoyable rather than to satisfy your unconscious psychological needs.

9 to 15 points: You may have a few quirks about money. They may not be interfering with your life, but you might want to examine them just to make sure any self-destructive tendencies you may have do not develop further.

16 to 23 points: Your attitude toward money is probably causing you some problems. This chapter could be important.

24 to 30 points: You probably have already alienated family and friends with the way you use money. This chapter is a must.

What Happened to the Five Dollars I Gave You on Monday?

Jean knows how to pinch a penny. While most of her friends complain about how difficult it is to make ends meet, Jean is able to put away two or three hundred dollars every month. Of course, it isn't easy to be so thrifty, but Jean believes that her efforts more than pay for themselves. So what if it takes her two days to do her biweekly grocery shopping? If you want to take advantage of coupons and specials, a few extra hours are well spent. And she likes to cook, so she doesn't mind making her own crackers and croutons. A penny here and a penny there can really add up.

Jean does not economize for any particular reason. She just likes to know that the money is there is case she or her family might need it. "I know my friends think I'm a little strange, but I just can't understand how they can be so unconcerned about the future. I would be a nervous wreck if I knew that every penny coming in was already spent. How can people live like that? Everyone seems to think I should have something I'm saving the money for. Well, just because there's nothing I want to buy doesn't mean that I don't have a reason for saving money. I'm saving it for the future! I think that anyone who does not plan ahead is either naive or stupid."

Although her attitude toward money affects her children's lives, they are mostly unaware of it. There are times when they feel bad because most of their clothes are hand-me-downs from their mother's sisters' families or come from garage sales, when their friends are wearing designer clothes. And they tend to avoid having their friends over because they are a little embarrassed about how the old, worn furniture in their house compares with that of their friends. But they have never known things to be any other way; they have come to accept their mother's assertions that there isn't enough money to go around.

Jack, Jean's second and current husband, was pleased to discover his wife's frugal ways when they were first married. "I was kind of worried about how things would go at first, because Jean had already had a taste of the middle-class dream. I had been in the service for a few years and then college, so even though I was thirty-one years old when we got married, I was just getting started with my career. So I was relieved when I found out that not only did she not pressure me into buying a new house full of expensive furniture, but she actually was able to save money on my meager starting salary. I'm basically a saver at heart too, so I was more than happy to turn over the finances to her, since she seemed to be so good at it."

It did not take too long before Jack realized that his wife was more than thrifty. "I should have done something about it earlier, because, God knows, she gave me plenty of clues that she had a few screws loose when it comes to money. I remember one time she got mad at me because I paid full price for a *New York Times* that didn't have the book-review section in it. She thought I should have gotten the guy at the newsstand to take a dime off the price. But I thought she would loosen up as I started to make more money. Boy, was I in for a surprise! When Christopher was born, I thought we'd use our nest egg to buy a nice house, but she wanted to keep on living in our apartment! I finally talked her into getting a house, but I had to compromise and get one in an old redevelopment neighborhood. She claimed that if we fixed it up ourselves it would be a great investment.

"The problems really started when I got my last promotion. Until then, I always took my lunch to the office and ate it in the cafeteria with some of the people I worked with. I never really needed any cash, so it didn't matter to me that Jean gave me five dollars on Monday and expected me to make it last until Friday. Well, now the people I work with go out for lunch, and I want to go with them. When I told Jean that I would need thirty dollars a week, she hit the ceiling. She said that there was no point in making more money if I was just going to spend it on lunches in fancy restaurants. Rather than make a scene about it, I got my own credit card and threw away the lunches she packed for me. Well, I realized that this couldn't go on when I had to give my five dollars for a shower present for my secretary one day. The next morning, I asked Jean for another five, and she asked me in her iciest, coldest voice: 'What happened to the five dollars I gave you on Monday?' "

Money is an interesting topic, because few people admit that they have a problem with it. They may admit that they don't have enough, or that the sour state of the economy has caused them some problems, or that they have been unlucky in their investments, but they do not seem to be able to recognize that they may be causing their own money problems. This is ironic, because it is easy enough to see how other people can be foolish with their money; we can all recognize when others are spending money impulsively for things they don't really need or, spot the miser who unnecessarily denies himself the pleasures of life and hoards his money for a rainy day that will never be rainy enough to make him dip into his accumulation of funds. We just cannot seem to see these things in ourselves.

The reason that it is so difficult to be objective about money is that we use it to satisfy our emotional and psychological needs. From any one person's perspective, the way in which he or she uses money is completely rational and logical. Being a tightwad or a spendthrift, however, does not occur in a vacuum; it serves a purpose. We use money in a way that is consistent with our view of the world and our view of ourselves.

Jean, for example, saved every penny that she could because she saw the world as filled with uncertainty. Should something go wrong, she was not confident of her ability to find her own place in it. Her first husband left her after less than a year of marriage, and she lived in fear that it would happen again. That her second husband was a completely different person than her first, and that they had saved enough money to make any transition comfortable, made no difference to her. Her basic insecurity made it impossible for her to feel that she would ever have enough money tucked away in the bank. Pinching pennies was the only way that she could feel safe and secure.

The problem for people like Jean is that the things they do to ward off their feelings of anxiety may serve to make their worst fears come true. Jean was driving her husband away with her tightfistedness; he was beginning to view her as a woman who was incapable of enjoying life. She seemed to care nothing about her family; she only cared about the bottom line of their savings account. So Jean managed to create a self-fulfilling prophecy. She was afraid that her husband would leave her, and the method she chose to cope with these fears made it all the more likely that he would.

Jean's husband, however, was on the mark with some of his observations. While she did care very deeply about her family, she did not get much pleasure from life. Her need to be on guard made it impossible for her to completely enjoy any activity that required spending money. She liked the idea of eating out, but the first thing she would notice when she got to a restaurant would be the prices on the menu. Jean would almost always pick the "Special of the Day," and she would feel vaguely annoyed when her husband got an appetizer along with his dinner. After all, why spend four dollars for a few shrimp when you could get so much more for the money at the fish store?

Price is always the foremost consideration for compulsive nonspenders like Jean. They are more than willing to sacrifice quality, as well as their own preferences, in order to get a good price. Larry was able to recognize this tendency in himself. "I hated to spend money on clothes, but about every two years, my wife would start to badger me to get some new ones, and because I knew she was right, I would reluctantly agree to go shopping with her. I was always attracted to the things that were on sale, even if they didn't fit quite right or even if I didn't really like them. Susan would try to tell me they were wrong for me, but I just wouldn't listen. I would convince myself that I really did like the pair of pants, and not just because they were fifty percent off. Well, what happened, of course, was that these things would find their way to the back of the closet and I just wouldn't wear them. We've reached a compromise of sorts. Susan buys all of my clothes for me, and I can take something back if I really don't like it. I know it doesn't make sense, but I just can't stand paying thirty dollars for a shirt even though I like thirty-dollar shirts and can afford them."

The compulsive nonspender has to be distinguished from the bargain hunter. While the former feels insecure with himself and his relationships, the bargain hunter uses money to prove how clever and superior he is. The old joke about the antique collector illustrates this nicely. It seems that this man prided himself on being able to spot a bargain when others could not. One day he was passing a secondhand store when through the window he saw a cat drinking milk out of a very old, very valuable saucer. He did not want to let the owner of the store know how valuable the saucer was, so he offered to buy the cat for twenty dollars. After this was agreed upon, he commented as casually as he could, "Just to make sure the cat feels comfortable in his new home, I'd better take his dish too." The owner, who was no fool, replied, "I may be superstitious, but I want to keep the saucer. It seems to bring me good luck; since I got that saucer, I've sold fifty cats."

Like the antique collector, many bargain hunters are motivated by underlying feelings of hostility and aggressiveness. The antique hunter was more interested in proving how smart he was and how dumb the store owner was than he was in owning the saucer; he didn't want it unless he could "steal" it from someone who was not as clever as he. It is not unusual for bargain hunters to fill an entire house with things they do not really want. The "bargains" are important only because they serve as a monument to their superiority.

These people can be difficult to live with, because they are capable of driving a hard bargain with family members as well as with strangers. Liz is married to a man like this. "Jim learned very early in our marraige not to try to make his deals with me, but I can't get him to stop doing it with the kids. He negotiates everything he does with them. If they want to go to a movie, he gets them to clean up the garage first. If they want to hear a story before bedtime, he is likely to ask them to wash his golf balls in exchange. He says he is just trying to teach them the hard realities of the world, but it's more than that. I know he gets some satisfaction from knowing that he has our oldest boy mowing our grass for two dollars when most of the other kids in the neighborhood get four or five. He just can't resist getting a good deal even if it's at the expense of his own family."

Many bargain hunters are perfectly harmless. Betsy is nearing fifty, and since her children have left home, she does not have much to do—or much to make her feel important. She spends much of her free time hunting for bargains, because she believes that if there is one thing in this world she is good at, it is shopping. She gives most of her bargains away to her children or to her friends. Her husband is a successful businessman, so he does not care about the money, and he feels that her shopping "keeps her out of trouble." So the only person who is hurt is Betsy. She does derive some momentary satisfaction from finding her bargains and being able to present them to family and friends, but mostly her life feels empty. While she continues to try to prove to others how clever she is, and how much she can help them by buying things for them, they view her efforts as little more than an eccentricity. After all, how many extra rolls of toilet paper does a person need?

At the other end of the continuum lie the compulsive spenders. These are the people who simply cannot live within their means. At times they may have some awareness that they have a problem holding on to money, but more often than not they blame their family, the economy, their boss—anyone except themselves—for their inability to satisfy their every whim. Sharon was one woman who had some insight into her pattern. "The day before payday, I start to think about how I can spend my money, and it's the very first thing I think about when I wake up that morning. If I can't think of something I really want, I start to feel tense. But I'll go shopping anyway and I'll end up spending most of my check. I must have a dozen purses that I don't really like and never use. My husband gets furious with me because we could use the money to pay some bills, but I just can't seem to help myself."

Linda is more typical of the compulsive spender. It is

clear to everyone except her that she is trying—with notable success—to live beyond her means. She and her husband both have good jobs, but there never seems to be enough money to last until the end of the month. In our credit-card society, this does not provide much of an obstacle, however. Linda still manages to spend one or two hundred dollars more each month than she and her husband earn.

One of Linda's biggest weakness is buying clothes for her family. Her two children and her husband are among the best-dressed people in the city. Her four-year-old daughter has more dresses than she can wear before she outgrows them. Once when her husband commented that he needed some new pajamas, she came home with a silk robe and matching pajamas that cost over two hundred dollars. She is just as generous with her sisters on birthdays and Christmas. Of course, she always feels hurt and rejected when her generosity (or grandiosity, as her sisters would say) is not returned. When her husband objects to her spending habits, Linda becomes angry with him; she accuses him of being a tightwad—even though their credit cards are extended to the limit and they have refinanced their house three times in ten years to pay off bills. Linda's only defense—and the only one she feels is necessary—is that "it costs a lot to live these days."

Linda would deny it, of course, but she is using money to try to buy love. She is a few years older than her two sisters, who are only a year apart, and she always felt a little bit left out. As a child, she encouraged this distance between herself and her sisters, but after she left home, she began to regret being something of an outsider when the family gets together. She has always had a weight problem, and she fears that her husband will leave her for a more attractive woman someday. Her generosity is her unconscious way of trying to make sure that everyone will always love her, and shopping for others gives her a warm, contented feeling. Her husband finds it difficult to object too strenuously to her ways, because after all she spends most of the money on other people. So he mostly remains silent, but his bitterness about their financial situation is slowly but surely eroding the bond between them.

Sometimes the spendthrift's extravagance appears blatantly selfish. John feels that he deserves nice things, and he makes sure that he has them. He bought himself an expensive leather coat for Christmas one year, even though he already had several coats and his wife's coat was worn with age. Another Christmas, he bought himself a three-hundred-dollar watch and his daughter a second-hand bicycle. John gave his son plenty of advance notice that he would have to pay his way through college on his own, because John planned to buy a sailboat. Yet he refused to be put on the spot about his spending habits. "I deserve these things. After all, I'm the one who earns the money to pay all the bills. Besides, kids can't really appreciate nice things, and my wife doesn't like it if I spend a lot of money on her." Of course she doesn't. They couldn't make it if he spent half as much on her as he does on himself.

What John cannot see is the connection between his spending patterns and his feelings about himself. John is a professional person, but he has never believed that he is as smart or as competent as his colleagues. He confirms his beliefs by not working as hard at his job as he should. Rather than trying to compete directly with his co-workers, he tries to prove his superiority by accumulating things; wearing expensive clothes and jewelry is his way of proving that he is just as good as they are.

If we exclude those people who really do not have enough money to pay for the basics, it is a safe bet to assume that people who consistently live beyond their means have inner doubts about their self-worth. Everyone gets in over his or her head now and then, so simply being short of money on occasion does not in itself indicate a psychological problem. But people who are chronically worried about how they are going to pay their bills and who continue to buy things that they know they cannot really afford do need to take a close look at themselves. Not everyone believes that it is necessary to compete with the Joneses.

The biggest problem with money sickness, as it has been called, is that the people who have it never feel satisfied. The compulsive nonspender may feel some temporary satisfaction after making a bank deposit, but no matter how large the balance, it is never quite enough. Often these people start out by saying, "I just want enough money in the bank to deal with an emergency that might come up." But when they reach that level, then they have to have enough to pay for their children's college education. Once that goal is met, they worry about what would happen to them if they were in an accident or got sick and never could return to work. There are lots of people in the world who have more money than they could ever spend, yet continue to resent having to spend money. The person who is trying to tuck away a thousand dollars is no different from the person who needs a million to feel secure. The money itself is mostly irrelevant. The feelings that motivate the compulsive nonspending actually cause the chronic dissatisfaction.

The same is true of the bargain hunter and the compulsive spender. They can never feel more than fleeting happiness from the bargains they find or the things they buy. No matter how many things they have or how many bargains they are able to find, they will still feel a gnawing sense of dissatisfaction. Of course, they can never be convinced of this. They continue to believe that "if only I could have a house with a formal dining room, I'd be perfectly satisfied" or "I'd never want another thing if I could have a Mercedes." The sad truth is that buying a larger house or a more expensive car has never transformed an unhappy person into a happy one.

Although few people would admit to thinking that money can buy happiness, the money-sick base their lives on this premise. How we spend our time has much more to do with our happiness than how we spend our money. The person who uses money to make spending time more pleasurable is the one who will feel content. The person who believes that the road to contentment is spending or not spending money will never make it.

Development of the Money-Sick

It is hard for anyone not to have at least a touch of money sickness; our society promotes it. We may not like to admit it, but we pretty much accept without question the idea that people who make a lot of money are somehow superior to those who do not make as much. We may give lip service to the notion that the vagrant has as much worth as a human being as the successful business person, but we don't really believe it. Money is the yardstick for worth that most of us use.

Money is equated with love as well. It is not just a coincidence that Cinderella ended up marrying a rich, handsome prince. Nor do we question the fact that the poor but lovable Hansel and Gretel end up with the witch's treasures so that they can live happily ever after with their kind but browbeaten father. After all, who can live happily ever after as a pauper? We all assume, at some level, that money and love go together. The lessons begin very early in life.

Although it has probably reached the status of a cliché,

it is true that many parents use money as a substitute for their time and love when their children are growing up. Linda, the woman who was so extravagant with her family, remembers that the times she felt closest to her mother were when they went shopping together. "I know I was a difficult child to be around. By the time I was in junior high school, my weight problem was getting bad and I felt terrible about myself. I don't blame my mother for being angry at me so much of the time, but I do remember wishing she would just sit down and talk to me. Well, she just couldn't seem to do it. Anyway, whenever we had a particularly bad fight, she would usually suggest that we go out shopping then she would buy me something extravagant and I would feel sure that she really did love me after all. Now I can see her do the same thing with my children. She buys them all kinds of expensive gifts, but she doesn't seem to want to spend any time with them. I understand her well enough to know that she can't be any different, but it doesn't make the hurt go away completely."

Other parents may not have the same problem of being close with their children, but they do use money as a way of soothing hurt feelings or as a reward. Wally's parents spent a lot of time with him, but their solution to every problem was to buy him something to cheer him up. If he got pushed around by a bigger kid at school, his mother would give him a dollar and take him to the store so he could spend it. If he received an A on his report card, his father would do the same thing. His parents were not using money as a substitute for love, but they did want Wally to have the things that they could not have when they were children. No wonder Wally now goes on a spending spree when he feels down; buying something brings back his childhood feelings of knowing his mother and father love him. Parents who use food as the universal pacifier will have fat children; likewise, parents who use money will have children with money sickness.

Children also learn at a very early age that having expensive things is a way of measuring up to their friends. Kindergartners are now asking for—and getting—expensive shirts and blouses, Nike sneakers, and designer jeans. John, whose parents were more indulgent than most, was one of the fortunate kids who had all the rights labels on his clothes, and he had the most expensive baseball glove and tennis racket in the neighborhood as well. The envy and admiration of his friends did a lot to build up his self-esteem. Of course, it is tragic that as an adult he still relies on possessions to make him feel good about himself.

The child who does not get the right labels may try to make up for it in later life. Although Linda's mother would buy her something extra-nice on occasion, Linda got most of her clothes from J.C. Penny and a majority of the kids she went to school with wore designer labels which made her feel out of place. She intends to make sure that her children will never experience those feelings of not belonging, regardless of the cost. What Linda does not realize is that wearing the right clothes is no guarantee of feeling accepted. Lots of children do manage to grow up feeling good about themselves even though they own less than their friends.

The bargain hunter and the compulsive nonspender learn their styles more directly. There is a good chance that their parents had the same feelings about money. Andy, who has used his bargain-hunting ways to his advantage as a real estate investor, remembers that his father "talked a lot about the importance of getting a good deal. My wife and I had a terrible fight when our eight-year-old came home filled with excitement one afternoon and announced that he had sold a broken truck to the six-year-old next door for five dollars, his birthday money. My dad was always proud of me when I did something like that, and I felt proud of Zach, too. Well, my wife was furious with me for encouraging our son to take advantage of other people. It never really occurred to me that fairness was an issue. I had always lived by my father's advice that if you don't take advantage of them, they'll take advantage of you."

Most compulsive nonspenders grew up believing that financial disaster was imminent. This feeling may have been evidence of sensitivity to their parents' plight, or it may have been encouraged by the parents without any real justification. A lot of people who were children during the Depression developed into compulsive nonspenders with good reason; having to skip meals and move out of an apartment in the middle of the night to avoid the landlord would make most people feel that financial security is important. But even in these cases, the parents play a crucial role. Edith, who now has a dozen grandchildren, doesn't believe that she was affected by the Depression at all. "I don't think I realized that my parents were poor. They certainly never talked about their money problems in front of me. We had some pretty skimpy meals, and over a period of two years we moved eight times, but I somehow never made the connection between these things and being poor. I know that I never worried about what was going to happen to us."

On the other hand, the chronic pessimism and insecurity of some people compels them to talk constantly about problems even if they do not exist. Jean finds herself doing this to her children. "I know I have used 'we can't afford it' as a standard excuse for telling my children no. And I'm sure they must be sick and tired of hearing that money doesn't grow on trees when they don't finish their dinner or they don't take care of their things properly. I never realized what I was doing until I overheard my youngest child telling one of his little friends how poor we were."

It may be nearly impossible at times, but it is important to remember that the money-sick are not really happy being the way they are. They can be frustrating because they do not know why they feel chronically dissatisfied. Remember that while they are likely to attribute their feelings to not having enough money, their attitudes reflect their poor self-esteem and their need to feel loved and secure. Let's look at some suggestions for how these people can be turned around.

Living with the Money-Sick

Even in relationships in which neither person has so much as a hint of money sickness, there are bound to be disagreements about money. Do we buy new furniture or use the money to take a vacation? Do we try to keep the old car going for another year or do we splurge and get a new one? So it is important to distinguish between those inevitable situations in which the only solution is to work out some compromise and those conflicts that stem from the money sickness of your partner. Just because the person you live with does not agree with you about a money issue does not mean that he or she has "a problem." Always try compromise first. If, however, your partner never seems to be able to make any adjustments, then you may very well be facing a case of money sickness.

Q. My husband is a chronic worrier about money. He really doesn't like to spend money for anything. We've worked out most of our differences, but there is one thing that he continues to do that just drives me crazy: When he talks to other people, he always tries to give the impression that we're just barely making it. At the last party we were at, a group of us were talking about what we would do if we inherited a million dollars. My husband said he didn't care about being rich, he just wanted to reach the point where he didn't have to worry about it if we had to buy new tires for the car. Well, we certainly can afford new tires if we need them. What can I do to get him to stop this?

A: I would make two guesses about your husband. First, I'm willing to bet that he felt that his family was poor while he was growing up. Whether they were or not is not as important as what he thought. My second guess is that your husband tends to be low in self-confidence. A lot of people with this combination of characteristics tend to feel that they do not deserve to have money. They are not aware of this, of course; in fact, they may be obsessed with wanting more of it. Like your husband, they tend to be compulsive nonspenders, but when they accumulate a tidy little nest egg, all it does is make them feel uncomfortable.

On the bright side, many people with this problem deal with it in much more destructive ways than your husband. Some make chronically poor investments; others may develop a gambling problem. The unconscious strategy is to get rid of the money that they do not believe that they deserve.

If you have been able to work out most of your differences, then I would say that your husband is doing very well in trying to deal with his quirk. Although it is difficult to understand (remember, he doesn't understand it either), your husband feels more comfortable if he gives others the impression that he does not have much money. As long as he enjoys the things that he has and feels generally satisfied with his life, I would say that he does not have much of a problem.

The first thing I would try is simply to ask him to stop doing it. Apparently he is responsive to your feelings, or you would not have been able to work out all the things that you have. (You might want to ask yourself why it bothers you so much when he does this.) If this doesn't work, try a little humor. When he makes a comment like the one about the tires, you might say "Don't worry, dear, I'll always buy your tires for you." Given the fact that your husband has done as well as he has, I bet it won't take long before he begins to see the humor in his poor-talk. Once he realizes how silly it is, he won't feel the need to keep on with it.

Q: My wife has no appreciation for money. Our monthly bills are a couple hundred dollars more than my income. We've taken out several bill-consolidation loans the past few years, but she never seems to learn her lesson. Once the credit cards are paid off, she gets them right back up to the limit within a year. It won't be much longer before all of this catches up with us.

She's a good person in every other way, but being constantly in debt is getting to be more than I can take. After trying to juggle the bills on the first of the month, I'm depressed for a week. I have a good income, but I just cannot support her in the style she would like. If I can't get her to change, I will have to leave her to preserve my sanity.

A: Married, nonworking women—which I take your wife to be, since you mention your income only—have it tough in many ways. The biggest problem they face is that their feeling of being needed, of making a worthwhile contribution, and of being a competent person is so dependent on their families. This strain is reflected in statistics that show that married women have more psychological problems than single women. (Just the opposite is true for men; single men have more problems than do married men.) I think it would be safe to say that your wife's spending patterns are related to her sense of not being an important person. People who feel a need to keep up with the Joneses are missing something important in their lives—a productive and adaptive source of self-satisfaction.

There are exceptions to this notion that poor self-esteem can contribute to spendthrift tendencies. Some people have led such a sheltered life that they simply have never learned the connection between income and the things that money can buy. Women, as well as men, who come from a family in which everything was provided for them learn to expect that everything will *always* be provided for them. Intellectually, they know better, but deep down they assume that things will work out just fine. People who are like this do not misuse money in an attempt to build up their sense of self-importance; they simply do not know any better.

If your wife fits into this category, it sounds to me as if you have helped to keep her money-ignorant. You have continued to pay the bills, even though you obviously hate doing it, and you have bailed her out by getting the bill-consolidation loans. From her perspective, you can afford the life-style that you currently have. I wouldn't be surprised if your wife views you as a tightwad and a worrywart.

People who feel secure with themselves but are simply money-ignorant can usually change in short order when they have to face the consequences of their spending habits. Many people do manage to avoid this idefinitely by having a spouse or parents who continue to help them over the "rough spots" which never seem to end. Regardless of whether your wife is money-sick or money-ignorant, I would suggest turning over the household finances to her as a first step. Don't expect miracles. It may take her several months before she can do it competently. People like this have a tendency to "forget" to pay bills that put a crimp in their budget. But don't belittle her efforts, either. If you tell her that you knew that she couldn't do it and take over the task again the first time she makes a mistake, she will never learn.

Many women have become much better money managers than their husbands once their husbands relinquished the responsibility. Too many husbands keep their wives in a dependent role because they feel that their masculinity demands that they handle the finances. Remember, you want a partner, not just another dependent.

If your wife shows no aptitude for managing money after six months and her attitudes remain the same, then it is safe to assume that it is more than a case of money ignorance. She has a touch of money sickness, and more drastic measures will be needed. The first step is—as always—to talk to her. Tell her how you feel and why you worry about your situation. Do it in a calm, reasonable way. If you start making accusations, you won't get anywhere; you have to convince her that there really is a problem, and you won't be able to do this by fighting. If things are as bad as you say, the facts should speak for themselves. Don't expect her to accept everything you say immediately or uncritically, however; remember, she has a psychological stake in wanting things to continue as they are. Be gentle, but be persistent.

Once she accepts the fact that a problem exists—and I don't mean that she acquiesces just to shut you up, but really seems to understand the situation—then ask her for her ideas about how to turn things around. It is crucial that any plan that you develop result from a mutual effort. Most family budgets fall apart because they are unilaterally imposed by the partner who worries the most about money. If it is indeed a mutual effort, it will mean that you will have to make some sacrifices as well, so be prepared. Even if your wife were not a spendthrift, it would still be unlikely that the two of you would be in complete agreement about how to spend your money.

The plan that the two of you develop is only the short-term solution; the long-term solution is to help your wife feel better about herself. Until she can, the chances that she will stick to the plan are slim. Many women go through a period in which they feel compelled to spend a lot of money on clothes for their family and on furnishings for their house. Remember that for many women who stay home with the children, how well they can take care of their family is the only proof they have of their competence. Once their children grow older and require less of their time, they go back to school or find a job, and if they meet with success, they will look back and wonder why it ever was so important to them to have just the right oriental lamp in the living room.

Perhaps your wife needs a nudge in this direction. Many women who enter the job market when they are in their thirties or forties report a big boost in their self-esteem. Even if their paychecks are paltry compared to their husbands (after all, their husbands have had a ten- or twenty-year head start), they often discover how important it is for them to find out that they have something to offer that someone will pay for. Perhaps it is a sign that money sickness is rampant in our society, but the self-esteem of most men is tied in with their ability to earn money, and men should not assume that women are any different.

Try to view your wife's spending habits for what they are—a sign that she is not happy with herself. As long as you are willing to try, I think the odds are good that you will be able to help her find the solution. And there is nothing more meaningful that a person can do than to help another person grow and develop.

Q: My wife and I started our own business over thirty years ago when we were just kids. Thanks in large part to my wife, the business has done extremely well and we have reached the point where we could sell it and be financially independent.

Now that our kids have all finished college, I want to start enjoying life; I would like to take more time off. But my wife insists that Saturday is the most important day to be in the store; she hasn't been away from it for more than a week, and then it was only because she was in the hospital. I've tried to talk to her about what is important in life, but it's no use. She won't spend the money to take a nice vacation because she says that we'll need it to open another store. When I tell her I don't care if we have another store, she accuses me of being selfish; she says I should care about what we will be able to leave our children after we're gone. Well, we've worked sixteen hours a day, six days a week for most of our lives, and I want to take advantage of the success we've had. I'm beginning to wonder if there is any chance that I can get her to leave the business. What should I do?

A: It is ironic, but often the characteristics that are so useful in helping us get ahead at one stage of our life turn out to be our undoing later on. As sad as it is, partnerships can be the same way. A relationship that is perfect for us at one stage in life may simply be unworkable later on. I hope this does not apply to your case, but the chances are not good that your wife will change much at this point.

Most successful people have difficulty letting go. Their success has reinforced their willingness to sacrifice their time, and their identities become intertwined with their careers; what would they be if they were to walk away from it all? Also, retiring means acknowledging one's mortality; if one's life work is over, can the end of life be far behind? Your desire to walk away from a thriving business in order to enjoy life makes you more unusual than your wife—healthier, in my opinion, but more unusual.

Since talking to her has not worked, there are two other strategies I would suggest that you try before giving up on her. First, try to get her to see a therapist, and if she won't go alone, go with her. Sometimes just hearing a neutral person's perspective can be sufficient to get people to examine their values. If she does see someone, however, don't expect her to sign up for a world cruise immediately. The best you can hope for is that she will loosen up a little. She may be willing to try a few short trips, and if she enjoys those, she will probably want to try others. You must prepare yourself, however, for the possibility that after taking a few vacations she will decide that she would rather spend her time with the business.

The second suggestion is for you to take the trips by yourself. This will give her a chance to see if she cares more about the business or about being with you; also, you may decide that this is an acceptable compromise. Most people do not like traveling alone, but some do enjoy it; they like the freedom of not having to please anyone but themselves and they view it as an opportunity to make new friends.

If neither of these strategies works, and you decide that you want someone to enjoy your success with, then as sad as it is, you owe it to yourself to dissolve your partnership with your wife. One of the most difficult things that all of us have to do is to achieve a balance between our obligations to others and our obligations to ourselves. From the way you asked your question, I suspect that you have been sacrificing your desires in order to please your wife for some time now. I think you owe it to her to give her a chance to change, and to do what you can to help, but you do not owe her the rest of your life.

Q: The man I've lived with for the past three years seems to be perfect except for one little thing. He is cheap in small ways. As just one example of the kind of thing he does that bugs me, when we go out to dinner with another couple, he is never content to just split the check. He adds up what everyone's meal cost and then he prorates the tax and tip. We've been talking about getting married and having children, but I really don't like his cheapness. Am I making a mountain out of a molehill?

A: Some people do develop habits regarding money that have nothing to do with their overall attitudes. It could be that his father handled the check that way and it simply doesn't occur to him to do it any differently. On the other hand, most compulsive nonspenders are cheap in small ways, so it also is possible that he does have a few quirks when it comes to money.

Even if there were nothing about his behavior with money to give you pause, you should have a good long talk with him to explore your respective attitudes toward money. When marrying for the first time, most people think that it is almost in poor taste to talk about money. But people who are marrying for the second time and have a little experience under their belt spend a lot of time discussing money issues before making any final decisions. In short, I don't know if you are making a mountain out of a molehill, but you owe it to yourself to find out. Talk to him; ask him what his goals are. Ask him what he would do if he inherited $25,000, and whether he intends to save for the children's education, or feels that they should pay their own way. Then you must decide if you can live with his answers. There aren't any guarantees that he won't change his mind about some things as he gets older and makes more money, but at least you will know what you are getting into at the beginning.

Some Final Thoughts

There is a tendency, I think, to dismiss money problems as superficial. We may spend a lot of time worrying about it or fantasizing about it, but we don't like to admit that our view of money says something very important about us as people. And when we select someone to share our life with, compatibility regarding money is every bit as important as compatibility of religion, or politics, or attitudes about children. For some reason, though, we seem to think that money differences will work themselves out over time.

It still amazes me that my wife married me. Shortly before our wedding, I told her that I wasn't very ambitious and that all I wanted to do was to make six hundred dollars a month. She didn't say anything, so I assumed that her goals were similar. Several years later, she told me that if she had really believed me, she never would have married me. She was lucky in that our differences about money did work themselves out over time, but I would never recommend trusting luck when it comes to making such important decisions.

Because there is plenty of room in the normal range for disagreements, even those couples who have basically healthy attitudes about money need to come to terms with their money differences. This does not mean that they must agree about everything, but they do have to understand and appreciate their partner's feelings and wishes. They must be willing to make compromises. All too often, one person sets the standard by default; the other may not mind giving in at first, but the resentment will inevitably build. I once knew a woman who threatened to get a divorce because her husband wanted to give their six-year-old an allowance for doing a few chores around the house. She believed the child should be expected to help out because he was a member of the family and should not be paid for doing his duty. Obviously, no one would get a divorce if this were the only issue; this woman had gone along with her husband's way of doing things for eight years, and the allowance was the straw that broke the camel's back. It was just too late for her and she ended up divorcing her husband. So even if your partner does not have any signs of money sickness, do not sweep your differences under the rug. Talk about them!

8

THE HEALTH WORRIER

The Health Worrier Test

1. **During the past two years, I have seen my physician:**
   a. a dozen times or more.
   b. maybe five or six times.
   c. once or twice.
   d. I don't have a physician.

2. **During the past two years, I have visited:**
   a. at least three different doctors.
   b. my family doctor and one other specialist.
   c. just one doctor.
   d. I already told you, I don't have a physician.

3. **When I do visit a doctor:**
   a. I'm told that there is nothing wrong with me or that I just need to take better care of myself.

b. I usually get a prescription that helps me within a day or two.
c. I am usually just getting my annual checkup.
d. I don't remember the last time I did.

4. If I go to my doctor with a symptom that I'm worried about and he tells me it's nothing:
a. I think he is keeping something from me.
b. I get a second opinion.
c. I feel much better.
d. I never worry about symptoms.

5. When it comes to how the body works and what can go wrong with it:
a. I could probably pass the exam for a medical license.
b. I know more than the average person.
c. I know about as much as the average person.
d. I know very little and I don't want to know any more.

6. Cancer:
a. is something that terrifies me—I go to great lengths to check myself for any symptoms.
b. scares me a lot—I try to eat mostly natural foods and avoid people who smoke.
c. concerns me—I do what I can to reduce my chances of getting it.
d. is something that could never happen to me.

7. I get a stomachache or headache:
a. several times a week. My doctor tells me it's just nerves, but I think he just can't find what's causing it.
b. several times a week, especially when I'm upset.
c. not very often.
d. never.

8. **When I was growing up, I missed school because of illness:**
   a. so much I was almost held back a few times.
   b. much more often than most children.
   c. when I had the usual childhood diseases.
   d. virtually never.

9. **When I'm not feeling well, other people:**
   a. seem to be impatient with me.
   b. don't seem to be interested.
   c. tell me that they hope I feel better soon.
   d. I always feel well.

10. **When my partner asks me to do something I really don't want to do:**
    a. I seem to get sick—isn't that a coincidence?
    b. I do it, but my stomach gets tied up in knots.
    c. I try to work out some kind of compromise.
    d. I tell him or her to get lost.

The Health Worrier Test Scoring Key

1. a. 3 points.
b. 2 points.
c. 1 point.
d. 0 points.

2. a. 3 points.
b. 2 points.
c. 1 point.
d. 0 points.

3. a. 3 points.
b. 2 points.
c. 1 point.
d. 0 points.

4. a. 3 points.
b. 2 points.
c. 1 point.
d. 0 points.

5. a. 3 points.
b. 2 points.
c. 1 point.
d. 0 points.

6. a. 3 points.
b. 2 points.
c. 1 point.
d. 0 points.

7. a. 3 points.
b. 2 points.
c. 1 point.
d. 0 points.

8. a. 3 points.
b. 2 points.
c. 1 point.
d. 0 points.

9. a. 3 points.
b. 2 points.
c. 1 point.
d. 0 points.

10. a. 3 points.
b. 2 points.
c. 1 point.
d. 0 points.

Interpretation of Test Scores

0 to 7 points: Perhaps you are just unusually healthy, but I wouldn't be surprised if you have some real fears about your health. Please read the last few paragraphs of this chapter with an open mind.

8 to 16 points: Whatever your problems may be, you do not seem to have any tendencies toward expressing your conflicts through your body. Go on to the next chapter.

17 to 23 points: You could be a little frail, but there is a chance that you express your feelings through your body. This chapter could be important.

24 to 30 points: You are either very unhealthy or, more likely, you are a health worrier. This chapter definitely applies to you.

Do You Think It's Cancer?

Beth knew that she was the luckiest woman in the world. She was married to a man she loved very much, she had a job that could really take her places, and after being married for only two years, she had a house that was nicer than she had ever dreamed of owning. True, she had had some medical problems the last couple of years, but these seemed to be taking care of themselves. She used to have intense stomach pains, and one surgeon had even recommended that she have her gall bladder removed. But ever since she and her husband moved to a new city, her stomach pains were mysteriously fading away. Perhaps the change of climate agreed with her.

Her husband, Paul, has his own theories about Beth's stomach problems. "It took me a while to realize it, but I'm pretty sure her problems are related to her mother. It dawned on me that she usually had one of her attacks shortly after we visited her mother. Since we've moved, she's had only a couple of attacks, and those occurred after she talked to her mother on the phone. The last one happened after she got a letter from her mother; I don't know what was in the letter, because Beth wouldn't let me read it. Her mother had an unhappy marriage, and I think she was afraid that Beth would let me take advantage of her. She was probably giving Beth lots of advice that was putting her in a bind—advice about how Beth should be doing things in her marriage. She's getting a little more assertive with her mother now, and I think that's why her stomach isn't bothering her much anymore. I sure don't think her gall bladder healed itself all of a sudden."

Beth is relieved that she doesn't need an operation, but

she does worry that something else is lurking around the corner. "I never used to be this way, but I'm scared to death that I'll get some serious disease and I'll die. I think it's because I'm so happy—I'm worried that something will happen to Paul. If he's fifteen minutes late from work, I'm sure he's been in a terrible accident. I bet if I were not so happy, I wouldn't be having these problems."

Paul is mostly amused by Beth's hypochondriacal tendencies. He was worried about her stomach problems, but now that he thinks he understands the situation, he doesn't take it too seriously. "It seems that about once a month Beth thinks she has some new disease, but it usually doesn't take much to convince her that she's okay. Once, her wrist felt stiff and she was sure she had arthritis. I asked her if her other wrist was stiff, and when she said no, I said that it couldn't be arthritis; arthritis, I told her, is symmetrical, and if she didn't have it in both wrists, then it couldn't be arthritis. She was happy with that explanation, but later that week she told me that her boss, who is sixty-two years old, was complaining about the arthritis in his knee. She told him that unless his other knee hurt, it couldn't be arthritis. After I told her I had just made that up to reassure her, she admitted that her boss had given her a strange look. This month, she's worried about lumps. One night she found one on her side, and she made me feel it. I felt around for ten minutes, but it was so small I never could find it, but I told her I did just so I could get to bed. I didn't think that even Beth could be taking this seriously, but she asked with real panic in her voice: 'Do you think it's cancer?' "

Beth is one of millions of Americans who express their psychological conflicts through their bodies. She is a health worrier. While everyone knows that our feelings can have an effect on how our bodies feel (our stomach can be tied up in knots, or we can have a splitting headache), few people realize just how intimately our bodies and our minds are related to each other. Psychological factors have been implicated in illnesses that range from the common cold to cancer. In fact, experts generally agree that almost all diseases are influenced to some degree by our minds. The American Psychiatric Association has deleted psychosomatic disorders from its most recent diagnostic manual because of the recognition that virtually all physical illnesses are influenced by psychological factors. Add to this the countless people who have physical complaints without any physical illness, and you begin to get some idea of the scope of the problem. It has been estimated that perhaps as many as 80 percent of those in physician's waiting rooms would be more appropriately treated by mental health professionals.

I like to call the kind of problems that health worriers experience "mind-body problems." There are two major kinds of mind-body problems, and the technical terms for them are hypochondriasis and conversion disorders. Both kinds of health worriers express their psychological conflicts in bodily symptoms or concern about the body. Beth's concern about her lumps was one of the signs of hypochondriasis. Hypochondriacs have a tendency to interpret unusual bodily sensations, regardless of how minor or slight they may be, as a symptom of some dreaded disease—usually fatal. When most of us wake up with a sore neck, we might think to ourselves that we must have slept in a funny position. Not hypochondriacs. They will be convinced that it is the early warning of some degenerative muscle disease.

A second sign of hypochondriasis is a disease phobia. None of us would like the idea of getting cancer or any other serious disease, but we do not spend much time worrying about it, either. For people like Beth, the fear of some dreaded disease is something that they live with on a day-to-day basis. They spend a lot of time looking for symptoms, and just as much time fretting about how unlucky they are to be so prone to sickness. Their fear motivates them to learn as much as they can about the body and medicine; they can't wait for the next issue of *Reader's Digest* to come in the mail so they can learn about the disease or the organ of the month. Some of them even become quite knowledgeable; many a physician has had the experience of having a patient diagnose his own problem as some rare disease the physician hasn't heard about since medical school.

Finally, hypochondriacs cannot be convinced that there is no reason for them not to worry. Those with just a touch of hypochondriasis, like Beth, can be temporarily reassured. Her husband's kidding and his refusal to take her symptoms seriously would make her feel better for a little while, although before the month was out, she would have a new set of symptoms to go with a new disease. Others, however, refuse to be reassured even by experts. Many of these people will go from doctor to doctor until they find one who can find "the cause" of their problem. Many doctors will recognize the real problem as hypochondriasis, offer reassurance and perhaps some minor medication, and send these people on their way. Sadly, there are too many doctors who, when in doubt, will operate. Even physicians are becoming alarmed at the large number of unnecessary operations performed every year. Hypochondriasis can range from the mildly amusing to the deadly serious.

People who experience the second class of mind-body problems, conversion disorders, *do* have real symptoms, but there is no identifiable physical cause for their problems. The symptoms can range from the dramatic to the ordinary. There have probably been a million television detective shows that have used conversion disorders in the plot. In these stories, a person witnesses a terrible crime, then gets bumped on the head, only to wake up to discover that he is blind. The doctor can't do anything about it and concludes with a sad look in his eye that "perhaps it's psychological." (As you already know, our key witness gets his sight back just in time to identify the criminal before he strikes again.)

Freud got his start by treating conversion disorders. In his time, "good women" were horrified and disgusted by sex, so the prospect of the wedding night was extremely frightening. Many of these women (at least enough to keep Freud's appointment book filled) developed paralysis of the legs; if they were paralyzed, then it would be impossible to get married and they would not have to face their sexual fears. Hysterical paralysis, as it is called, is rare today, but there are less dramatic variations. "Writer's cramp," an involuntary contraction of the fingers, has been a favorite of authors who could not face the possibility of having their manuscripts rejected; perhaps with the advent of word processors, writer's cramp will be replaced with numb finger tips. I've had my share of days, when the words were not flowing, when my fingers felt a little stiff. (Luckily for me, a round of golf always seems to get my fingers back in shape so I can face the keyboard again.)

Most conversion disorders involve much more ordinary symptoms. These can include stomachaches, headaches—in fact, pains anywhere in the body. They also include such general complaints as chronic weakness or constant fatigue. The dividing line between conversion disorders and hypochondriasis can be blurry. But in general, people with conversion disorders have some symptom that they can point to and that is causing them some pain. Hypochondriacs tend to see symptoms in every little twinge or bump. When they are asked to describe them, they tend to be rather vague.

Health worriers do not make up a relatively consistent personality type as do the other styles we have described. Mind-body problems cut across all of the other diagnostic categories. Beth, for instance, could also be classified as a cling-on personality. It is not unusual for compulsive personalities to develop frequent headaches, and mopers often feel chronically weak or fatigued.

However, health worriers do have two important things in common. First, they have trouble expressing their feelings about at least some issues. They may be very assertive about most things, but there is usually some aspect of their lives that they find it difficult to be open about. Beth had no trouble at all letting Phil know when he wasn't doing enough to help her around the house, but she could not talk to him about her fears that he would lose interest in her one day and leave her. Because these feelings remain unexpressed, they either take their toll on one's body or are expressed in concern about one's body.

The second common trait is that these people have learned that they can use their symptoms to help them get what they want. They may be like Freud's patients who used their paralysis to avoid sex. (Headaches and fatigue seem to be more popular today, for both men and women.) Jim was living with a woman who had strong needs to be around other people; the only problem was that Jim did not feel comfortable in groups larger than four or five. He did not like to admit this to himself, much less anyone else, so he would always be agreeable when his partner mentioned plans to go to a party. Eight times out of ten, however, Jim would become nauseated a few hours before the party and would actually vomit. The first few times this happened, his partner was appropriately sympathetic and would stay home to take care of him. Jim not only got out of going to the party, but managed to have company while he stayed at home. It did not take long, though, before Jim's "sensitive stomach" began to cause a real strain in the relationship.

The underlying motives for developing body problems can range from the simple need to be noticed to the need to express feelings of hostility and anger. Beth's concern about getting cancer was her way of expressing her insecurities about her relationship with Paul. She had no desire to control or manipulate him, but secretly, she wondered just how much Paul cared about her. Paul's interest in and concern about her physical problems offered her some reassurance that he really did love her; even his teasing her was better than being ignored.

Neale is a good example of someone who uses his body to express his anger. Although he likes to think of himself as a modern husband who doesn't have strict ideas about the respective roles of men and women, he is still influenced by what he learned while he was growing up. He saw his father sit in front of the television reading the paper night after night while his mother scurried about cooking, cleaning, and caring for the children. He does pretty well with his conflicts, except on those rare occasions when his wife wants to take a short trip to visit her family. Neale knows that he feels irritable when she is planning these trips, but rather than trying to understand why, he assures his wife that he and the children will be just fine while she is away. But more often than not, just before his wife is due to leave, he comes down with a "bug." Of course, the only alternative for his wife is to cancel her plans and take care of her family.

It is important to remember that these people are not faking; their aches and pains are very real to them. Also, they seem to have a stake in believing that they are just unfortunate to be in such poor health. If you were to suggest to them that they were faking or that their problem was psychological, the chances are that they would be indignant. Some people may be aware of their mind-body problems; a part of Beth knew that her fears of dying from some terrible disease were not rational. But more often than not, they will be hurt and angry at any suggestion that they are using their illness to avoid something or to manipulate others.

Because health worriers are such a diverse group, there is no one particular style of person whom they can or cannot live with. The degree of their problems will vary depending on the overall level of conflict in their lives. When things are going well for them, they will not have as many health problems, and when things are not, then you can expect a noticeable increase in their bodily complaints.

Development of the Health Worrier

Because so many different kinds of people have mind-body problems, it would take an entire volume to describe all the different ways that they could have developed them. So let's take a close look at the two patterns that these people tend to have in common: the inability to talk about or recognize certain kinds of feelings, and their use of their problems to get what they want.

Much of the training that sets the stage for mind-body problems is similar to what nice guys receive—and nice guys, by the way, are often health worriers. The only difference is that the training is more selective. Remember the parents of the nice guys? They are the ones who taught their children that other people's feelings are more important than their own, so if they felt angry or hurt or mistreated, they would never dream of saying anything about it.

Parents who inadvertently teach their children to have mind-body problems may allow them to express their feelings about most issues, but there is likely to be a sore spot that they refuse to talk about. Beth's mother, for example, left her husband when Beth was only four because he was impossible to live with. Because she did not have a job or any special skills, it took her many years before she could provide for her children comfortably. She was determined to teach Beth to be strong and independent so that Beth would never get herself in the same situation. As Beth remembers it, "My mother used to tell me that I could never count on anyone, so I had to learn to take care of myself. Whenever I came home from school crushed because something had happened to hurt my feelings, my mother would get a little irrational. She would tell me I had to be strong, that if I let people know I cared what they thought, they wouldn't have any respect for me. I think the result of all that was that now I just can't allow myself to think that I really need Paul." Beth couldn't see it at first, but after spending many hours in therapy, she learned that she was afraid Paul would turn out to be as undependable as her father was.

A common blind spot that parents have with their children concerns fears about competence. When their budding little genius comes home from school worried because he is having some trouble learning fractions, they tell him, "Don't be silly—you're smart enough to learn anything." John received a heavy dose of this while he was growing up, and now he finds that his colds seem to hit him just when he is beginning to feel overwhelmed at the office. He sees this as a coincidence, but it is much more than that. His colds allow him to avoid having to feel that any mistakes he might make are really his fault. After all, he wasn't feeling well.

Virtually all children take a stab at using a physical complaint to get something from their parents at some point in their lives. Who doesn't remember trying the old tummyache routine on a day when it seemed it might be pleasant to stay home and watch a little television rather than go to school? I know I did, especially if there was a big test scheduled that day. And most parents will be more than a little indecisive about all this; after all, who wants the school nurse calling up and informing you that your child has just vomited all over the teacher's new shoes? I actually did receive such a call. But parents aren't dumb, so in most cases children can't try this trick too often.

There are, however, some parents who are a little dumb about it. Jan, for instance, remembers that she always had a great time when she stayed home from school. "I think my mother liked the company. If I said I wasn't feeling well, she would immediately tell me that I couldn't go to school. She would fix me my favorite breakfast, and then about ten in the morning—when the department stores opened—she would ask me if I was feeling better. Then off we would go shopping and out to lunch."

Other children, whose parents seem indifferent to them or perhaps even hostile, learn that being sick is the one way they can get them to show any interest or concern. It is not a conscious kind of learning, however, and they do not do it intentionally; to this day, Jan denies lying about not feeling well. But nonetheless, they have learned to be sick, because being sick means that they can get people to do things for them that they wouldn't do ordinarily. Being sick is also a safe way of getting back at people; a child who is angry because his parents are leaving him with a baby-sitter while they go off for the weekend may discover that he can use his poor health to make his parents feel good and guilty.

Psychologists' talk about the importance of paying attention to our feelings may be all too familiar, but the fact of the matter is that it is impossible to repress feelings out of existence. If we try to ignore feelings that make us uncomfortable, they will find a way of expressing themselves. In the case of people with mind-body problems, their feelings are expressed through their bodies. It can be very frustrating to live with someone who is constantly complaining about imaginary illnesses or who always seems to be getting sick at the most inopportune times. But the good news is that many of these people can be nudged in the direction of giving up their old ways of handling their conflicts.

Living with the Health Worrier

One thing that makes it difficult to live with health worriers is that even they are not always aware of what is bothering them. They may be harboring some resentment about the relationship that they can't let themselves in on, let alone their partners, or they may have conflicts about things that are completely unrelated to the relationship, but their need to avoid facing these conflicts squarely makes it impossible to recognize them or to ask for their partner's help and support. If your partner fits this description, you can't have too much patience and sensitivity if you are going to be of any help.

Q: My husband was a manager for a discount department store when it went out of business. He seemed to handle that okay; in fact, he got another job in a similar store within a month. But a year later, that store closed down, too. Ever since then, he has been complaining of not feeling well. I don't blame him for being discouraged, but he won't admit that his losing his job has anything to do with how he is feeling. But it's obvious that that's what it is; he's canceled several interviews because he was too sick to go, and when our friends call, he doesn't feel well enough to see anyone. I've tried to get him to see a doctor, but he insists that it's just a bug and there's no need to spend money for something that will go away in a day or two. He was always such a take-charge person before, so I don't understand why he is reacting this way now. Is there anything I can do to help him?

A: As children, when we are faced with situations that

scare us, most of us learn ways of making ourselves feel better that are not the most productive ways possible. But as we get older and a little more sure of ourselves, we learn that we can deal directly with these uncomfortable situations; we no longer need our childish defenses. So everything goes along fine until something really scary happens. Then our childish defenses don't seem so childish anymore; they are downright comfortable.

I would guess that this is what has happened to your husband. He may have had tendencies to use illness as an excuse to avoid some of the harder moments of his childhood, and then, as he got older, and better at dealing with these things, he lost his need to avoid problems. But now that he has had a really big blow, being sick doesn't seem like such a bad alternative. It's certainly better than facing the possibility that the nightmare of finding a job only to lose it a few months later will happen all over again. Even though he knows it's irrational, I wouldn't be surprised if a part of your husband felt that it was his fault that two stores in a row closed on him. At the very least, he must feel embarrassed and ashamed—even though there is no reason for him to. That's why he uses his poor health to avoid seeing friends.

Because he hasn't used his health as a means of avoiding serious problems before this trauma, I don't think there is much point in trying to get him to realize what he is doing. Once he gets another job and get his confidence back, I expect that he will revert to his old take-charge ways. So you don't need to try to "cure" him; just help him find a new job.

Since he has gone back to his childhood ways, the most effective strategy might be for you to take on the role of a kind, loving, but firm parent. Reassure him, even though he claims he doesn't need reassurance. Tell him that you think he blames himself for his predicament, but you know he has always done the best he could for his family. Let him know that you're with him, that you don't think any less of him because he is out of a job. He may get mad at you for saying these things, but keep it up anyway. He wants to divert attention—his own, as well as yours and your friends—from his job situation to his health, but deep down he is worried about whether he is destined to be a chronic loser.

The firmness is especially called for when he tries to use his "not feeling well" excuse to avoid looking for a job and seeing friends. When he starts to talk about feeling sick on the day of an interview, tell him that perhaps he should go anyway; after all, you can't go on forever without any money coming in. If he wants to duck out when friends come around, let him know that you think he is being inconsiderate. Remind him that his friends care about him and that it hurts their feelings when he refuses to see them. Don't accuse him of using his illnesses to avoid these situations at this point; this will only make his strategy more entrenched. Try to be like a kind, supportive parent who will not let her child stay home from school every time he mentions a tummyache.

Expect some hostility on his part. People don't like to be told what to do, especially when they know that's exactly what they should be doing. You have to walk a fine line; on the one hand, you want to push him hard enough so that he will begin to feel uncomfortable with his half-hearted attempts to find another job, but on the other hand, you do not want to talk about it so much that he begins to view you as a nag. If you overdo it, it may take him a while to forgive you, but if you push him just hard enough to get him moving, then I think he'll realize once he is back at work that you were trying to help him. I'm willing to bet that it won't be too long before you have your old take-charge husband back again.

Q: Kathy, my wife, feels very uncomfortable around my family; she comes from a working-class background, while most of my relatives are pretty well off. I admit that my parents weren't very nice to her when we first got married—they thought I could do better—but they've come to accept and like her. Kathy gets so nervous when there is a family occasion that she throws up before we leave the house and again shortly after we arrive. She acts friendly when we're there, but I know that she's really suffering. I've tried to talk to her about it, but she says that it's something she has to learn to deal with and she refuses to discuss it further. I want to help her. We've been married only a year, so she has a lot of time left to spend with my family.

A: I think time will take care of your wife's problem. It sounds to me as if she has a clear idea of what's going on and is determined not to give in to it. As long as she can keep this attitude, she is almost certain to win out over her problem in the end.

Since she is aware of what is causing her problem and it is not affecting your relationship, I would give her the room she seems to want to work this out on her own. It can be a little patronizing to force your help on someone who does not want it if the problem is not affecting you. This is not to say that there is nothing that you can do; you can let her know how well she fits in with your family and tell her when you know that one of your relatives likes her. Be subtle about it, though; you don't want Kathy to get the idea that you or your family are being condescending toward the poor girl from the wrong side of the tracks. With her determination and your support, I would bet that in a year's time, her problem will be a thing of the past.

Q: If you could hear my husband talk, you would think he was about to keel over from a heart attack at any moment. Every time I ask him to do something he doesn't want to do, he gets chest pains. If we have an argument, he cluthes his chest until I give in and let him have his way. I've accused him of being melodramatic, but he insists he has a bad heart and if I really cared about him, I would try to understand. The only evidence that he does have a bad heart is that he had a slight murmur as a child. How can I deal with someone who virtually accuses me of trying to kill him every time we have a difference of opinion?

A: It's very hard, but be assured that your husband knows this every bit as well as you do. I'm not suggesting that he is faking or consciously trying to get you to keep your opinions to yourself, but nonetheless, he has learned a very effective strategy for getting his own way.

From your comment about his childhood murmur, I take it that he has not been getting regular checkups. Don't take this as a sign that he knows there is nothing wrong with him. Some hypochondriacs do make monthly trips to the doctor's office in search of a cure for their imaginary illnesses, but others avoid them like the plague. Even though they fear that they are seriously ill, they rationalize that it is better to be uncertain than to know for sure. Or it may be that they have some concerns about the treatment, perhaps your husband is afraid that if he had the operation he "knows" he needs, he will never come out from under the anesthetic.

The first step is to get him to see a heart specialist. If he has managed to avoid doing this for so long, this won't be easy, but be persistent; there is always the chance that he does have some physical problem that is treatable. It may have nothing to do with his heart, but because of his fears, he has a tendency to interpret any signs of discomfort as related to his "heart problem." Talk to a physician yourself; ask about the possible explanations for his symptoms. Perhaps you can get the physician to call your husband to try to schedule an appointment. If your husband can be convinced that there is a good chance he has some minor problem that is treatable, he may very well go see someone.

When you are working on him to go, do it from the angle that you care about him and are concerned about his health. Don't let your feelings about his using his health to manipulate you get in the way at this point. If he gets the feeling that you don't believe he has a heart problem and that you are trying to take his excuse away, he will become even more resistant to getting a checkup. Always keep in mind that his fears are real even if they seem silly to other people. I wouldn't be surprised if he was frightened when he learned about his heart murmur as a child; all he could understand was that there was something wrong with his heart, and that people who had heart problems died. Even though as an adult he is capable of being more rational, his childhood fears may still be with him.

As for his manipulating you, don't let him get away with it. If you do, you have only yourself to blame. Even if he were dying, it would not justify his intimidating and controlling those around him. People who are trained to feel guilty have a lot of trouble understanding and believing this, but no one should be asked to sacrifice his or her entire life for another person regardless of the circumstances. I'm not saying that anyone should put a dying spouse in a home to get him or her out of the way, but it is important to achieve some balance between doing what you can for the other person and going on with your own life. Loving, caring people do not want to use their frailties to control others, so remember, when your husband is pulling his act on you, he is expressing his anger and hostility.

After you take away the power he gets from his heart problem, try to help him express his feelings more directly. For instance, when you have a disagreement and he starts to clutch his chest, tell him that you are not going to change your mind, but you would like to know what he is thinking. He is not going to tell you the first time you ask, but if you do not allow him to manipulate you, sooner or later he will begin to talk to you.

My experience has been that it does not take too long for people to stop using their physical problems to control others once they learn it doesn't work. But you have to be consistent. The analogy of training an infant to go to sleep without crying may be useful. If you decide that you will not pick up the child when he cries one night, he will cry even harder; if you pick up the child then, all you have done is train him to cry louder. Don't back down with your husband. If he is like other people I have known, he may begin to be "secretive" when he is experiencing his "chest pains." But he won't be so secretive as to keep you from seeing him clutch his chest; he will want you to think that he is trying to be brave. But be patient with him. Remember, you will be taking away a strategy that has worked for him all of his life. It will take him some time to learn a more mature way of dealing with conflict. He will, however, be better off in the end if you help him to learn.

Q: Our youngest child left for college last year, and I thought this would be the time that my wife and I could start to do all of the things that we've been putting off for so long. But instead of taking trips to Florida, my wife has been taking trips to the hospital. She hasn't been sick a day in the last twenty-five years, but all of a sudden, she believes she is falling apart. She's had thousands of dollars' worth of tests and several hundred dollars' worth of prescriptions. She's been told she is healthy as a horse, but she still won't go out of town because she wants to be close to her doctor "just in case anything happens." How could she turn into such a hypochondriac after all these years?

A: I think the answer might be in the first sentence of your question. If your wife has stayed at home all of her life to take care of her children, she may fear that her purpose in life is over now that all the kids are on their own. It is not unusual for full-time mothers to have a reaction like this when they view their job as completed. Men often experience a similar reaction when they retire.

Your wife is going through a very difficult time in her life. Not only has her job been taken away from her, but her body is going through some pretty dramatic changes as well. I assume that her physician is helping her with any problems that may be associated with menopause, but along with that, it is generally harder on women than men to accept the fact that before too long, "middle-aged" will be nothing more than a euphemism for elderly. In our society, there is a double standard of aging. A few gray hairs indicate that a woman is becoming matronly while they make a man look distinguished; a few extra pounds go unnoticed on a man, but they make a woman appear to be "letting herself go." Women are taught to place a high value on their looks, so when they begin to fade, it should come as no surprise that they may begin to feel worthless. Your wife is probably translating these fears into concern about her health.

You can help your wife by helping her to verbalize some of these concerns. She is probably unable to allow herself to think about these issues now; that's why she has "chosen" her health as a way of expressing her fears. Start by sharing some of your fears with her. Tell her that you understand how hard it must be for her to make this transition in her life. Be there when she needs to cry.

Also talk to her about the positive things you have together. Let her know that you still find her attractive. Ask her to help you make plans about how the two of you will spend your time. If you want to get her started on taking trips, perhaps it would be a good idea to plan the first few so they include a visit with your children.

I would guess that with your support and love, your wife will make the transition before too long. It could speed things up quite a bit if you could get her to talk about her feelings with a professional, even though she probably will be reluctant to do this. Remember, people who use their bodies to express their conflicts do so because it is hard for them to face their fears. Talk to her doctor about this. Since she seems to have a lot of faith in him, he could be helpful in helping her to realize that it would be a good idea for her to give it a try. Good luck! With you on her side, I think she has an excellent chance to enjoy this period of her life.

Some Final Thoughts

There is another side to the coin of mind-body problems that can be deadly. There are some people who will never admit that they have a physical problem regardless of the evidence to the contrary. Richard Lazarus, a psychologist who has extensively studied how people react to illness, has described men who in the midst of a heart attack began to exercise vigorously. They want to prove to themselves that they just have a case of gas pains. Tragically, their refusal to "listen" to their bodies kills them.

People who refuse to admit that something could be wrong with their bodies are often just as intolerant of others who complain of aches and pains. I remember one man who accused his wife of being a sissy because she complained that her leg hurt after taking a fall. After three weeks of being a sissy, she insisted on going to her doctor, and it turned out that she had a fracture. Another woman was admitted to a psychiatric hospital where I worked because she was having psychotic delusions. Her "delusion" was that she had cancer "inside her body somewhere." To prove she was wrong, her psychiatrist ordered tests, and as you can guess, she turned out to be right.

The point is that we do have to listen to and take care of our bodies. Often people who have noticed subtle signs that something was not quite right turn out to have caught a serious illness in its early stages. Not everyone who has vague complaints about his or her health is a health worrier. Complaints should be taken seriously, even if the first physician consulted can't find anything wrong. It's when the complaints are a lifelong pattern, or when they occur in response to a major crisis, or when they seem to be used to some purpose, that the possibility of a psychological problem becomes stronger. Do give your partner the benefit of the doubt.

9

THE CHRONIC DIETER

The Chronic Dieter Test

1. **The first thing I think about when I wake up in the morning:**
   a. is the good time I had the night before.
   b. is what I have planned for the day.
   c. is whether or not I will be able to get up.
   d. is what I plan to eat that day.

2. **I can really stuff myself on:**
   a. nothing—I rarely overeat.
   b. my favorite foods.
   c. anything that I don't absolutely dislike.
   d. anything that is edible.

3. **My weight has been stable:**
   a. since I was twenty years old.
   b. for the last several years.
   c. for the last several months.
   d. for the last several hours.

4. **When I think about my weight:**
   a. I get depressed about how fat I am.
   b. I realize I could stand to lose a few pounds.
   c. I'm surprised—I rarely think about my weight.
   d. I'm proud that I have been able to keep it steady.

5. **When I see other people who are overweight:**
   a. I wonder how they could do that to themselves.
   b. I don't think much of anything—I usually don't notice overweight people.
   c. I think that I could be like them if I don't watch it.
   d. I think that I am bigger than they are.

6. **If I were to eat one potato chip:**
   a. I wouldn't stop until every last chip in the house was gone.
   b. I wouldn't stop until I was full.
   c. I would end up eating a handful.
   d. I might have another one, depending on my mood.

7. **I think about eating:**
   a. almost all the time—it's always in the back of my mind.
   b. when I see food—for example, when I see pictures of it in magazines or when I'm in the grocery store.

c. when I am hungry.
d. rarely—I have to remind myself to eat.

8. I can control my eating:

a. always—I virtually never overeat.
b. most of the time—I only have trouble with a few favorite foods.
c. most of the day, but the late evening hours are hard for me.
d. for a few hours at a time.

9. If at the end of the day I realize I have not had very much to eat:

a. I will have a snack so I don't wake up hungry in the middle of the night.
b. I will wonder if I am coming down with something.
c. I will pat myself on the back for sticking to my goals.
d. I will pat myself on the back for being good.

10. For this item, use the five-point scale below to rate how you feel about the following parts of your body and your overall appearance.

1 means you feel very bad about it.
2 means you feel somewhat bad about it.
3 means you feel neutral about it.
4 means you feel somewhat good about it.
5 means you feel very good about it.

______ Hair
______ Face
______ Shoulders
______ Arms
______ Chest (for men), breasts (for women)
______ Stomach

______ Hips
______ Thighs
______ Lower legs
______ Height

______ Total

______ Your overall appearance

The Chronic Dieter Scoring Key

1. a. 0 points.
   b. 0 points.
   c. 0 points.
   d. 3 points.
2. a. 0 points.
   b. 1 point.
   c. 3 points.
   d. 2 points.
3. a. 0 points.
   b. 1 point.
   c. 2 points.
   d. 3 points.
4. a. 3 points if you are less than 20 percent above your ideal weight, otherwise 2 points.
   b. 1 point.
   c. 0 points.
   d. 2 points.
5. a. 0 points.
   b. 0 points.
   c. 2 points.
   d. 3 points if you are less than 20 percent above your ideal weight, otherwise 2 points.
6. a. 3 points.
   b. 1 point.
   c. 2 points.
   d. 0 points.
7. a. 3 points.
   b. 2 points.
   c. 1 point.
   d. 0 points.
8. a. 0 points.
   b. 1 point.
   c. 2 points.
   d. 3 points.
9. a. 0 points.
   b. 1 point.
   c. 2 points.
   d. 3 points.
10. For this item, divide the points listed next to "Total" by 10 and subtract from this your

rating of your overall appearance. The scoring is based on this number.

+2 or more—3 points.

+1 to +1.9—2 points.

0 to +.9—1 point.

-.9 or less—0 points.

Interpretation of Test Scores

0 to 5 points: You do not really care about food and do not receive much pleasure from eating it.

6 to 12 points: You are not and have never been a chronic dieter. You are like most people who enjoy food but do not worry about their weight.

13 to 22 points: You have some tendencies toward the chronic dieting pattern.

23 to 30 points: You are a chronic dieter; this chapter is an important one for you.

I'll Start Again Monday Morning

Lisa is a chronic dieter. Although at 125 pounds and five feet five inches tall she has a very attractive figure, she thinks of herself as being plump. In reality, she has been overweight only once in her life; in her early teens, when she was only about five feet two, she had gotten up to 140 pounds. The weight had come off as she matured, but it was enough to instill a lasting self-image. Nothing anyone could say to her would convince her that she did not have "fat, ugly hips and thighs."

During high school, dieting was a game she played with her friends. They would talk about their weight incessantly, and it was a status symbol to have nothing more than a carton of milk and a piece of fruit for lunch in the cafeteria. There was a sense of competition among them as to who could come up with the most unusual diet. Lisa's favorite was the period in which she ate nothing but a can of baby green peas for dinner each night. By the end of two weeks her parents, who had thought it would all pass over in a few days, demanded that she eat with the family. Lisa's mother and father never took her protests that she was fat seriously; they dismissed them as something all teenaged girls felt obligated to say. But the issue was real to Lisa.

During college, Lisa continued to monitor almost everything she ate, but it still was not terribly important to her. "It wasn't quite the same as it was in high school, but most of the girls I knew were doing the same thing I was—eating a piece of toast for breakfast, a salad for lunch, and skipping the starches and dessert at dinner. It wasn't a big deal, it was just a way of life. We pretty much had to eat like that during the week because we were all eating a lot of pizza and drinking a lot of beer on the weekends. We all talked about how fat we were, and even though I really believed it, I think it didn't bother me then the way it did a few years later because we all seemed to be in the same boat."

Her feelings about dieting began to change after she was married. She and her husband, Bruce, both liked to eat out, and since they both worked, they could afford to do so often. It did not take long for the combination of increased calories and decreased activity to have an effect, and within a year she was up to 135 pounds. When she realized what had happened she went on a severe diet and lost ten pounds within six weeks. She wanted to lose five more so that she would weigh the same as when she was in college, but that proved to be an ongoing struggle. Her husband was supportive and understanding while she lost the ten pounds; they ate at home most of the time, and he was willing to skip desserts so that Lisa would not be tempted. But when Lisa began to struggle with the last five pounds, his advice was to forget it; he thought she looked great at 125 pounds and there was no reason to suffer so much for a few more pounds. But Lisa still thought of herself as she had been when she was thirteen and weighed 140 pounds at five foot two.

Lisa became obsessed with food and dieting. "I would wake up in the morning and the first thing I would think about would be what I could eat that day. If I'd had a big dinner the night before, I would plan on skipping breakfast, then having an apple for lunch and a salad for dinner. By dinner I would feel weak because I was so hungry, and I would usually eat more than I had planned. Then I would spend the evening depressed because I would be stuck with my fat thighs for the rest of my life. Bruce was getting sick of my moods and my diets, and now I wonder how he stood it as long as he did. At the time, though, I accused him of not understanding."

Bruce remembers those times well. "She was really driving me crazy. She looks good at 125 pounds, and I could not understand why she felt she had to get down to 120. At first I tried to be helpful, but she seemed to be getting more and more irrational about it. She would cry about how fat and ugly she was, and she would accuse me of not being honest with her when I told her she looked fine. Her diet seemed to take a lot of fun out of our relationship. We couldn't go to certain restaurants because they didn't have any low-calorie meals; at home, we no longer prepared elaborate meals together. I don't care if I never see a baked chicken again! Added to all that, she was getting boring. A lot of our conversations concerned new diet ideas she had read about or how many calories were in every bite of food I ate. I finally told her that she was a lot more fun to be around when she weighed 135 pounds than when she was trying to reach 120."

Lisa doesn't remember exactly what helped her to place her weight in better perspective. "I think it was a combination of things. I knew that Bruce was getting pretty exasperated with me. At first he was supportive, but he started to snap at me when I would talk about my diet. I think I just decided that my relationship with him was more important than being a little pudgy. Also, I was getting sick of myself. During my rational moments I would wonder how I could get so upset about something as trivial as my thighs being a little bigger than I wanted them to be. I got tired of thinking about food all the time, too. I remember one particular incident well; it convinced me how crazy I was being. We went to a party on a Saturday night, and that day, I had eaten very little because I knew there would be lots of good food at the party. I did have a fair amount to eat at the party, although I didn't stuff myself. But rather than enjoy the food, which included several of my favorites, all I could think about was my diet, and I kept telling myself, 'I'll start again Monday morning.' "

Chronic dieters come in all varieties. Many are like Lisa, who are well within normal limits; even though others perceive them as being just right, or even slender, they cannot be convinced that they are not unattractively plump. Others may be slightly overweight according to the weight charts, and they spend much time and energy trying to reach the elusive ideal. Still others may be obese; they may need to lose a considerable amount of weight for health reasons as well as to improve their appearance. They spend a lot of time trying, and usually are either gaining or losing weight; they find it almost impossible to remain at a stable weight.

Chronic dieting and obesity do not necessarily go together. Lisa, for example, was far from being obese; in fact she was not even overweight. An extreme example of how the two do not always go together is anorexia nervosa. This is a very serious condition in which people, usually adolescent girls, actually starve themselves, sometimes to death; these girls will still point to areas of their body that are they consider too fat when they weigh only 75 percent of their ideal weight. On the other hand, there are many people who are obese according to generally accepted standards, but have little interest in losing weight and never go on diets. Ted was about fifty pounds over his ideal weight, but he had not been on a diet for years. "I used to make annual attempts to lose weight; every New Year's Day I would go on a diet. My heart was never in it, but I always felt an obligation to feel bad because I was fat. Finally, I just gave it all up, and I'm glad I did. Food is one of my most important pleasures in life, so why shouldn't I enjoy it?"

Regardless of their actual weight, chronic dieters have

one important thing in common: Weight is an emotional issue for them. They are unable to be rational about their situation. They have distorted perceptions of their bodies, and are not able to be logical about approaches to losing weight. Ask anyone who is not a chronic dieter how to lose weight and the answer is likely to be simple: "Get more exercise and don't eat so much." But chronic dieters believe there is a magic solution, and if they search hard enough they will eventually find it. It is this irrationality that makes it possible for totally absurd and even dangerous ideas to turn into best-selling diet books. People actually have drunk salad oil or eaten nothing but grapefruit for weeks at a time in their attempts to lose weight. They really do know better, but they feel desperate.

Joan was a chronic dieter who admitted to buying every available diet book. "I think part of me knew that what I was doing was stupid. At least, after I had tried—and failed—with each latest fad, I could look back and wonder why I had ever thought it would work. But when I heard about a new book, it would always seem like such a good idea. I would get excited about it because it seemed to be so painless, and actually believe things like how I would have thin thighs in thirty days. I finally just got sick of it and promised myself that I would never buy another diet book. I feel chunky at 140 pounds, but people tell me I look good. And my husband and children tell me I'm a lot more pleasant to be around when I'm not dieting."

The desire for a magic solution causes chronic dieters to distort information they hear in a way that will fit in with their desire to find an easy answer. Francy had been trying to lose the same twenty-five pounds for a number of years. Her latest strategy was to attend Weight Watchers' meetings. This was a good choice, because Weight Watchers offers a sound and sensible plan for losing weight. She liked the idea of a structured diet; however, she did not like the idea of getting more exercise. So when asked by a friend what kind of exercises she was doing, Francy replied that they had told her at the meetings not to do any exercises until she had lost fifteen pounds. Of course, no such advice was ever given, but the idea of exercise did not fit into Francy's scheme for a magic solution, so psychologically she distorted the message to suit her needs.

Weight becomes a moral issue for chronic dieters. They see themselves as either being "good" and in control or as "bad" and out of control. The chronic dieter who says "I was a good girl today—I had only eight hundred calories" is not merely using a figure of speech. She means it when she describes herself as a "good girl" just as she means it when she describes herself as a "bad girl" on the days she does not do as well.

The "I'll start again Monday morning" syndrome results from this black-and-white perspective. Ray was very familiar with the pattern. "I'd do well all day, and then if I had even one cookie during the evening it would be enough to send me over the edge. If I had one, then of course one more wouldn't hurt. And before long, since I had blown my diet anyway, I would finish off the bag. Then I would always swear to start again Monday morning."

Nondieters go on binges too, but because they do not see it as a moral issue, or as all-or-nothing, they do not do it with the same compulsive intensity. I've been known to eat a whole pizza as a late-night snack, but I have never thought of myself as being out of control. Ray, on the other hand, could not stop eating once he had labeled himself as "out of control"; he would continue to eat even after he began to feel uncomfortably full. "I wouldn't even enjoy the damn cookies. I just couldn't stop until they were all gone."

A common stereotype of the dieter that happens to be false is that they love food and have gourmet tastes. Some do, but a majority of chronic dieters have the most difficulty with foods that they do not particularly enjoy. Ray's weakness with cookies is far from an isolated example. The act of eating seems to be much more important than what is eaten. Anne, who was never more than ten pounds over her ideal weight, would eat almost anything when she felt a craving for food. "One of my biggest weaknesses was bread, so at one time I started to keep it in the freezer. If the urge to eat hit me, though, it wouldn't make any difference; I would eat it frozen, without even waiting for it to thaw. If I wanted something sweet to eat, and there wasn't anything in the house, I would stand by the sugar canister with a spoon. I certainly didn't enjoy it; in fact, it made me feel terrible. But I just couldn't help myself."

One of the most perplexing features of chronic dieters is distortions in how they perceive their bodies. Bruce, for example, simply could not understand how Lisa could believe that she had fat hips and thighs; at 125 pounds, she seemed just right to him. Anorexia nervosa, as we mentioned earlier, provides an extreme version of distorted body image. These girls will say that they look about right when they are down to about 65 to 75 percent of their ideal weight, while anyone else would be horrified at their emaciated state.

For those chronic dieters who are overweight, the excess weight is exaggerated and becomes the focal point of self-evaluation. Patty, an attractive thirty-three-year-old woman, seemed to have everything going for her. Although she had been out of school for only four years, she was the controller for a medium-sized company, and she had a close relationship with a man she had lived with for two years. Most people would be happy to change places with her; but Patty was continually depressed over her "weight problem." Her weight fluctuated between 130 and 140 pounds, and she wanted to weigh 115 pounds.

Nothing could convince Patty that she was not grossly obese. She claimed that she did not know one person who was as overweight as she was; once, after returning from a week's vacation at the beach, she reported that she did not see a single person there who had legs as fat as hers. She took the fact that her boyfriend never mentioned her weight to her as evidence that he was ashamed of her, and his comments about other women who were fat as his subtle way of trying to get her to lose weight.

Patty was sure that her career was affected by her weight: "How can anyone think that I am competent as an accountant if I have so little self-control over my eating?" She was not about to give up this belief, even though she was more successful than most of the people she had gone to school with. On those rare occasions when her boss made a mildly critical comment about her work, she was convinced that he would not have found fault with her if she weighed 115 pounds.

Any problems she had with her boyfriend were also interpreted as resulting from her weight problem. If he did not want to go to a party, it was because he was ashamed to be seen with her. If he did not feel like having sex on a particular night, it was because he was turned off by her fat. It did not matter that he would deny these accusations; she was sure that "he just doesn't want to hurt my feelings."

Even people who are indeed excessively overweight can be accused of losing perspective. They frequently conclude that they are completely worthless as human beings because of this one problem. They may be competent in their occupation, loving parents, and caring friends, yet their self-evaluation is based only on how much they weigh.

The effects of chronic dieting on family members can be variable. Some dieters, like Patty, rarely talk about their diets and would never think about asking family members to settle for nothing but salads, fish, and baked chicken. Others will make sure that there is plenty of snack food in the house, using the rationalization "Why should my family have to suffer simply because I have a problem?" Of course, this serves as a handy excuse to have the tempting foods around. Often, too, the family of the chronic dieter will become accustomed to talk about diets and simply tune it out.

There are, however, many chronic dieters who involve their family members in their diets to the point where it can become an annoying issue. Ray would demand that his wife plan meals according to whether he was "in" or "out" of control. When he was in control, no one in the house was allowed to have desserts or fried food; when he was out of control, he would insist on having plenty of both available. This irritated everyone, but they all felt obligated to comply with his requests because it meant that they were helping him with his problem.

It is not unusual for the chronic dieter to come to blame his or her spouse for the problem. Elaine had always had to watch her weight, but it never got more than a few pounds above where she wanted it to be until she had been married for a few years. "The problem seemed to begin when I announced to Richard that I was going on a diet. He was supportive and tried to be helpful. I had asked him to remind me of my diet when he saw me eating something that wasn't included in the plan, and boy, was he good at it! He didn't do it in a nasty way, but after a few weeks I resented his saying anything about it. I started to eat behind his back so I wouldn't have to listen to his comments. On the way home from work I would pick up a couple of candy bars so he would tell me how well I was doing when I ate a small dinner, and during the evening I would sneak out to the kitchen for a snack. I ended up eating more than I would have if I had been eating in front of him. I actually gained six or seven pounds while on the diet! I was feeling very angry at him; I thought it was all his fault that I had a weight problem."

Living with the chronic dieter can be frustrating, because the pattern is so irrational in the eyes of those who have no difficulty maintaining their weight. Add being blamed for the problem to this sense of frustration, and it becomes clear how chronic dieting can lead to friction. On the hopeful side, this is one problem which family members have a good chance to help with. Chronic dieters want to change. They may not know the best way to do it, and they may not be able to do it alone, but their desire to change increases the chances that others will be able to help them accomplish their goals. There is reason to be optimistic.

Development of the Chronic Dieter

It is not a coincidence that most of the case examples used so far involve women. Women are much more likely to be caught up in the chronic dieter pattern than are men. The reasons for this are obvious. There is much more pressure for women to be slender than there is for men. It is a tired but true observation that women tend to be evaluated in terms of their appearance, men in terms of their accomplishments.

The media ensures that women have impossibly high standards to meet; even the women shown scrubbing floors on television commercials are slender and attractive. So it is not surprising that so many women feel insecure about their appearance. It is interesting to note that even attractive women are not free of these pressures; psychological studies have found that there is no relationship between how attractive a woman is, as judged by others, and how she feels about her appearance. So even those women who are a "perfect 10" are just as likely as the truly unattractive to feel bad about their appearance.

Weight becomes a focal point in one's concerns about appearance because it seems to be one thing that we can do something about. A woman cannot do exercises to raise her cheekbones or change the contours of her lips, but she *can* have the same weight as Bo Derek—or so she believes. Of course, she may be programmed biologically to weigh twenty pounds more than Bo, but she wants to believe that through willpower and hard work she can become the neighborhood sex symbol, if not an internationally known model. So she strives to reach a state that simply is not natural for her, and the more her body rebels, the more emotional she becomes about her weight. She is doomed to feel like a failure.

Chronic dieters can be divided into two categories. The first consists of those who perceived themselves to be overweight during childhood. (Remember, perceptions of one's weight are more important than how much one actually weighs.) Self-concept becomes relatively stable by the time one reaches adolescence, so these people may go through life believing that they are fat regardless of their actual weight. Recall Lisa, who had great difficulty believing that she was not fat at 125 pounds. Her feelings about her body resulted from her experience of being a little pudgy around the age of twelve and thirteen.

This first category includes many men as well as women. Rich, for example, was chubby throughout his early childhood. He was teased by other children for being "fat," and his refuge became television cartoons and snack food. His parents indulged him, since they felt sorry he was so lonely. When he reached adolescence he became interested in sports, and to his delight, found that he was good at them. He became much more active, spent less time nibbling, and slimmed down in short order. But now, at age thirty-five, he still thinks of himself as a fat person who could lose control at any time. "On the one hand I know it is irrational, but I think about my weight every day. I have the feeling that if I do not continue to exercise and watch what I eat closely, I could balloon up in a matter of days. My wife mostly accepts the way I feel, but there are times when it irritates her. I am pretty rigid about jogging, and there are times when it would be more convenient if I skipped a day—but I'm afraid to. The other thing that gets her is that no matter what she fixes for dinner, I never have a second helping; she says she wonders why she even bothers trying to make things that I like. But I vowed that I would never be fat again."

The second category of chronic dieters is made up of those people who develop a sense of being overweight after they reach adulthood. For both men and women, there is a tendency to become less active without making a corresponding change in eating habits as one gets older. The natural result is to put on a few pounds over the years. The thirty-two-inch waist that I had when I was twenty has expanded to thirty-six inches now that I'm approaching middle age (I don't know when I'll be able to admit that I've actually *reached* middle age), but it has never occurred to me that I'm going downhill.

So when the woman who has had a child or two and has put on a few pounds decides she is going to get herself in shape, she does not think in terms of being in good shape for a middle-aged woman; she wants her body to be as it was when she was eighteen years old. She goes on a diet, may even join an exercise class, and makes some progress, but she still does not look like Victoria Principal. She thinks she has to try harder, so she limits herself to seven-hundred calories a day. This puts her body in a constant state of deprivation, and before long she is obsessed with food; she wakes up every morning thinking about what she can eat that day and whether she will be a "good girl." She develops the all-or-nothing outlook. When she is "bad" she continues to eat beyond the point of satiety, and she is out of control.

Donna remembers well the three years she spent locked in the chronic dieter pattern. "It started when my youngest child entered the first grade and I went back to work as a secretary in an insurance agency. I knew that I had gained weight while I was staying home with the kids, but I never thought much about it until I was around all those slender women in their early twenties. All of a sudden I felt old and fat. I lost ten pounds without much trouble, but the second ten that I wanted to lose just would not come off. It didn't take long before I became obsessed with my diet. I would do well for a week or two, and then I would go crazy and stuff myself for the next week. Sometimes when I would start a diet, I would become so obsessed with food that I would actually gain weight. I'm not sure how I finally got over all that, but I think I finally accepted the fact that I couldn't compete with women who were fifteen years younger than I was. I still try to watch what I eat, but since I gave up diets it is a lot easier for me to maintain my weight. And I don't have to feel guilty every time I eat something sweet."

Dieting rarely becomes an emotional issue for men who make it to adulthood without a weight problem. They may think that they could stand to lose a few pounds to improve both their health and their appearance, but their heart is not in it in the same way as it is for women. Societal pressure to be slim is not nearly as great for them, so their self-esteem is not likely to be so dependent on the size of their waistline. Paradoxically, because weight is not as likely to be an emotional issue for men, it is usually easier for them to lose weight; most weight-loss programs find that men do better than women.

Living with the Chronic Dieter

Living with the chronic dieter is not likely to be as difficult as living with some of the other patterns described in the book. Feelings about one's body are a personal problem rather than an interpersonal one. There can be frustrations, such as putting up with another person's bizarre menu or seeing someone you care about being irrational and unhappy, but for the most part, chronic dieting does not have too much impact on family members.

It is, however, one problem for which family members can make or break the pattern. No one can, or should, take on complete responsibility for another person's problems, but an insensitive spouse can contribute to chronic dieting while a sympathetic and understanding spouse can help the dieter get past it. Let us look at some specific cases.

Q: My wife's goal is to weigh 110 pounds. She has only been there a couple of times, and when she was there I thought she looked gaunt; I think she should settle for the 125 pounds she usually weighs. She has tried every diet imaginable, and now she says she wants to see a psychiatrist to understand what is blocking her from reaching her goal. This seems crazy to me, but do you think it will help her?

A: I think there is a good chance it will, but not for the goal she has in mind. A competent therapist will recognize that the importance she places on being so slender is the real issue rather than her weight. The most important step in getting past the chronic dieting pattern is learning to have realistic goals. As hard as it may be, she has to accept the fact that her body may not have been designed to weight 110 pounds. I don't think that anyone is justified in using biology as an excuse for being obese, but the fact of the matter is that people come in different shapes and sizes. We seem to be able to accept this for men, but we forget that it applies to women as well. Men can range from slender to stocky and still be viewed as attractive; the acceptable range for women in much narrower—and much more unrealistic.

Her therapist should be able to help her accept herself even though she may never reach her ideal weight. You could do a lot to help her along as well. Tell her frequently that you think she looks good the way she is; people do not give up irrational ideas easily, but if she hears your opinion often enough, she may gradually come to accept it. Try not to make comments or be too obvious in your appreciation when you see attractive slender women. Many women, regardless of how intelligent or rational they are, have grown up with the belief that they can attract and keep a husband with their looks only. If your wife is already feeling bad about her body, any comparisons, however subtle, will make her feel more insecure.

The chances are good that time alone will help her feel better about herself, and her need to be a chronic dieter will fade away. This pattern often becomes part of the transition into middle age. When people come to the realization that they are not twenty years old anymore, they can accept more realistic standards for themselves.

Q: I would like my husband to lose weight. He has put on about fifty pounds over the twenty-two years we have been married, and he looks sloppy. If I nag him enough, he'll say that he will go on a diet, but it never lasts more than a few days. Is there anything I can do to get him to stick to one?

A: I don't think so. Losing weight has to be a personal decision; I doubt that more than a handful of people have ever lost weight because someone else wanted them to.

The chances are that he does not feel that his weight is much of a problem. If he was slender as a child and as a teenager, he probably still thinks of himself that way. Of course, he realizes that he has put on weight when he looks in the mirror, but he just does not think of himself as being fat. Until he does, there will be little chance that he will be able to sustain enough motivation to follow through with a diet.

Your nagging probably hurts the situation more than it helps. Even if he says that he will do as you ask, the chances are that he resents your comments and may actually be eating more as a result of them. Even if he wanted to lose weight, it would be best not to continually remind him of his overeating. In his situation, the most that you can do to help him is to make subtle changes in his diet that he will not resent—things like broiling rather than frying, and taking the skin off of chicken. Try not to make any changes that are so dramatic that he will realize you are putting him on a diet; it will only make him resentful. These small changes won't have any great effects on his weight but they may make you feel better, since you will be doing something to help him. All you can really do is to wait and hope that he decides to do something about his weight.

A: My wife has gained seventy-five pounds since we were married. I am thoroughly disgusted with her. In fact, I went to see a lawyer, but he told me that obesity is not grounds for divorce. She knows how I feel; I told her that I don't want to have sex with her because she looks so repulsive, but she still won't do anything about it.

She is always dieting, but nothing seems to work for her. I think she has bought every diet book ever written, and I know she has tried every weight-loss clinic in our city—I have the bills to prove it. Actually, she doesn't eat all that much for meals, but I think she must eat from the moment I leave in the morning until I get home at night. How else could she weigh more than I do? Is there any hope for her? If there's not, I will leave. I'm not going to live the rest of my life with someone whom I'm ashamed to be seen with and who repulses me.

A: Yes, there is hope for her. It is crucial, however, that you try to adopt a helpful attitude. If she is as aware of your anger and hostility as you say she is, it will be very difficult for her to do anything about her weight. The first step to successful dieting is to develop a rational view of the problem. Your anger and threats of divorce, make this impossible. I would suggest that you set some time limits in your own mind—two years would be reasonable. Don't tell her about it. She won't succeed if she feels under pressure. But give her your help for that period of time, and then if she has not made progress, decide what you want to do.

The first step is to get her to adopt a realistic plan. Try to convince her that fads do not work in the long run and that the only way she will lose weight, and keep it off, is to eat less and exercise more. This does not sound very appealing, but it is a fact of life. Eating nothing but grapefruit or canned diet drink is unhealthy, and no one can live the rest of her life in this way. People have to learn to make decisions about how they are going to use food, and many gimmick diets are just a way of avoiding such decisions. Sooner or later, such dieters go back to their old habits and regain any weight they have lost.

If you can persuade your wife to eat less and exercise more, there are three simple techniques that will help. First, ask her to do all of her eating in one place—namely, sitting at the kitchen or dining-room table. If she works, she should pick one place there where she will do all of her eating during the day. This serves several purposes. First, it eliminates what we psychologists like to call "automatic" eating, or eating that people do without really being aware of what they are doing. For instance, many people like to snack while they are watching television; it is easy to finish off a whole bag of potato chips or cookies without even realizing it while your attention is divided. So she should do all of her eating in one place and do nothing but eat at those times. (She is allowed to carry on conversations at meals.) If she does this faithfully, it will not take more than few days before she begins to break the associations that she has acquired between eating and other activities.

The second reason this technique works is that it gives her something that she can do actively rather than forcing her to focus on things she is giving up. What would happen if you told yourself that you would never eat something you really liked—say ice cream—again? I know that I would have an immediate and constant craving for ice cream. That's what happens to dieters when they tell themselves that they are going to eliminate something from their diet. The chances are they will begin to think about it even more. With this technique, she can eat what she wants, as long as she eats it at the table. Eating it there will make her more aware of what she is doing, and she will probably eat less of it. And most people decide that they really don't want it that much in the first place if it means getting up and going away from the television set and eating it in the kitchen or dining room.

Third, it will help her develop a sense of control over her eating. Most chronic dieters begin a diet believing that it is only a matter of time before they fail, and with good reason. They've had quite a history of failure. Sitting at a table to eat is something anyone can do, and it will help her to develop confidence in herself. Success breeds success.

The second technique is even easier. Ask her to put her fork down between bites of food. This is also intended to help her develop a sense of control. Most chronic dieters think of themselves as compulsive eaters, and this will help them to feel that they are not completely helpless when it comes to food. Also, many people with weight problems tend to eat faster than they should. Putting their fork down between bites will slow them down.

The third technique is the hardest, but it may be the most important. She needs to get more exercise. When people begin to eat less, the body tries to protect its weight by slowing down the metabolism. It is thought that this is a leftover from our evolutionary heritage; at one time, people did have to go a while between meals—until they could find another mammoth or something—and those who could adapt were the ones who survived. The more people go on diets, the better their bodies get at slowing down the metabolism. So it is true that chronic dieters can eat a lot less than other people and still not lose weight.

The only way around this is to increase activity levels, which in turn increases the metabolic rate. Regular exercise tunes the body at a higher level, so that people who do it will be burning more calories even while they are sleeping than people who do not exercise. You should encourage your wife to do something that she enjoys. Walking is often the best choice; if she were to walk for thirty minutes a day, she could expect to lose fifteen to twenty pounds a year even if she did not reduce her eating. If she makes even a modest reduction in what she eats, she can expect to lose about a pound a week.

Getting more exercise is the one area in which you can be the most helpful. Offer to do it with her; suggest a walk after dinner, or perhaps you can get her interested in tennis or golf. It doesn't matter what it is as long as she enjoys it. If it is fun to exercise, then she is likely to keep up with it.

Don't expect her to master these techniques immediately. Changing habits is hard, and it requires perseverance and practice. You wouldn't expect her to learn to play the piano in a month, so don't expect her to learn to change her life-style in a month, either. Do encourage her to stick with this plan; if she slips for a few days, do not write it off as another diet plan that does not work. It *does* work; it just takes time for people to master it.

One last concern that I would have is that she may be eating because it is the only thing in her life that is bringing her any pleasure. To take food away from some people leaves them with little to live for; it is not true that all fat people eat to satisfy some deep psychological need, but it is true that some of them overeat because they have nothing better to do with their lives. Talk to your wife about this. If this does apply to her, perhaps with your help she can find something more satisfying to do with her time.

Q: My wife has been on one diet or another for the last ten years. She is pretty big—she weighs about two-hundred pounds—but I think she should just accept the fact that she was meant to be that way. I don't mind, so why should she? Her diets cause more problems than they are worth. Every time I bring home something that's good to eat, she accuses me of trying to sabotage her diet. If I ask her if she wants seconds at dinner, she gets mad at me. I just don't understand why she bothers.

A: It sounds to me as if the problem could be yours, not hers. The obvious question is, why is it so important to you that she not lose weight? Her desire to is certainly justified. Wanting to live longer is one pretty good reason.

I think your wife could be right; it does sound as if you may be trying to sabotage her efforts. Perhaps you need to look at yourself and try to understand why having a slender wife might be threatening to you. Some men fear that if their wife were slender and attractive, she would become involved with another man. It has also happened that men have encouraged their wives to maintain their obesity because the men themselves were involved with other women; having a fat, unattractive wife can be a good rationalization for having an affair.

Unless you have a thing for big women, I would suspect that you are somewhat insecure about your relationship with your wife. Try to be honest with yourself. Were you ever the jealous type? Did your jealousy begin to fade as she began to grow bigger? Perhaps her obesity is your insurance that other men will not be interested in her.

If you can help your wife rather than hinder her, and she manages to lose weight, I would bet that your relationship would get better rather than worse. If she is able to be happy with herself, then I would predict that she will be happier with you. Why don't you give it a try and see what happens?

Some Final Thoughts

As I have suggested several times in this chapter, family members can make or break the chronic dieter. There are few patterns with the same potential for others to have an impact. This does not mean that chronic dieters have a right to blame family members for their problem, but they do have a right to expect emotional support and practical help.

If the chronic dieter you live with does not need to lose weight, try to keep in mind that the bad feelings he or she has about her body are real. Telling a chronic dieter that he or she is foolish is not going to help. Be generous with compliments. Be reassuring. Encourage him or her to have realistic expectations. If you do this, the chances are excellent that he or she will develop a better self-image as time goes on. It will be a gradual process, but it will happen.

If your chronic dieter does need to lose weight, do not give up on him or her. It is tempting to accept the notion that obese people are never going to change. I have heard psychotherapists say that curing obesity is harder than curing cancer, and the fact is that in any particular program, 90 percent of the participants will be back to their original weight within a year.

There is good reason to be optimistic, however. Recently, psychologist Stanley Schachter interviewed every person in three small communities about weight and smoking problems; his goal was to get some idea of how many people were able to solve these problems on their own. His results were surprising. He found that nearly 65 percent of those people who identified themselves as once having a weight problem were within the normal range when they were interviewed. What seems to happen is that any one particular attempt to lose weight does not have a very good chance of being successful; maybe fewer than 10 percent of those who go on a diet will succeed. But the fact that such a large percentage eventually succeeded suggests that as long as one keeps trying, the chances are good that he or she will make it eventually. Family members can play a crucial role in helping those with a weight problem keep up their motivation and their will to succeed, and as long as one does not give up, success is virtually inevitable.

10

THE CLING-ON

The Cling-on Test

1. **If my partner forgot me on Valentine's Day, I would think:**
   a. he or she didn't love me anymore.
   b. he or she doesn't care about me as much as I care about him or her.
   c. he or she is being a jerk.
   d. nothing of it—I probably wouldn't even notice.

2. **If my partner were to leave me:**
   a. I don't think I could make it alone.
   b. I could never find anyone to love me ever again.
   c. I'd be hurt, but I would get on with my life.
   d. it would do wonders for my sex life.

3. **My partner needs me:**
   a. much less than I need him or her.
   b. a little less than I need him or her.
   c. as much as I need him or her.
   d. not at all.

4. **When my partner is out of town for a few days:**
   a. I would never let my partner leave without me.
   b. I have trouble getting through the night.
   c. I can't wait for him or her to get back.
   d. I thoroughly enjoy having some time to myself.

5. **If I were offered a new job I would:**
   a. ask my partner what I should do.
   b. ask my partner for his or her thoughts.
   c. tell my partner what decision I had made.
   d. forget to mention it at all.

6. **If, at a party, I saw my partner talking to an attractive member of the opposite sex, I would:**
   a. feel sure that they were planning to meet later.
   b. feel bad that he or she wasn't talking to me like that.
   c. think nothing of it.
   d. be pleased that my partner is having a good time.

7. **While I was growing up, my parents:**
   a. seemed to have mixed feelings about me.
   b. told me they loved me, but never spent much time with me.
   c. spent a lot of time with me but never said a kind word to me.
   d. expressed their affection toward me openly and spent a lot of time doing things with me.

8. **While I was in high school, my parents:**
   a. selected my courses for me to make sure I didn't do anything foolish.
   b. made it clear what courses they thought I should be taking.
   c. were interested in what courses I was taking.
   d. didn't know if I was in school or not.

9. **When I think about living by myself:**
   a. a chill runs down my spine.
   b. I know how lonely I would feel.
   c. I think it could be fun—at least for a while.
   d. I get a warm feeling all over.

10. **If my partner was not home two hours after I expected him/her, I would:**
    a. be sure that he or she was never coming back.
    b. be scared that something terrible had happened to him or her.
    c. enjoy the extra time to myself.
    d. never notice.

The Cling-on Test Scoring Key

1. a. 3 points.
b. 2 points.
c. 1 point.
d. 0 points.

2. a. 3 points.
b. 2 points.
c. 1 point.
d. 0 points.

3. a. 3 points.
b. 2 points.
c. 1 point.
d. 0 points.

4. a. 3 points.
b. 2 points.
c. 1 point.
d. 0 points.

5. a. 3 points.
b. 2 points.
c. 1 point.
d. 0 points.

6. a. 3 points.
b. 2 points.
c. 1 point.
d. 0 points.

7. a. 3 points.
b. 2 points.
c. 1 point.
d. 0 points.

8. a. 3 points.
b. 2 points.
c. 1 point.
d. 0 points.

9. a. 3 points.
b. 2 points.
c. 1 point.
d. 0 points.

10. a. 3 points.
b. 2 points.
c. 1 point.
d. 0 points.

Interpretation of Test Scores

0 to 6 points: You sound as if you have problems with intimacy or your relationship is in serious trouble. Dependency is the last of your worries.

7 to 14 points: The healthiest range to be in. These people are likely to have the view that while they want to have a close relationship, they know they can survive without one.

15 to 22 points: You have some tendencies toward dependency. If your partner has similar tendencies or if he or she has strong paternalistic tendencies, this may never cause any problems.

23 to 30 points: You are a dependent personality, and this chapter definitely applies to you.

Please, Just Tell Me What To Do

Jenny is a very loving woman. She has dedicated her life to her children and her husband, and she gets great pleasure from taking care of them. Her friends tease her about being a Kool-Aid mom, but she likes being that way; being there when her children arrive home from school is very important to her. Jenny takes her role as wife equally seriously. She makes sure that Stu, her husband, has half an hour to read the paper before sitting down to an elaborate meal every evening. After dinner, she cleans up the kitchen and gets the kids ready for bed so Stu has a little time to himself to unwind from his hectic day. She is only too happy to do anything she can to make his life easier. After all, she is very lucky to have a husband who takes such good care of her.

Stu has a slightly different perspective of the relationship. "I appreciate all the things Jenny does for me and the family, but at times, I feel a little claustrophobic. Jenny seems to have the idea that because we are married, we should do everything together. After the kids go to bed, she feels bad if I read, because that means I'm ignoring her. If I want to play golf on the weekend, she's hurt because I wouldn't rather spend the time with her. The few times I've had to go out of town on business trips, she doesn't understand why I don't take her along. I've tried to talk to her about it, but she just doesn't seem to appreciate that I need to have a life of my own. Being married shouldn't mean that you have to completely dedicate your life to another person."

Stu is right; Jenny does not understand him. "What I'm beginning to understand is that Stu just doesn't love me as much as I love him. I want to make him happy; I do all the things I do for him to show how much I love him. All I want in return is for him to show me that he thinks I'm someone special. I've begged him to start playing tennis with me, but he would rather play golf with his friends. It couldn't be much clearer where I stand. I know that he's a good person, and that he works hard for our family, but I don't think he really wants me. If he did, he'd find more time for me."

Things became steadily more tense between Stu and Jenny until they decided to get some help. As Stu tells it, "I decided that we might as well try therapy, because we had nothing to lose. I thought that our expectations about what marriage should be like were different and that nothing could be done about it. I even thought I might have a problem, since I did not seem to be able to feel the same way about spending time together as Jenny did. However, it finally became clear to me, when she was offered a part time job, that she just depended too much on me. She asked me what I thought, and I tried to point out the pros and cons of taking it; I wanted her to do what *she* wanted to do. Our discussion seemed to frustrate her more and more until finally she pleaded, 'Please just tell me what to do.' "

Moving from dependence to independence is something we all have to do. We come into this world totally dependent on others, and if we did not have other bigger, stronger, more capable people to take care of us, we wouldn't make it. It does not take long, however, before we start to reach out and learn that there are things that we can do for ourselves. This process begins when we discover that we can get from one place to another on our own. It ends, for some people, when we realize that we can not only survive, but be happy without depending on others to do it for us. Unfortunately, there are a lot of dropouts, like Jenny, along the way; these people fall into a category that I like to call the cling-on, or what psychologists refer to as the dependent personality.

Jenny believed that people got married so that they could take care of each other. She defined her primary mission in life as being a good wife and mother. She wanted to take care of her family, and in return, she expected her husband to take care of her. This included not only the things that he was doing, such as earning enough money to pay the bills, making minor repairs around the house, and so on, but also taking care of her emotional needs; it was his responsibility to make her feel special, desirable, and appreciated for the things she did for the family. And if she did not feel good about herself, it was certainly his fault; after all, he was her husband, and who else was there to blame?

Of course, everyone who enters into a relationship expects to get something out of it; what would be the point of our making such a commitment unless our partner did allow us to experience feelings of being needed and wanted? In short, having a close, loving relationship with another human being should help us to feel good about ourselves, so the difference between what most people want from a relationship and what people like Jenny want is subtle—but nonetheless real.

The biggest fear that people like Jenny have is of being left alone to face the world on their own; they do not feel qualified for such a terrifying job. So Jenny is especially sensitive to any signs that Stu may not be totally committed to the marriage. If he is reading during the evening, it could be because he finds her boring to talk to. If he wants to play golf on the weekends, it must mean that he would rather spend time with his friends. And worst of all, if he won't take her on out-of-town trips, he may be meeting another woman.

Stu found that trying to provide Jenny with enough

reassurance was almost hopeless, and over a period of time, he began to feel suffocated. He tried to remind himself to say something nice to Jenny every day, to tell himself that it really did not take much to make her happy and the least he could do was be more romantic more often. But the more he tried to do these things, the harder it became. "How can you be romantic when you have to remind yourself to do it so your spouse won't feel neglected?" Stu's response was to withdraw even more, which in turn increased Jenny's fears of abandonment.

In extreme cases, the fear of abandonment is so strong that these people will do anything to hang on to a relationship. Some people may tolerate a spouse who is openly promiscuous, or verbally or physically abusive, or who makes it clear that he or she cares nothing for the other person. These people are, of course, miserable in the relationship, but they are too scared to try to go it on their own; having someone, regardless of what a snake in the grass he or she is, is better than being all alone.

A second characteristic of the cling-on is the willingness to let someone else make all the decisions, both big and small. This was the clue that made Stu realize that his wife might be a little too dependent on him. Jenny's inability to decide on her own whether or not to accept a part-time job is not at all unusual for people with this style; they like to have people tell them what to do. Again, the belief that these people have is that someone—anyone—is better qualified to make these kinds of decisions than they are.

Becky found that some of her tendencies toward dependency came out after her first child was born. "For the first few years after Kelly was born, I didn't have any confidence in my instincts as a mother. I would ask Dan if I should change her diaper or wait awhile. If she had a cold, I would ask Dan if we should take her to the doctor. As she got a little older, and I would get mad at her and punish her, I would ask Dan if he thought I had handled it all right. He finally told me that I could decide those things as well as he could, so I should stop asking him. I don't know how I ever became such a wimp. I never realized what I was doing; I just thought of it as asking for his advice. But he was right—I *was* asking him to make all the decisions for me."

Many cling-ons manage to find a partner who is willing to take on the role of decision maker. Bob was a professional man who was highly regarded by his colleagues and his clients. But the power in his family was his wife, who was more than happy to accept all the responsibility Bob was willing to give her. She decided what house they would buy, who they would socialize with, and even when Bob should change jobs. Bob went along with his wife's "advice" happily for many years until his wife left him for a man she could "respect."

In extreme cases, people with this personality style are fully aware of their self-doubts. They are willing to tell anyone who will listen how stupid they are and how they could never make it except for the person who takes care of them. Bob, who entered therapy for depression after his wife left him, realizes now that he put up with a lot of abuse because of his fears. "I was more like her slave than her husband. I did everything for her to try to keep her happy. I did whatever she asked—and she wasn't shy about asking—and I would try to surprise her by doing nice things for her just to get a few crumbs of approval. I was scared to death that she would leave me and I'd never find anyone else. I was sure that I was so homely and so dull that I'd never find another woman who could be interested in me. Now, I wonder why that should matter, because my wife was never really interested in me either. But I was frightened of being alone."

In other cases, the dependent person may appear to have a lot of self-confidence, and may indeed feel self-confident much of the time. In these cases, it is only when something triggers their fears of being abandoned that their self-doubts will surface. Jenny, for instance, gave the impression of being a self-assured, self-reliant woman; in fact, it was this quality of hers that first caught Stu's attention. Her self-doubts began to surface only after she began to question her husband's dedication to her. "I always felt pretty good about myself until I began to think that Stu was losing interest in me. At first I thought that his lack of interest in me must mean that there must be something wrong with me. Then I reached the point where I decided that I wanted a chance to find someone with whom I could have the kind of relationship I wanted; that's when I really panicked. I went back to thinking that there was something wrong with me and that no man could be interested in me for very long, so I was afraid to leave him. It became like a seesaw. I would decide to stick with Stu and then I'd start to feel unhappy with the way he was treating me. But as soon as I started to think about leaving him, I would go back to thinking that I would end up growing old all alone, and so I'd decide to stay."

It is quite possible that someone who has dependent tendencies could go through life without ever realizing it and without having any problems with them. If two people with mild degrees of this personality style get together, it is likely that everything will work out fine for them; each will have some concerns about the other's commitment to the relationship, so they will both spend a lot of effort to make sure that everything works out. The dependent person who gets together with a person with paternalistic tendencies will also have a good chance of feeling secure in the relationship; their complementary needs will make for smooth sailing.

So, although most mental health professionals, including myself, believe that people are generally better off without having dependency needs, there is nothing inherently bad or neurotic about them. Lots of people can, and do, live quite happily with them. They do cause problems, however, when the dependent personality gets matched up with someone who does not like the idea of being responsible for two adults. Sharing responsibility is one thing; taking on all the responsibility is quite another.

Development of the Cling-on

People who fear being abandoned as adults often grew up with those fears. Either through circumstances or because of the quirks of their parents, these people were never able to feel confident that they would be taken care of as children. They may never have had reason to believe that they would be abandoned, but there was always an element of uncertainty in their minds, and the uncertainty, is more important in the development of dependent personalities than abandonment itself. In fact, many children who are actually abandoned learn at an early age that they have to fend for themselves, and may grow up to be fiercely independent.

The circumstances that these individuals experienced as children can range from the heartbreaking to the very subtle. As an example of the former, Tom's first six years were spent with a mother who tended to view him as something of a nuisance. She left his father before Tom was born, and Tom spent much of the first five years of his life with baby-sitters. Lots of children survive that without any psychological scars, but Tom's mother would never tell him when she would be back to pick him up. His earliest memories are of his crying while wondering if his mother would come to get him. "If my mother got a better offer, which wasn't hard from her perspective, she would just take off after work and forget all about me. I remember one time when she hadn't picked me up by ten, and the woman who was taking care of me was furious; I was sure my mother was dead and I'd never seen her again. She always did get me sooner or later, but I know that these experiences have taken their toll. If my wife is twenty minutes late, my stomach gets tied up in knots; my fears range from her being killed in a car crash to her running away with another man. I know it's crazy, but I just can't help myself."

Jenny is an example of a person who never experienced anything obviously traumatic, but she remembers having a vague sense of fear that her mother never loved her. Her mother thought of herself as an ideal mother, and in many ways she was; she saw to it that all of her children had clean clothes and nourishing food even though it was difficult to do so on the family budget. She also made it a point to tell Jenny and her sisters regularly how much she loved them and what special children they were; she was determined that her children would feel good about themselves, since she never had.

Her mother's failing was that she really did not like to spend time with her children. Although Jenny's mother would deny it, she lived the cliché that children should be seen and not heard. She would buy them books and games for Christmas, but then she would never read to them or play games with them. She would tell her children how proud she was of how well they were doing in school, but she would never take the time to listen to what it was they were doing so well. Jenny remembers that the first time her mother actually did something with her was when she was eight years old, when she tried to teach Jenny and her sisters how to play bridge.

Although many people would see Jenny's childhood as uneventful and even rather ordinary, she did have something in common with Tom. She had the same sense of uncertainty about how much her mother really cared about her. Obviously, Tom's fears were justified. His mother never bothered to reassure him, and he survived by telling himself that she must really care or else she would just leave him with the baby-sitter. But Jenny operated under another cliché, that actions speak louder than words. She never had the distinct thought "Does my mother really love me?" but she did develop a hunger for genuine affection, and so it is not surprising that she is so sensitive to any signs that her husband may not really love her after all.

Other people are taught to be dependent more directly. Lots of children with medical problems have no choice but to assume a dependent role. Children with asthma, for instance, grow up with the feeling that their very ability to breathe is dependent upon having someone bigger and stronger to look out for them. Parents of these children cannot be blamed for encouraging them to be dependent.

Some people were, to put it very simply, overly protected as children. Bob falls into this category. He was the youngest child by five years in a family of five children, and he had lots of people who were happy to help him with anything he tried. Everyone in the family considered him to be "the baby," so Bob had two brothers, two sisters, and two parents who all wanted to make sure that nothing happened to him. Bob remembers that while his family's protectiveness sometimes embarrassed him, part of him still liked it. "When I was a sophomore in high school I joined the band, and one of the things we would do was take trips to play for football and basketball games. My parents didn't want me riding on the bus with the other kids because there weren't any seatbelts, so they would drive me to all the games. At first I didn't think anything about it, because I had always done everything with my family. But then I started to realize what a nerd the other kids thought I was, so I put my foot down before my junior year." It was perfectly natural for Bob to let his wife take over his parents' job after he got married.

People like Bob who develop a dependent personality

as a result of being overly protected tend to have slightly different feelings about their style than people like Tom and Jenny, who experience a constant fear of abandonment. People like Bob generally do not worry about being left until it happens; because they have been smothered with love and concern, they usually assume that that's the way things will always be, and they never doubt that someone will always be there to take care of them. When something does happen to upset the apple cart, like Bob's wife leaving him, their first reaction is likely to be one of being lost: What are they going to do? How can they manage things on their own? How could this happen to them? The long-term effects are the same in both cases; unless something happens, unless they can be reassured, or unless they can find someone new to take care of them, their underlying feelings of being unlovable will come to dominate their sense of self, and feelings of depression will take over. Let's take a look at some ideas about how one can live with this kind of person.

Living with the Cling-on

Most of the styles we have talked about are difficult for people to see in themselves. (I still believe that I'm not like anyone described in the entire book, regardless of *what* my wife says!) But cling-ons have more trouble than most recognizing that their way of viewing the world might not be the best. If it is pointed out to them that they might be happier if they were a little more self-sufficient, they might respond that everybody needs other people. And they are right; everyone does need other people. It is all a matter of degree, and there is a lot of gray area when we talk about dependency issues.

Whenever I see a couple who have complaints that focus on this gray area, I am very careful not to jump to the conclusion that one person is too dependent on the other. It is equally possible that the other partner has some conflicts about being intimate or close to another human being. The point is that if you believe your partner is too dependent on you, you should be willing to examine yourself. Could it be that you have a need to maintain an unhealthy distance from your partner? The following cases should help clarify when the problem is too much dependency and when it is too little intimacy.

Q: My husband is a good man in almost every way except that he can't seem to cut the apron strings from his mother. His father died when he was twelve, and since he was the oldest child he took over responsibility for the family. I understand that he has an obligation to her, but he visits her four or five times a week. If she sees a mouse in the middle of the night, he runs over there to set a trap and calm her down. Even that wouldn't be so bad if it didn't come at the expense of his own family. He's painted her house twice in the time I've been trying to get him to paint one room in our house. If he's scheduled to go to a Scout meeting with our son and his mother calls with some trivial problem, he goes to see her instead. I've tried to talk to him about it, but all he'll say is that she won't live forever. Well, she's only fifty-nine years old and she's healthy as a horse. Am I justified in feeling that he's got a problem?

A: There is no doubt he has a problem, but it is one that will be very difficult for you to do anything about. I would guess that your husband never felt loved by his mother as a child, whether he recognizes it or not, and is still trying to be the perfect son in order to win his mother's love. One common situation I have seen in people like your husband is that the mother did not try to hide her preference for a brother or sister. Because people who feel secure with themselves cannot be manipulated by guilt, the preferred child generally won't put up with nonsense like trying to catch a mouse in the middle of the night; it is the child who feels unloved who is driven to prove that he or she deserves to be loved just as much as brother or sister. There is usually a fair amount of guilt mixed in with all this; at some level, such people believe that they must have done something wrong to be rejected by their own mother, and for these people, no request is too unreasonable.

The reason I don't think there is much you can do about it is that it will be nearly impossible to convince him that he is not doing the right thing by his family. As you said, people who can't sever the apron strings from their parents have the best excuse in the world—"they won't live forever." While this cannot be denied, they cannot see that it is not sufficient justification for asking "How high?" every time they are told to jump.

One point that I make with these people is that their children won't be children forever, either; in fact, their children will probably stop being children before their parents stop living. I also ask them to think about the people who mean the most to them, and then to think about the things they do with and for these people. Because the ties to the parents are based on such negative feelings—guilt and feelings of rejection—it's usually the case that they don't really like the controlling parent. So after they make their lists, they see that they are spending the most time with people they care the least about.

Try using this line of reasoning with your husband. It might help him to start thinking about things. Don't get your hopes up, though. These people hardly ever decide to take a close look at themselves on their own; the people I've seen who are like your husband rarely come to therapy voluntarily, but are usually coerced in by a disgruntled spouse. Your best bet is to try to get him to see someone—in marital therapy with you, if he won't go by himself. Don't be afraid to use a little coercion.

There are some things you should not be doing. First, don't let his feelings of obligation to his mother control your life. If the family has plans to do something and he gets a call from his mother just before you leave, go on with your plans without him. Even if just the two of you have plans and he cancels at the last minute because of his mother, you should go out alone. Seeing the family carry on without him may help him to recognize the fact that he is losing that which means the most to him—which indeed he is.

Second, don't nag him about his mother. To do so would put you—in his eyes—in the same boat as his mother; he would start to feel guilty about neglecting you, and then the things he did do would be done out of a sense of obligation. Try to make your wishes known in a calm, rational way. His desire to do things with you and the kids has to be stronger than his guilt feelings about his mother if things are going to work out. You do not want him to spend more time with you simply because you can make him feel guiltier than his mother can; if this turned out to be the case, the quality of the time you spent together would be pretty poor.

Since you sound as if you are happy with your relationship except for this one sore point, it might be best if you decide that this is his one big flaw and you have to live with it. Of course, you are bound to feel very angry at times, but you have to decide whether the situation is so bad that you simply cannot live with it. From the way you described your husband, it does sound to me that his good qualities outweigh his bad ones.

If you can accept his relationship with his mother, neurotic as it is, it may help him to demand a little more slack in the apron strings on his own. Remember, chastising him will only cause him to mobilize his defenses. If you can let him deal with his feelings by himself, while offering your support when he asks for it, he will have a better chance of seeing the situation a little more clearly. Good luck!

Q: I've been living with Sean for nearly two years now. We plan to be married in a few months, but I've been having second thoughts. Sean is the most jealous man I've ever known. At first it made me feel good, because I thought it showed how much he loved me, but now I'm beginning to think it's sick. If I get home ten minutes late, he grills me about it for an hour. If I talk to another man at a party, he accuses me of flirting. If I want to spend a weekend visiting my family, he thinks I'm meeting another man, and he'll call half a dozen times. Will he get over this after we're married or will he always be like this? If there's no chance of his changing, I don't think I can stand being with him.

A: Most people feel at least a little bit jealous when they first get involved with another person. When you care about someone else but don't have any history to fall back on, it would be unusual not to feel a little insecure, and hence a little jealous. In most cases, as the relationship goes on and the people learn that they can trust each other and count on each other, feelings of jealousy begin to fade.

Intense jealousy, such as your partner has, is a sure sign of a cling-on. It is a safe bet that Sean has had experiences that have taught him that you can't be too sure of other people. So he approaches his relationship with you filled with uncertainty as well. His jealousy is "sick" in the sense that he feels insecure about himself, so he cannot feel secure in his relationships with other people.

The chances are good that his jealousy would fade with time, but it is starting at such a high level that unless something is done, it could take years before it reached a level that you could tolerate. What happens in many cases like yours is that the jealousy drives the partner away before it has a chance to dissipate. So the time to do something about the situation is now. A marriage ceremony will not transform him into a secure, tolerant, understanding man, so don't marry him until you feel confident that he has resolved his feelings to the point where you can live with them.

Start by trying to get him to talk about his feelings. Encourage him to speculate about why he reacts the way he does. Be patient. As always, people like Sean tend to believe they are perfectly justified in feeling the way they do. But if you let him know that you can't live with his jealousy, and that you love him and want things to work out, he may be willing to give it a try.

Be sure you emphasize your feelings of love for him when you talk to him about the problem. Remember, his jealousy stems from his insecurities; his first reaction might be that you are using this issue as an excuse to dump him. You have to make it clear to him that you want him, but as painful as it will be to you, you cannot marry him unless he can get over his jealousy.

The tragedy of intense jealousy is that many people do believe that it will go away after the marriage ceremony, only to learn that it doesn't. I have known more than one client who felt like a virtual prisoner in the marriage because they allowed their partner's jealousy to control their lives. Don't let this happen to you. Get things settled before you take the next step.

Q: Please settle an argument between me and my wife. I'm at a crucial step in my career and I have to put in a lot of hours if I'm going to get anywhere. I usually don't get home until eight or nine during the week, and have to work most Saturdays, so on Sundays, I like to just sit around and regroup. My wife has been on my back because we don't spend enough time together. She says if I really loved her, I'd find the time to do things with her. I think if she really loved me, she be supportive of my career and do everything she could to make things easier for me. Anyway, she thinks that I have the problem—that I'm a workaholic. I say she needs to be more independent. Who's right?

A: I'm not sure that it should be a question of who is right and who is wrong. It could very well be that you have different ideas of what a marriage should be like and that your ideas simply are not compatible.

I don't see anything in your description of your wife that makes her seem to be a cling-on. From the way you tell it, it's not that she can't cope with your being gone all the time, she just doesn't like it. This does not make her a dependent personality. She has a right not to like the way things are going in your relationship.

You are not necessarily wrong, either, because there are lots of women who would be happy to have the kind of relationship you describe. Some people are perfectly content to have fairly separate lives from their spouse. In the extreme, there are couples who work and live in different cities and see each other only a few times a month; they believe that such an arrangement makes their time together that much more enjoyable.

I do wonder, however, whether you and your wife have any of these enjoyable times together. It sounds a little as if what you want is someone who will take care of your house and kids but won't bother you. If what you mean when you say that you want a wife who is supportive of your career is that you want a wife who won't demand any of your time, then I think you are the one with a problem. If that is what you want, why bother being married? You would be happier with a live-in maid.

In either case, I hope you take a close look at your need to devote so much time to your career. My experience has been that people who spend as much time as you do working face a real crisis when their careers begin to level out. Those lucky few who make it to the very top never have to face this, but most of the rest of us will reach a point when we realize that we are never going to be president of the company. What will you do if you find yourself in that situation? If you are like most people, if you do not have other people that you truly care about and other activities that you enjoy, you will feel that your life is pointless. In other words, don't put all of your eggs in one basket.

Q: I've been married for only four months, but I feel as if I have absolutely no privacy. If I don't say anything for ten minutes, my husband asks me what I'm thinking about, and I don't want to feel I've got to tell him every thought that's on my mind. Worse than that, he won't let me go anywhere alone. I can't even go the laundromat by myself; he insists on "keeping me company." He follows me around the house, and has even followed me into the bathroom. I love him, but how can I get him to give me some room to breathe?

A: Most couples have a touch of the cling-on when their relationship is brand-new, but in most cases, their need for an independent identity begins to reassert itself, and their wanting to spend every waking moment together begins to fade away. In most relationships, this process takes place at about the same pace for both partners, so there is no problem. It sounds as if it might take your husband a little longer to adjust, but I think he will adjust sooner or later.

The best thing you can do to speed things up a little is to tell him what you told me. Let him know that you need some privacy and some time to yourself. Be sure to say these things in a nonthreatening way, because it is a good bet that he still does feel a little insecure about your relationship. He is probably thinking that if you loved him as much as he loves you, then you wouldn't want to spend any time without him. It is hard for anyone to understand another person's definition of love.

I think the short-term prospects are good. I don't think it will be too much longer before your husband begins to give you a little more room, especially if you can talk to him openly about your feelings. Be careful, though, of the long-term implications of the difference between your styles. Even after your husband gets used to being married, he is still likely to have different ideas about what being married means. So continue to be open with him; don't let him make you feel guilty about not wanting the kind of relationship he does, because as soon as you start doing things to avoiding feeling guilty, your relationship will be in trouble. I don't mean to sound unduly pessimistic; I do think you have a good chance of working out your differences. But don't be complacent, either. The difference between you and your husband is important enough to warrant keeping close tabs on your relationship.

Some Final Thoughts

It is never possible to draw precise lines between what is normal and what is not, but it is more difficult than usual to make these distinctions when it comes to dependency issues. One thing I do know is that in this case, what is typical is not necessarily desirable. There have been a number of surveys that show that the average couple who have been married for ten years or so spend about two minutes a day talking to each other. This suggests to me that the average person who has been married for ten years must feel quite alienated from his or her partner.

The problem is that many people with a spouse who wants more intimacy accuse their spouse of being too dependent. Such a charge, when only two minutes of conversation per day is the rule, is absurd.

The point is that dependency, at least in its mild forms, is not necessarily bad. One person's dependency is another's need for intimacy. I'm sure you have read of couples who pride themselves on never having spent a night apart in thirty or forty years of marriage. While this would seem a little much to me and a lot of other people, it isn't bad as long as both partners like it that way. In fact, some of the happiest couples I've known were happy because both partners had a touch of the cling-on in them.

Dependence-independence is a crucial factor when it comes to long-term relationships, and when the partners differ on this factor, it is bound to cause problems. The problems may be expressed in any number of ways—money problems, affairs, depression, and on and on and on—and it is often the case that neither person is aware of what the real problem is. The only way to work out these differences is to talk about them; blaming the other person, ignoring the problem, or blaming yourself won't work. If you can be open about your needs, whether they are for more space or for more intimacy, then at least you have a basis for deciding if you want to make your relationship work.

11

THE AVOIDER

The Avoider Test

1. **If a piece of furniture I had bought was delivered to me and I noticed that there was a big scratch on it, I:**
   a. wouldn't pay any attention to it.
   b. would try to think how I could cover it up.
   c. would point it out to the delivery men and ask them to bring me another one.
   d. would raise such a ruckus that they would get that piece of furniture out of my house fast.

2. **If I'm at a party and I don't know anyone, I:**
   a. sneak out the door.
   b. wait for someone to start talking to me.
   c. look for some interesting people and talk to them.
   d. think of it as an opportunity to really let loose.

3. **When I weigh my accomplishments against my abilities:**
   a. I feel bad because I've made so little use of what I have.
   b. I realize I could have done more.
   c. I feel good about what I've done.
   d. I marvel at both.

4. **If I received a raise or a bonus that was not as large as I expected, I would:**
   a. be happy with anything I got.
   b. be disappointed, but I wouldn't say anything.
   c. talk to my boss and find out why there was the discrepancy.
   d. demand that I get what I deserve and threaten to quit.

5. **Other people tend to view me as:**
   a. an uninteresting blob.
   b. harmless enough.
   c. a fairly typical person.
   d. the superior person that I am.

6. **My parents often told me:**
   a. how I would never amount to anything.
   b. nothing—they didn't talk to me that much.
   c. that they loved me and I was a special person.
   d. that I could do no wrong.

7. **When I was in high school, I:**
   a. virtually lived in my room.
   b. had one good friend.
   c. enjoyed myself, although I was never a star.
   d. was admired by everyone.

8. **If someone said something very nice to me, I would:**
   a. wonder what he or she was after.
   b. think he or she was just being nice.
   c. thank him or her for being so thoughtful.
   d. take it in stride.

9. **If I saw an job advertisement for which I was qualified and which would mean a big boost in pay, I would:**
   a. probably never get around to doing anything about it.
   b. suspect that a hundred people more qualified than I would be applying.
   c. send in my résumé and hope for the best.
   d. call and let the employers know how fortunate they are that I was available.

10. **Procrastination is:**
    a. a way of life for me.
    b. something I do when I'm not sure how things will turn out.
    c. something I do when I have to do something I don't like—such as cleaning the bathroom.
    d. something I have never been guilty of.

The Avoider Test Scoring Key

1. a. 3 points.
b. 2 points.
c. 1 point.
d. 0 points.

2. a. 3 points.
b. 2 points.
c. 1 point.
d. 0 points.

3. a. 3 points.
b. 2 points.
c. 1 point.
d. 0 points.

4. a. 3 points.
b. 2 points.
c. 1 point.
d. 0 points.

5. a. 3 points.
b. 2 points.
c. 1 point.
d. 0 points.

6. a. 3 points.
b. 2 points.
c. 1 point.
d. 0 points.

7. a. 3 points.
b. 2 points.
c. 1 point.
d. 0 points.

8. a. 3 points.
b. 2 points.
c. 1 point.
d. 0 points.

9. a. 3 points.
b. 2 points.
c. 1 point.
d. 0 points.

10. a. 3 points.
b. 2 points.
c. 1 point.
d. 0 points.

Interpretation of Test Scores

0 to 8 points. If you scored in this range, there is a good chance that you have unrealistically high self-esteem. Go back to Chapter 5.

9 to 16 points: The healthiest range to be in. Well-adjusted people feel generally good about themselves, but they do have some self-doubts.

17 to 23 points. You have a mild case of the avoider in you. You could learn something from this chapter.

24 to 30 points: You are definitely an avoider. This chapter is a must.

I'll Get to It Tomorrow

Clark is the kind of man whom everyone likes, but few really know. He is a quiet, kind, unassuming person who seems to be able to get along with all different kinds of people, and who would do anything in the world for you but never ask for anything in return. His wife certainly appreciates this quality in him; Clark always seems happy to do anything she asked of him. He is the same way with the kids; all they have to do is ask and Clark would play with them, read to them, or take them practically anywhere they want to go. Everyone in the neighborhood thinks Clark is the ideal father.

There are, however, a few things about Clark that get on his wife's nerves. First of all, Clark doesn't seem to make much of an effort to be sociable when she invites friends over to the house. He is always polite, but mostly he just sits around and smiles and says very little. Then there is the matter of his letting people walk all over him. If they bought a piece of furniture and it was delivered damaged, Clark wouldn't dream of calling to complain, so Terri has to take on the role of the family complainer. And worst of all is Clark's tendency to put off important things. He has been eligible for a promotion in his civil service job for some time, but he just won't submit his paperwork in time to be considered.

Clark realizes that he could stand "to be a little more assertive," but he believes that his is not necessarily a bad way to be. "I know that there are things I could do differently, but what's the point? I don't like to complain about things like a little chip in a piece of furniture, because it doesn't bother me. So why should I do it? If it bothers Terri so much, she should be the one to call the store and complain. I know I could talk more when I'm around other people, but I don't like to have to compete to say anything. If people are interested in what I have to say, they'll ask. And as for my job—which Terri is always nagging me about—I like what I'm doing now. I don't think I would be as happy if I were made a supervisor. Don't I have a right to earn a little less money if it means I'll be happier?"

Terri has a different view of Clark's behavior. "I think Clark just needs a little more self-confidence. He is a very intelligent, capable man with a delightful sense of humor, but he just won't give other people a chance to find out what he's really like. I know he would really like the promotion at work, but he's afraid he will be humiliated if he applies for it and then doesn't get it. He won't admit it, but he's said enough to let me know that he would like the recognition, to say nothing of the extra money, that goes along with being a supervisor.

"Something happened recently that proves to me—and I think even to Clark—that he's not as satisfied with himself as he says he is. Clark loves to play golf, and a few men at work were organizing a trip to a resort for a few days to do nothing but play golf. Clark really wanted to be invited, and so I encouraged him to ask if he could go along. At first, he had all kinds of reasons why he couldn't make the trip, but I wouldn't let him get away with them. So he finally said that he would ask them the next day if he could go. When he got home the next day, I asked him if he had talked to them about the trip, and he replied weakly, 'I didn't have a chance to talk to them. I'll get to it tomorrow.' "

Clark is a mild version of what I call an avoider, and Terri's assessment of him is right on the mark. Clark *does* need more self-confidence. He does not like to admit it to himself, but he believes that other people are somehow more competent, more likable, more intelligent, more *everything* that is desirable than he is. It is something of a paradox, because Clark knows that he is a very smart person, and that he is better at his job than most of the people he works with; he also knows, based on his relationships with his few close friends, that he can be charming, funny, and likable. But his gut reaction is quite another matter. He approaches every new situation with the vague feeling that he will end up being rejected and appearing to be the fool. He really wanted to go on the golfing trip, but the possibility of being told he could not go along was a risk he could not bring himself to take. Objectively, he knew the chances were the other men would be glad to have him along, but a part of him was holding back. What if, just what if, they told him he could not come along?

Avoiders differ in terms of how much awareness they have of their problem. Many, like Clark, are able to rationalize away most of the self-defeating things they do. This allows them to present a facade—to themselves as well as to others—of a reasonably self-assured individual. Clark tells himself that he doesn't enter into conversations because he doesn't like to have to compete in order to say something. He never complains about poor service or defective products because these things supposedly never bother him. These rationalizations, or excuses, keep him from having to face the fact that he is afraid to do these things.

Defenses rarely work perfectly, so there are times when people like Clark feel uncomfortable with themselves. Clark has moments when he wishes he could be more outgoing. He would like to go out to lunch more often with some of the people he works with, but he finds it difficult to take the initiative; even when others ask him, he sometimes declines because he suspects they are only being polite and do not really want him to come along. And every now and then, something like the golf trip comes up when he cannot deny that he is just plain scared. But all in all, Clark works hard to maintain the illusion that he is content with himself, and he resents it when Terri tries to encourage him to be more assertive.

In more severe cases, the feelings of inferiority are much closer to the surface. These people readily admit that they have trouble getting along with others; they believe that people do not like them, and they can find evidence to prove it. The only way they have of coping with their feelings is to carry their avoiding tendencies to the extreme; if they stay away from other people, then there will be no chance that they will be rejected.

Linda is a good example of an extreme avoider. She had lived her whole life in the same small town and was very happy; she had her family there and a few close friends, and she was married to the high school football star, whom she had known since the first grade. Her world started to come apart when her husband, who was both ambitious and gregarious, was transferred to a large city in a different state. Linda "knew" that she would not be accepted there because of her unsophisticated small-town ways.

Linda mostly stayed at home to make sure she did not suffer any humiliations at the hands of the big-city sophisticates. When she was forced by her husband to be around other people, she only confirmed what she already knew—people did not like her and were not interested in her; after all, she was just different from them. "I had to go to a party for the people my husband works with, and it was the worst evening of my life. It was obvious that everyone there thought I was a jerk. No one really talked to me more than to say hello; as soon as they could, they would drift off to find someone more interesting. A couple of people even ridiculed me by saying something about what a change it must be living in the big city. Do they think we had outhouses back home?"

Linda was partly right. The people she met at the party did not particularly like her, but not for the reasons she imagined. They thought of her as being standoffish and hard to talk to; when they asked her about her move, she hardly responded at all. They concluded that because her husband was a bigwig in the company, she must think herself to be better than they.

So Linda found herself in a bind that is common to people who are shy or who find it difficult to be around other people. They avoid social situations because they feel so uncomfortable in them. They would love it if other people would seek them out, and they wish that at least one person would realize that they need some help in getting started. But others often interpret their quietness as lack of interest and their keeping to themselves as a sign of rudeness or conceit, so the more withdrawn people like Linda become, the more convinced others are that they consider themselves to be too good for the rest of the world. It is a vicious circle from which escape is extremely difficult.

Procrastination is one thing avoiders do very well. Most everyone is, or has been, guilty of engaging in a little procrastination, so in itself, it is not a sign of psychological problems. Most men can remember—at least I certainly do—the first time they wanted to call a girl for a date. Putting off for a few weeks the fateful call that could result in devastating rejection was the easiest thing in the world to do; I managed to put it off for three months. Avoiders, however, have developed the art of procrastination to the point where it seriously interferes with their opportunities to use their talents. They are scared to death of the possibility of failure or rejection, so they simply put off doing anything that could result in failure or rejection.

Clark's inability to get his application in on time to be considered for a promotion is typical of avoiders.

Like Clark, most avoiders have little understanding of why they procrastinate. They find all kinds of good reasons why they do not really want to do the things they could be doing, or reasons for why it is so hard to get these kinds of things done. Lillian provides a good example of this. She always was a good student, but she never believed she was as smart as the other kids in her class. She convinced herself that she got good grades only because she worked so much harder than anyone else. She was relieved when she could put off her plans to go to college when her steady boyfriend asked her to marry him after she graduated from high school. She was sure that college would be the final proof that her only talent was to memorize her textbooks.

Ten years later, after her two children were in school, she decided that she would get her college degree. It was something she had always wanted, and even though the idea of competition frightened her, the ten years since she finished high school had provided her with enough good experiences to convince her that she really was as smart as most people. In college, she did very well her first two years, but then started to run into trouble once she got into the advanced courses. She found that she just could not get her papers finished on time. Like many avoiders, she had plenty of good reasons why she was having this trouble. After all, she was still a mother; she had a family to take care of, and it wasn't fair for them to have to suffer just because she had to spend time in the library. And to top it off, she just didn't like deadlines. If she didn't have that pressure, then she wouldn't have any trouble.

These are all good, logical reasons except for the fact that they are wrong. Lillian had made the time to study for the exams she had taken for the first two years, and deadlines had never slowed her down before, either. She also had plenty of evidence that her family were more than willing to fend for themselves when she had work to do. What stopped Lillian was her fear that her "intellectual shallowness" would show through in her papers. Taking exams was one thing; it was easy enough to regurgitate the class notes and reading. But when you wrote, you were left without structure; you had to bare your soul. She had "fooled" her professors up to now, but they would find out she was nothing but a fraud once they read her papers.

Lillian was like many avoiders in that she was able to enlist several people who wanted to help her. Her husband was sympathetic and offered many times to do whatever he had to so she could have time to do her papers. Her professors knew she was a very capable student, so they were sympathetic as well; they extended due dates and offered their support and encouragement. All this help only made things worse. Lillian interpreted the support and encouragement of her family and professors as pressure to perform, and once she felt this pressure, it was all the more impossible to her to get started. At first she wished that they would just leave her alone, and when they wouldn't, she started to accuse them of nagging her. Procrastinators are good at enlisting rescuers, but they often end up accusing them of being tormentors.

Avoiders can make great partners. Because they are so sensitive to the possibility of being rejected, they will usually bend over backwards to be "nice." Like Clark, they are often thought of as being the kind of people who will do anything for you and never ask anything in return; they won't ask, of course, because they are afraid of being turned down, not because they are so unselfish. And because they tend to be somewhat isolated socially, they invest most of their energy in their families. It is not unusual for an avoider to be seen by others as the perfect parent, or the devoted spouse.

The most common reaction of the partners of avoiders is a mixture of sympathy and frustration—sympathy because avoiders could be so much more than they are if they would only have a little more confidence in themselves, and frustration because they seem to be refusing to take advantage of what they have going for them. Terri felt this way about Clark. "Sometimes I feel very sad about Clark. In many ways he is an exceptional man; he is extremely intelligent and he has a sensitivity for other people that I think is truly exceptional. I know that if he felt just a little better about himself, he could really go places, and I know he would get a lot of satisfaction from that. Then other times, I get really angry at him. If I had as much ability as he does, you can be sure that I wouldn't be satisfied with a dead-end job. I just can't understand why he won't at least try."

If the sympathy is stronger than the frustration, then there may be few problems in the relationship. Terri would never think of leaving Clark. She has times when she is annoyed by his refusal to take risks, and she resents having to be the complainer for the family, but she loves Clark for his sensitivity and his caring, and she is grateful for the ways in which he has helped her become a better person. Terri is more than willing to go on trying to help Clark feel better about himself, but even if he never changes, she isn't going to give up a relationship that works so well for her.

There are partners of avoiders who feel more frustration than sympathy. If they choose to focus on their partner's weak points, it is not hard to find plenty of evidence of an ineffectual, unambitious, stick-in-the-mud individual. If this perspective is taken, then there may seem to be little reason to stay with the relationship. If you find yourself feeling this way about your avoider, you may be encouraged to know that they can change. And once they begin to change, their more endearing qualities are likely to become obvious again. Remember, you saw them once—you can find them again if you are willing to try. Before we talk about how to live with an avoider, let's take a look at how they got to be the way they are.

Development of the Avoider

The background of avoiders is not very much different from the background of many of the personality types we have discussed up to now. The core of their problem is poor self-esteem. They grew up hearing the message that their efforts did not measure up, their parents may have had all the right intentions, but somehow they failed to help their budding avoider develop a sense of competence and self-worth.

The important difference between avoiders and people with other styles is that avoiders never learn a coping strategy. Compulsive people learn to submerge themselves in a world of detail to keep their insecurities under control; ladies' men and coquettes build up their feelings of self-worth by adding to their string of romantic or sexual conquests. But avoiders have nothing. They failed to develop a method for warding off the feelings of inferiority and worthlessness that plague them.

The background of many avoiders is remarkable only because it seems so ordinary. At first glance, it may appear that there is nothing about their childhood that would lead one to predict they would have problems in later life. Upon closer inspection, however, the one thing that does stand out is that they often had parents who suffered from some degree of emotional constipation. Their parents did not do anything that could be considered wrong; they simply failed to provide the support, love, warmth, and encouragement that children need if they are to flourish. Their parents may have loved them very much, but love in itself is not enough—it has to be communicated. Emotionally constipated parents find it difficult to let their children know, in any but the most indirect ways, that they love them.

After I was able to help Clark learn more about himself in therapy, he came to understand how his insecurities were related to the feelings he had while he was a child. "Both my mom and dad found it easier to express disapproval than approval. It's not that they ever did or said anything that dramatic, but I remember wanting them to be proud of me and thinking that I never could do anything to deserve it. The one thing they were big on was respect for adults. Whenever I had a difference of opinion with any adult—a teacher, or even a neighbor—there was no chance that my parents would even try to see my point of view. I think the result of that is that I feel like a little kid whenever I'm around someone who I think is higher in status than I am. Whenever my boss asks to see me, I panic; I wonder what I did wrong and if I'm going to get in trouble. That's a crazy way for a grown man to feel, especially when he's as good at his job as I am."

The degree to which parents failed to provide an atmosphere of love and acceptance is closely related to the severity of the avoider's style. Clark's parents loved him even though they had trouble letting him know it, so while Clark's tendencies to avoid do interfere with his life, he is still able to get along pretty well. Other people are not nearly as fortunate. There are parents who do not hesitate to tell their children in no uncertain terms that they are worthless and will never amount to anything, and as you might imagine, these children grow up to be extreme avoiders. Their feelings of insecurity are right on the surface, and they will be very suspicious of anyone who claims to like them; they cannot believe that anyone would find anything worthwhile about them.

One pattern that is common among people with a mild

case of the avoider is that they suffered a shock to their developing self-esteem from which they never recovered. Art falls into this category. His parents were a lot like Clark's, but he was very bright and a better-than-average athlete. His first fourteen years were good ones; he did not receive much emotional support from his parents, but he did not know things could be any different, so he did not miss it. He did very well in his schoolwork through junior high school, so he received a lot of praise and attention from his teachers, and he was a good football, baseball, and basketball player, which meant that he was admired by boys his own age. Art felt he had the world by the tail when he started high school. He was placed in an accelerated class because of his grades and test scores, and he thought he was sure to make the basketball team and maybe the baseball team.

Slowly his world began to fall apart. He found that a high school with over three-thousand students was a lot different from his junior high school of five-hundred students. Even though his test scores placed him in the top 5 percent of sophomores, he found that he was in the bottom fourth of his accelerated class. He did not come close to making the baseball team, but he did manage to survive to the last cut when he tried out for basketball. Lots of people suffer from similar setbacks with no lasting effects, but Art's parents had not helped him develop a sense of self-worth to fall back on. He made it through college and got a master's degree, and was able to do well in a challenging job, but he never recovered from the shock of being just one of the crowd when he started high school. He entered every new situation afraid that he would fail, and even after achieving some success, he continued to feel that someday it would all fall apart again. Let's look at a few specific examples of how to live with people like Art and Clark.

Living with the Avoider

Most people have just a touch of the avoider in them. None of us like rejection, and we tend to tread carefully on ground where it is a possibility. We may be hesitant to approach someone we would like to get to know because there is always the possibility that our feelings will not be reciprocated; we may feel a little apprehensive about presenting new ideas to the boss because there is always some chance that the fatal flaw in our plan will be discovered and we will end looking foolish.

The difference between these very typical and normal reactions and the things the avoider does is only a matter of degree. While most of us may have some anxieties about being rejected, we do not let those feelings stop us from taking action. We still make overtures to others and offer our ideas to the boss, and even if it all turns out badly, we are not devastated; we may even laugh about it and go on the next new situation, willing as ever to take a chance. Avoiders, on the other hand, cannot bring themselves to take these risks. If you feel frustrated and angry with the avoider you live with, try to keep this in mind. They are not being stubborn—they are just plain scared.

Q: I want to help my husband, but I don't know how. He is an accountant, and he is very good at it; the firm that he works for has given him more and more responsibility over the years, and now his accounts bring in more money than anyone else's. The problem is that his salary hasn't even come close to keeping up with the work he is doing. I have encouraged him to either ask for more money, find another job, or open his own office; if he went out on his own, I bet he could take a lot of business with him, so he wouldn't be taking much of a chance. When I try to talk to him about this, he gets mad. He says that he could never be so disloyal. I think he is unhappy but won't admit it. He seems to be depressed much of the time, and recently he has been complaining a lot about his job—which he never did before. Is there anything I can do?

A: I have the feeling that you are doing a pretty good job already, and it won't take too much longer before your efforts begin to bear fruit. If your husband is indeed an avoider, it is not surprising that he would do more and more work over the years without complaining or demanding corresponding increases in his salary. Almost everyone wants to be treated fairly, but avoiders often believe that they should consider themselves lucky for whatever crumbs are thrown their way; your husband has probably felt fortunate to be considered competent enough to be given the responsibility at work he has, and he fears that he really does not deserve any better treatment than he has received.

The reason I think you have been on the right track in how you have been dealing with his fears is that it sounds as if he is beginning to tire of being a doormat. His recent depression and complaints could be signs that he too is beginning to believe that he has been treated unfairly and deserves something better. Your husband is fortunate in that he is so good at his job. Avoiders who have some special ability often gain confidence in themselves over time—admittedly, over a long period of time, but they do usually make progress on their own. Avoiders who do not have any ability that stands out need much more help to get them moving in the right direction.

Your talking to him about alternatives is probably contributing to this slow but sure change. Avoiders have a set of beliefs and perceptions of the world that they use to maintain their low self-esteem. Some of the beliefs that your husband has had might include something like "They could find a thousand people to do what I do in a minute," or "If I quit this job, I'd never be able to find another one." But as he gets more experience and finds out how much his clients value his work, it becomes more difficult to maintain these beliefs. Also, his statement about loyalty doesn't make any sense either; as I'm sure you've pointed out to him, loyalty is a two-way street. What sense does it make to be loyal to someone who is exploiting you?

So the answer is yes, I think you can do things to help him. Continue to let him know when you think his reasons for not taking action do not make sense. Do it in a gentle but persistent way. Avoiders are quick to accuse those who are trying to help them of nagging, so expect some anger. But if you talk to him about these issues in a loving and supportive way, it will have an effect. They won't have an immediate effect because it takes time to heal damaged self-esteem, but if you don't give up, I think the chances are excellent that your husband will eventually gain enough self-confidence to take some action.

To speed things up a little, encourage him to do things that are not threatening, but could give him more evidence of his competence. He might go to an employment agency that specializes in placing accountants to find out what the chances are of finding another job at a higher salary. Or look through professional newsletters or business papers in which positions for accountants are advertised to get a feel for how much money he could earn given his experience. If he has any clients that he is close to, he might talk to them about his feelings. It would not surprise me if he was offered a job by one of his clients if the client knew that he would consider taking it. Also, his clients might be able to give him some encouragement about opening his own office. The chances are your husband will never be a high-powered, completely self-confident man; things just don't work that way. But with your support and encouragement, I do believe that you can help him achieve a level that will bring him much more satisfaction, and satisfied people make the best partners.

Q: My husband is a terrible procrastinator. The list of things he has promised to do around the house is endless. The paint is peeling off our house and we have had leaky faucets for two years. Every time I tell him I am going to hire someone to do those things, he promises me that he will get to them the very next weekend. But come Saturday morning, he is on the golf course. On Sunday, he has to relax before starting back to work. I'm really fed up with him. How can I get him moving?

A: I wouldn't even try. Nothing you said suggests to me that your husband has a problem. The chances are he simply doesn't like doing those kinds of things, and there is really no reason why he should; I don't like doing those kinds of things either. So, I wouldn't classify him as a procrastinator just because he avoids doing things that give him no satisfaction and that he dislikes doing.

I would encourage you to do what my wife does—pay someone to do the jobs around the house that need to be done. (Why are *you* procrastinating?) But try not to do it in an angry way. This issue is one of those trivial things that can build until it causes a real crack in a relationship. There are enough important things that couples have to work out without looking for more problems.

Tell your husband that it is very important to you to have these things done, then have one job a week done until you are caught up. This will give him a chance to do a few things if he wants to. Lots of men feel obligated to do home repairs because they saw their fathers doing them. So even though they can afford to pay to have them done, and even though they hate doing them, they still feel as if they "should" be doing them because that's the kind of thing a man does. Your husband's ambivalence is not unusual, but don't let him use it to drag things on indefinitely.

Q: My wife has no self-confidence. She is a very intelligent, talented, and attractive woman, but she is convinced that no one likes her and that she could never succeed at anything. I know she contributes to her own problems, because when she is feeling insecure, she can be abrasive, but she is really a very sweet, nice woman. It frustrates me because she won't listen when I tell her all that she has going for her. It's demeaning to me. Does she think I would marry someone who was the nothing that she thinks she is? Is there anything I can do?

A: I think you can help her, but you have a tough job ahead of you. Your frustration about her not listening to you when you try to build her up is understandable—and typical. Even though it is irrational, people like your wife tend to discount anything positive that people who are close to them have to say. Somehow, your compliments don't count. She probably could not tell you why, but she thinks that you're not an objective judge; you love her and so you are willing to overlook what she is sure are her numerous fatal flaws. The best way to help her is to try to get her in situations in which other people will give her approval as well.

This can be difficult to do with a hard-core avoider; they don't like to be pushed into anything new. One man in a similar situation entered his wife's paintings in an art show; his wife was convinced that she had no particular talent and refused to show her work to anyone outside of the family, but when her husband came home with a prize and a couple of sales, it was the boost she needed to start a gratifying career. Think about what your wife is especially good at. Encourage her to try out some things that would result in some success experiences. If she is intelligent, some evening courses might be just the thing for her. If she objects, offer to take a course with her. It doesn't matter what specifically she does, as long as she gets some irrefutable evidence that she is not the loser she believes she is.

To help her feel more comfortable around other people, give her plenty of practice. Invite your friends over; make the gatherings small at first, but keep it up. Tell her later how much your friends liked her; I have seen an offhand remark like this have quite an effect. Once she begins to believe that other people do like her, then her abrasiveness will come to an end. People who like themselves have no need to put down other people.

You might talk to your wife about seeing a professional therapist. As you said, she tends to discount anything good that you have to say about her. So hearing the same thing from an authoritative source might have a much stronger impact. Problems like this can be treated with a high degree of success, so with your help and the help of a competent therapist, your wife would have a good chance of turning her life around.

Q: My husband is very shy. He knows that he is an intelligent person who has worthwhile things to say, but when he is around strange people, he can hardly get a word out. He says he wants to change, but he just has the feeling that because he is so nervous around people, he would end up saying something stupid. Because both of his parents are shy people, he's convinced that it's hereditary and it's hopeless to try to change. Is it possible for him to do anything about his problem?

A: Yes. It is true that "nervousness" is in part inherited, but shyness is learned. There are lots of very nervous people who never stop talking; in fact, the more nervous they get the more they talk. So your husband may have inherited his nervousness, but he learned to be shy, and he can learn to be a better conversationalist.

The fastest way to help him with his problem would be to find an assertiveness training workshop for him to attend. Lots of organizations, including mental health clinics and colleges, offer these periodically, and if you can't find a specific workshop, phone a few psychologists and ask if they offer such groups. I have seen such people change dramatically in weeks as a result of such experiences.

The essence of these groups is practice, so you could help your husband do it on his own if he is willing. One example of the kind of thing that is done in these groups is "small-talk practice." The group leader picks two group members to carry on a conversation for a few minutes about some silly topic—say, breakfast cereals. The leader gives a few pointers, such as maintaining eye contact, asking the other person about his or her thoughts, talking in a loud enough voice to be heard, and so on. Before the end of the first session, virtually everyone learns that he or she can carry on a conversation about any topic with no trouble at all. This gives them the confidence to try their newfound skills out in real-life situations.

You could practice with your husband, and I think it could help some. It works better in a group setting specifically intended for this problem because it is closer to real life. Shy people feel pretty nervous when they are asked to practice these skills in a group, so the lesson they learn is more meaningful; they learn that even when they are feeling scared, they can speak up and carry on a conversation. Even if your husband was willing to practice with you, he probably would not feel nervous about doing it, so when he found himself in a social situation, it wouldn't quite be the same.

Encourage your husband to join one of these groups. If he is getting along well in other areas of his life, he could experience dramatic changes in a very short period of time. Remind him that he is not alone. About six out of ten people consider themselves to be shy. Extreme shyness is a self-imposed prison that no one should live in.

Some Final Thoughts

I once saw an artful avoider in therapy who could not be convinced that he would be happier being any other way. He entered therapy for what he called a midlife crisis, and he refused to see that his holding back had anything to do with his feelings of unhappiness. He was a highly skilled engineer, and he worked for such a small company that there was no room for advancement. He had turned down several offers from larger companies that carried with them added responsibilities because, in his words, "Who needs it?" He claimed he liked his job, and he just did not want the hassles that would go along with being with a high-powered company. And why should he do something he did not want to do? I agree that on the whole, people should avoid doing things that they don't want to. But I also know that many of us have a remarkable capacity for fooling ourselves. Our fears and our insecurities can blind us when it comes to deciding what it is that we do want to do.

Avoiders live by the motto "Nothing risked, nothing lost." They allow their fears to convince them that they would be happiest sitting back and doing nothing. The engineer was afraid that he would not be able to handle the added responsibilities that would go along with the new job, but he could not admit that to himself; it was easier to "believe" that he didn't want any new hassles. I finally convinced him that there was something holding him back from taking on new challenges, so he agreed to try a different job for one year. To his surprise, he had more energy and felt happier than he had in years.

One benchmark of good psychological adjustment is the freedom to try new experiences and to take risks. This does not mean that everyone who does not get ahead or who is not constantly meeting new people is an avoider; lots of people keep jobs for which they are overqualified, or spend much of their time with only a few people. But the key is choice. Avoiders do not have a choice; they allow their fear to remove all of their choices from them. So if you can help your avoider remove the chains of fear, you will have an eternally grateful partner.

12
THE IMPERFECT LOVER

The Imperfect Lover

1. **When I'm in the mood to make love:**
   a. my partner senses my feelings and we just seem to begin.
   b. if I offer a few hints, my partner will go along with me.
   c. if I do a really special favor for my partner, he or she will grudgingly go along with me.
   d. I might as well take a cold shower for all the good it will do me.

2. **When my partner is in the mood to make love:**
   a. I sense my partner's feelings, and will gladly cooperate.

b. all my partner has to do is ask, and I will cooperate.
c. I cooperate, if my partner would agree to do a favor for me.
d. if I'm not in the mood, which is a safe bet, my partner may as well take a cold shower.

3. **Making love with my partner is:**
   a. as exciting as it ever was.
   b. not as exciting as it used to be, but it's still pretty good.
   c. just about as exciting as watching the *Tonight Show*
   d. not quite as exciting as washing the dishes.

4. **If my partner suggested to me that we try something a little different in our lovemaking:**
   a. I would get excited about the idea.
   b. I would listen to my partner's idea, but might not go along with it.
   c. I would look at my partner with more than a little disgust.
   d. I would know that my partner was ready for the funny farm to make such a suggestion.

5. **My partner's sexual tastes are:**
   a. okay, but a little on the conventional side.
   b. just right for me.
   c. a little too adventurous for me.
   d. downright perverted.

6. **The last time my partner told me what he or she liked:**
   a. I was glad to know.
   b. I was willing to try it.
   c. I was offended.
   d. was the only time my partner ever suggested anything.

7. **I have trouble responding sexually to my partner:**
   a. only when I am in intense pain.
   b. only when I am worried about something.
   c. if we have had sex within the past week.
   d. if we have had sex within the past year.

8. **If my partner told me his or her sexual fantasies:**
   a. I would want to act them out.
   b. I would feel a little uncomfortable.
   c. I would feel very threatened.
   d. I would tell my partner to have his or her head examined.

9. **If my partner were not able to have an orgasm while having sex with me:**
   a. I would be patient and would help my partner to have one sooner or later.
   b. I would tell my partner that things would work out better the next time.
   c. I wouldn't say anything about it.
   d. I wouldn't notice and wouldn't care.

10. **If my partner were to talk to me about our sexual relationship:**
   a. I would be interested in anything my partner had to say.
   b. it would make me feel uncomfortable.
   c. I would listen if he or she were really serious about it.
   d. I would listen if my partner tied me to a chair.

The Imperfect Lover Text Scoring Key

1. a. 0 points.
b. 1 point.
c. 2 points.
d. 3 points.

2. a. 0 points.
b. 1 point.
c. 2 points.
d. 3 points.

3. a. 0 points.
b. 1 point.
c. 2 points.
d. 3 points.

4. a. 0 points.
b. 1 point.
c. 2 points.
d. 3 points.

5. a. 1 points.
b. 0 point.
c. 2 points.
d. 3 points.

6. a. 0 points.
b. 1 point.
c. 2 points.
d. 3 points.

7. a. 0 points.
b. 1 point.
c. 2 points.
d. 3 points.

8. a. 0 points.
b. 1 point.
c. 2 points.
d. 3 points.

9. a. 0 points.
b. 1 point.
c. 2 points.
d. 3 points.

10. a. 0 points.
b. 1 point.
c. 2 points.
d. 3 points.

Interpretation of Test Scores

0 to 7 points: You either have a very new or a very unusual relationship. Unfortunate as it is, it is a fact of life that sex is usually the most exciting with someone whom you are just getting to know and care about. If you have been able to maintain the intensity of your sexual relationship after the feelings of romantic love have begun to fade, consider yourself very lucky.

8 to 16 points: If you have been together for several years and obtained this score, then you are doing pretty well. While sex is not as exciting as it once was, feelings of closeness and security can more than make up for any decline in intensity.

17 to 23 points: You have some problems that you have to work out with your partner. Either the two of you have very different perspectives about sex, or you have allowed yourself to fall into a rut. This chapter is an important one for you!

24 to 30 points: You already know you have problems. In order to have reached this point, both you and your partner must be very inhibited about sex. Things could not have gotten this bad unless you both cooperated in allowing them to. Your situation is by no means hopeless, but it will take a lot of work to get things turned around.

Why Won't You Do What I Want?

Kim, an attractive mother of two, spent the night of her thirty-fifth birthday thinking about getting a divorce. She had hoped for a romantic evening with her husband topped off with some leisurely but exciting sex; however, as usual, she did not get it. Her husband, Mark, had taken her out to dinner, but he seemed almost formal; he was polite and attentive, but Kim had the feeling he was forcing it. Kim was determined to make the evening go well, so she did not let it bother her, but the disappointment that came later that evening in bed was more than she could bear. She was not going to stay married to someone who could show her so little warmth, either in bed or out.

In looking back, Kim believes that the problems with her husband started about the time their second child was born and he received a big promotion. "It was a gradual sort of process, but one day I realized just how much things had changed and how miserable I was. The first seven or eight years of our marriage, I was continually amazed at how happy I was. Mark was always a little reserved, but he was also a very warm, loving man. Our sex life was great; we had sex almost every night for the first couple of years, and about three or four times a week after that. During that time, I think I can count the number of times I didn't have an orgasm on one hand; I usually had two or three. He was a great lover.

"About a year and a half ago, it started to become clear to me that he was losing interest in having sex with me. At first, I thought it was just the pressure of his new job, or the fact that we were both tired a lot from getting up with the second baby. So I tried to do more. I'd make sure that he wouldn't have to help with the housework in the evenings, and I even cut the grass for a whole summer, but none of it seemed to have any effect. Next, I tried to be extra-warm to him. I'd go up to him and give him a hug and a kiss. But rather than returning my warmth, he would pull away. Sex was the biggest frustration of all. When he gave in, he would do it in a remote, mechanical way, and would always begin before I was ready. It got to the point where I had trouble having an orgasm; I always felt tense and frustrated."

Mark could not understand what had happened between him and Kim. "I admit that I did not take her complaints seriously for quite a while. I thought she was just going through a bad time because she was staying home all day with two young children, so I tried to be supportive and helpful, but it seemed to me that nothing I did was good enough. I was under a lot of pressure at work, and when I got home I wanted to just plop down and stare at the television. But Kim would greet me at the door with detailed stories of how bad her day was, so I would take over with the kids for the rest of the evening. By the time they got to bed I was really exhausted, because I was the one who had gotten up the night before to give the baby her bottle. When we finally crawled into bed, Kim would want to have sex when all I wanted to do was pass out.

"I thought things would be better once the baby started sleeping through the night and I got settled into my new job. But instead, they seemed to get worse. Kim was more and more insistent about having sex more often, which made it harder for me to do it. Who can have sex when you feel it's something you have to do to avoid an argument? I got to the point where I dreaded going to bed, and when we did have sex, I didn't really enjoy it. There were even several instances when I wasn't able to have an erection. I really felt I was at the end of my rope."

According to Kim, things are slowly getting back to normal. "When I told Mark that I wanted a divorce, I think he finally realized how bad I felt. After talking about the situation seriously, we both realized that we were doing things to make things worse instead of better. Mark admitted that every time I tried to hug or kiss him, he started to worry that I wanted to have sex and would withdraw from me. And I was placing demands on him in bed because I wasn't getting any warmth from him any other time. But I still don't understand things completely. I must have told him a hundred times that we didn't have to have intercourse; I just wanted him to show me some affection, and I would have been happy if he had only held me and caressed me; but he just would not do it. If you really love me, I'd think, why won't you do what I want?"

Sex may be the ultimate paradox. There is no other human activity that can afford such intense pleasure and yet can cause such profound grief and unhappiness. While sex can be playful and fun, it often turns out to be a battleground upon which men and women test their wills against each other. It is impossible to know about these things for sure, but most experts agree that over half of all marriages experience sexual difficulties, and sexual incompatibility is always near the top of the list of reasons for divorce. It is a rare couple indeed who experience nothing but pleasurable sex throughout their relationship.

One of the reasons that sex has such potential for conflict is that there is such a wide range of normal and healthy ways of expressing one's sexual interests and appetites. There are many couples who are perfectly happy having sex once a month, while many other couples enjoy it every day. For some men and women, sex falls into a pattern—if it is Sunday night, then it is time to make love.

Other couples value spontaneity and would never dream of having sex on a schedule. Yet, neither preference is inherently normal or abnormal. Many couples have never had sex in any way other than the "missionary position" and are perfectly satisfied; other couples are not happy unless they can discover at least one new position a month, and some couples enjoy using a variety of props—such as vibrators, special clothes, or even more elaborate paraphernalia, while many men and women cannot understand why anyone feels the need to improve on the basic equipment.

It would be ideal if we could find someone who had sexual tastes and preferences that were very similar to our own, but things are hardly ever ideal. Most people do develop relationships with others who have similar attitudes to their own, but when it comes to sex, what may seem to be minor differences can turn out to be very disrupting. Ginger, for instance, was surprised, and not pleased, to discover that the man in her life liked to have sex in the morning. "Before we started to live together our sexual relationship was great, so I wouldn't have guessed in a million years that six months later, we would be arguing about sex. It turns out that Scott likes to have sex when he first wake up in the morning. I don't like that at all. It is always rushed because we both have to go to work, and besides, I don't understand how anyone can even think about sex until after lunch. At first, I went along with it because Scott seemed to like it so much; he says that's when he feels the horniest and he thinks it's a great way to start the day. But after a couple of months, I started to resent it so much that I couldn't respond. I tried to be nice about it, but every time he reached for me in the morning, I would feel this intense anger. I couldn't get to sleep at night because I would be worried about what would happen the next morning. I finally had to tell him that I wasn't going to do it in the morning anymore. Then he accused me of not caring about his feelings; I don't know how he had the nerve to say that, since he obviously cared so little about mine. I guess he wanted to show me, because then we stopped having sex at night too."

Neither Scott's nor Ginger's reaction is unusual. Both had clear ideas about what they liked, and both seemed to be incapable of appreciating the other's feelings. Scott thought that if Ginger really loved him, she would be glad to have sex with him anytime he was interested. Her refusal made him feel a little insecure and also was a blow to his masculine pride; all men like to think that they are great lovers, so Ginger's inability to have an orgasm in the morning made him feel inadequate.

Ginger felt that she was being used. For her, sex was more than a biological function; Mark's argument that he felt the horniest in the morning was proof to her that he thought of her as nothing more than a convenient way of releasing his sexual tensions. She thought that if he really cared about her as a person, he would want to have sex at night after they spent some time just being together, since sex was something that you wanted when you felt close to another person.

Perhaps most common of all are differences centering on frequency of sex. When one person wants to have intercourse more often than the other, it is almost certain to result in hurt feelings for both. A generation or two ago, this used to be almost exclusively a male complaint, but now just as many women as men report that they would like to have sex more often than they do. In fact, jokes about tired husbands seem to be replacing the old jokes about wives with headaches.

Mark and Kim, whose story opened this chapter, are a typical case. Mark's interest in sex started to wane a little as he moved into middle age; he certainly had not lost interest completely, but now he was content to have intercourse once every five or six days. Sex was still fun, but it just did not have the same urgency for him that it did when he was twenty-five years old.

Kim's sexual needs, on the other hand, were a little more intense than when she was twenty-five years old. Not only had she learned to thoroughly enjoy it, but she was beginning to worry about the wrinkles that were starting to appear around her eyes. The double standard of aging was catching up with her; her husband seemed to be getting more attractive as he got older, but she just seemed to be getting old. Mark's declining interest in sex was more than enough proof to her that she was losing her appeal.

Her needs for reassurance, rather than her needs for sex, are what prompted her to step up her demands on Mark. She wanted to feel loved and to believe that she was still desirable. And because it was hard to ask for these things directly, she tried to get them through sex. When Mark did not respond to her overtures, she felt devastated.

Mark's reaction to his wife's sexual demands was anger; he felt inadequate because he simply was not interested in having sex as often as Kim was. Even though he told himself that it was just a matter of interest, he began to doubt his adequacy. Here was an attractive woman who was interested in making love and all he could feel was weariness. Was he getting old? Was he over the hill? Was this the beginning of the end of his sexuality? These doubts were too threatening for him to form them clearly in his own mind, much less express them to his wife, so he got angry instead. He blamed Kim for having unrealistic expectations; sex was not *supposed* to be very exciting after fifteen years of marriage.

The cases of Mark and Kim and of Scott and Ginger

involve relatively straightforward differences in preferences. You may have noticed that in these cases, it is impossible to say who is the "imperfect" one. If you have already decided who has the problem, then this says something about your preferences rather than anything about what is right or wrong. Questions of morning or night, once a day or once a week, do not, in themselves, suggest that one person is right or normal and the other person is wrong or abnormal. They are simple differences, in much the same way that a preference for Chinese over Italian food, or golf over tennis is a simple difference.

These differences become problems because sexuality is so closely tied in with our feelings about ourselves as men or women. While no one would feel inadequate or unloved because he or she preferred tennis while the spouse liked golf better, differences about sex usually lead to such emotional reactions. This makes it very difficult to talk openly about the differences and reach compromises.

Once couples can separate the sexual issue from what they believe it means about themselves, their partner, and their relationship, then they can usually work out solutions that are satisfactory to both. Scott and Ginger were able to do this in short order. After I was able to convince them that their sexual preferences had nothing to do with their love for each other, they did achieve a compromise. Ginger agreed to have sex in the morning on weekends and holidays when she did not have to worry about getting up and getting ready for work. Once she no longer felt the time pressures, she was able to enjoy these early-morning encounters. After Scott understood that Ginger's reaction to sex in the morning was not a rejection of him, he too was happy with the compromise. He missed the morning lovemaking during the week, but he did feel closer to Ginger when he saw how much she enjoyed sex in the evenings.

Mark and Kim had more difficulty working things out

because their problem developed over several years. But Mark was able to appreciate Kim's fears of growing old and undesirable, and because he really believed that she was even more desirable than when they were first married, he was able to provide her with the reassurance she needed. Kim was quick to understand how her husband could feel threatened by her desire to have sex more often than he wanted to. As a compromise, Mark caresses and shows affection to his wife when she indicates that she is in the mood, but they both understand that they will not have intercourse unless Mark feels that he wants to. As Kim begins to feel better about herself, she does not feel the need to have intercourse quite as much as she used to, and now that the pressure is off Mark, he feels the urge to have sex more often. There are still times when one of them ends up with hurt feelings, but they feel that they are making progress.

Sometimes when there are differences between a man and a woman in their sexual preferences, it is possible to identify the one with the "problem." These are situations when one partner's preferences result from guilt or anxiety about sexuality; in these cases, people prohibit themselves from doing things they might find pleasurable because they have strong beliefs about the rightness or wrongness of certain sexual activities.

The roots of sexual guilt and anxiety go back several centuries in western civilization, reaching their peak during the Victorian era in the 1800s. Then the prevailing view was that "good" women did not enjoy sex, but that it was their rather unpleasant duty to satisfy the animalistic urges of their husbands, and that their reward for doing their duty was having children. While very few people today believe that only "that kind of woman" enjoys sex, almost everyone does have pretty clear ideas about what is acceptable and what is not when it comes to sex. But even though everyone would agree that some kind of standards are necessary, there are times when one's definitions of right and wrong are so narrow that they get in the way of enjoying sex in a relationship.

Dick, for example, grew up in a working-class family in which the father was clearly the boss. Although neither of his parents ever said anything explicit about sex to him, he developed a clear idea that sex was a man's prerogative. "By the time I was in college I realized that some of my ideas were a little behind the times, but I couldn't help it; that was just the way I felt. It really hit home when I was a junior and fell in love with Susan. She was pretty, bright, and capable, and really a good person, and I fully intended to marry her. But after we had dated for about six months, she told me that she wanted to make love with me, and I felt as if she had kicked me in the stomach. Even though I knew I wasn't being logical, I just could not accept the idea that my wife-to-be was asking me to have sex with her. I wasn't pressing her to have sex because I loved her so much. I just couldn't feel the same about her after that."

Dick did marry a virgin two years later, but to his distress, his wife turned out to have the same healthy appetite for sex that Susan had. His guilt and anxiety made it impossible for him to accept the fact that his wife was just as likely to initiate sex as he was. Again, he had the feeling that he was being stupid, but he could not help but feel that his wife was somehow a little bit immoral.

Lynn provides a second example of how guilt can affect one's sexual relationship. "I grew up in a family that placed a very high value on modesty. By the time I was six, it was unthinkable that I would let my sisters see me naked, much less my brother, and I don't remember seeing either of my parents even in their underwear. So when I first got married, I would not let David see me undressed. I would change into my nightgown in the bathroom and I wouldn't make love unless the room was completely dark. Thank God he was patient with me or I don't think we would have made it. Now it makes me feel good that he enjoys looking at my body. I still feel uncomfortable about having sex when the lights are on, but I can forget about it once we get started."

When guilt and anxiety are responsible for the differences in views about sexual preferences, they usually can be overcome with a little patience and understanding. Both Dick's wife and Susan's husband realized that their spouses had some conflict about sex, and by going slowly, they were able to help them resolve it. As is often the case, both Dick and Susan realized that they were unnecessarily restricting themselves, and their openness to change made it relatively easy for them to do so. It's crucial to realize that the person who experiences these feelings is not being stubborn; the feelings are real, and they have an impact. Dick was not being vindictive or bullheaded when he refused his wife's sexual advances; he simply was incapable of responding to her, feeling the way that he did. And Susan was not being coy or obstinate when she refused to allow her husband to watch her undress when they were first married; she felt an intense sense of shame and embarrassment at the very thought of it.

It is not always clear when differences in preferences are just that—differences—or when they result from one person's feelings of sexual guilt and anxiety. There are, however, two keys that, while not foolproof, do help to distinguish between the two.

First, if guilt and anxiety are playing a role, the differences are almost always immediately obvious. Recall Ginger, who did not like to have sex in the morning. It is unlikely that her preference to have it in the evening resulted from guilt and anxiety, because she was willing to give morning sex a try, and it was only after several months that she decided that she could not continue with the pattern that Scott preferred. Susan, on the other hand, made it clear from the very start that she did not want to have sex when it was light in the room. Her unwillingness, or rather her inability to give it a try, was a clear sign that her feelings did result from restrictive sexual attitudes, and hence might be changed with a little patience on the part of her partner.

Kim's and Mark's different ideas about how often they should have sex are unlikely to be caused by the guilt feelings of either, since this difference did not show up until they had been married for several years. On the other hand, if one person in the relationship made it clear right from the beginning that once a week was going to be the norm, then I would suspect some negative attitudes about sex. Freedom from guilt and anxiety leads to a willingness, and even a desire, to be flexible and to experiment. Of course, people do fall into patterns as the years pass by, but an unwillingness to try new and different things when the relationship is just getting started is a pretty sure sign that guilt and anxiety are operating.

The second key is how a person explains his or her preferences. Using words like "right," "wrong," "moral," and "immoral" is a good sign that the person is motivated by negative feelings about sex. Dick's feeling that "it just wasn't natural" for his wife to be the one who got things started was a clear giveaway of his underlying feelings. Ginger, on the other hand, told Scott that she did not like to have sex in the morning because she felt rushed. While this could be just an excuse for her feelings of guilt, it is unlikely, since she never expressed any objections to the sex *per se*; what she objected to was the relation between the setting for sex and other realistic demands—namely, getting ready for work. In most cases, the extent to which feelings of guilt and anxiety are causing problems is clear to the people involved.

A third type of difference that some couples may have to face results from what might be thought of as the unusual tastes or preferences of one of them. Most people have some sexual fantasies that may involve some unusual elements, but for one reason or another, they never act on them; perhaps they are embarrassed to bring them up with their partner, or perhaps they are happy to have them as fantasies and would not enjoy them much in real life. But some people are drawn to these unusual elements so strongly that they feel that they cannot enjoy sex unless their partner goes along with their fantasies.

Sometimes these individuals find partners who are sympathetic and do not mind going along, so no problem exists. There are, for example, thousands of women who accept the fact that their husbands are excited by women's underwear; they do not mind their husbands' wearing women's underpants or having undergarments play a major role in their lovemaking. Thousands of men can accept, and perhaps come to enjoy, their wives' need to have them "talk dirty" to them, or to treat them roughly during lovemaking. Again, if both the man and woman can accept and enjoy such unusual or atypical patterns, then there is no problem.

But because almost all of us do have some ideas about what is and what is not proper, it is often the case that eccentricities like these cannot be tolerated. Fran is not sure that she will ever be able to accept her husband's tastes in sex. "The problems didn't start until after we had been married for about a year and a half. Until then, our sex life was okay, although I thought Jim didn't have a very strong sex drive. Then one night he told me that he thought it would be fun if I dressed up in some sexy clothes. When I agreed to try it, he brought out a costume that he had bought several months earlier but hadn't had the nerve to ask me to wear. It was kind of sleazy, but I went ahead with it, since I had already agreed. After I got dressed, however, he told me to put on some makeup, in a certain way and it dawned on me that he wanted me to look like a prostitute. Even though I was beginning to wonder what was going on, I went through with it and it turned out to be the best sex we ever had. I started doing it regularly, since it seemed to excite him, and then he started to ask me to do more and more outlandish things. I began to worry that he was really some kind of pervert and that he had just fooled me up until then. For quite a while, I was making my plans to leave him. In the end I decided to stick with the marriage, because in all other ways, he is a good husband and a very good father. I don't know, though, if I can get used to his ideas about sex."

Most people are similar to Fran in that they simply cannot understand how their partner can be excited by things that leave them cold. Fran wondered why regular lovemaking was not exciting enough for her husband. The fact that he wanted her to dress up like a cheap prostitute made her feel inadequate; if she were really desirable, then she would not have to play some bizarre role to get her husband excited. She also worried that his sexual tastes might be like a progressive disease. This week he was satisfied to have her dress up like a prostitute, but would he feel that he had to have the real thing next year? Maybe he would turn out to be the kind of person who liked to kill women after having sex with them as his "perverted ways" became more pronounced.

We really don't know very much about why people develop the kinds of preferences they do, but we do know that Fran's fears that her husband might end up to be a woman killer are groundless. He would be no more likely to end up killing prostitutes than a man who had ordinary sexual experiences for all of his life. People develop sexual scripts—patterns that they find to be exciting—and they generally stick with the same script for most of their lives.

We do not know precisely how these scripts are determined, but we do know that they are established early in life and tend to be very stable. So Fran's husband probably had fantasies about prostitutes as a teenager, and it is extremely unlikely that he will develop a set of new and dangerous scripts.

Sexual differences can have a devastating effect on a relationship. If both people are assertive enough to voice their dissatisfaction about the differences, the relationship may end up to be little more than a constant source of friction. If one or both of the partners decide to go along with the other's preferences and suffer in silence, it won't take too long before that person's love turns into anger and resentment. It is a rare couple that can work out their differences without one of them going through some tough times.

Development of Sexual Preferences

People who have a lot of guilt and anxiety about sex almost certainly had parents who were guilty and anxious as well. Attitudes about sex are learned in the same way that attitudes about anything else are; just as Republican parents tend to have Republican children, guilty parents tend to have guilty children. Naturally, there are exceptions; just as many politically conservative parents are distressed to learn that their children favor deficit spending, guilty parents are often horrified to learn that their children are enjoying premarital sex. The analogy between political and sexual attitudes does break down, however, if you reverse it. While Democratic parents are sometimes surprised to learn that their children favor cutting back on entitlement programs, it is extremely rare that parents with liberal attitudes regarding sex have children who believe sex to be dirty and disgusting. The reason is that guilty parents are likely to make sure that their children are not exposed to "corrupting" influences.

Don came from such a family. "My parents didn't have a whole lot to say about sex, but they managed to get the idea across that it was something 'nice' people didn't have anything to do with. They wouldn't let me go see a movie that was rated PG until I was fourteen years old—and then only after they made sure that it didn't have any sex in it. Violence was okay, but sex was a no-no. They were quick to label all of my friends, and the ones that showed any interest in sex were off limits for me; they were 'low-class' people. I had my birds-and-bees lecture when I started the ninth grade; it was pretty confusing, but the point seemed to be that there were two kinds of girls in the world—nice girls and not so nice girls. The nice girls would be horrified if you so much as touched them.

"My mom and dad pressured me into going to a small church college, and most of the girls I met there seemed to be 'nice girls.' When I finally got up the nerve to try to kiss a girl goodnight—on the third date—she told me she didn't know me well enough to do that sort of thing. I felt like a real degenerate. Thank God I finally did find a woman who helped me get over all that craziness."

Some people never do get over it. They are convinced that their attitudes about sex are a result of a highly developed standard of morality rather than guilt and anxiety. Leonard and Harriet fit into this category, and they are dismayed because their children do not seem to share their values about sex. "Leonard and I have always tried to provide a strong moral foundation for the children, and we can't understand where we went wrong. Sex is a gift from God and should not be cheapened; we would never have dreamed of having sex before we were married, and we can't understand how they can do it. They are adults, so we can't do anything about it, but it is depressing. Sex should be an expression of love, and it's wrong to do it out of lust; there are a lot more important things in life than momentary pleasure."

Leonard and Harriet illustrate that it can be difficult to distinguish between sexual guilt and sexual morality. Most people would view their preference to have sex no more than once a week so as not to give in to lust and their refusal to try anything but intercourse and then only in the "standard" position as evidence that they have a lot of guilt about sex. But Leonard and Harriet believe that to behave in any other way would be immoral; they would feel guilty experimenting with each other. Who can say if they are right or not? (Although I do admit that it is hard for me not to give in to the temptation to say that they are wrong.)

It is fortunate that they were able to find each other, because if either of them had married someone with more typical ideas about sex, they would certainly have problems. People without restrictive attitudes, regardless of whether the attitudes result from guilt or morality, are not likely to be patient with a partner who wants to place limits on their sexual activities because it is "wrong" to do some things.

The difference between Don on the one hand and Leonard and Harriet on the other is one of degree. Don's parents did teach him to have negative attitudes toward sex, but they were not completely convincing; he felt as if he were doing something wrong even when he had sexual fantasies, but part of him knew that it was possible to feel differently. Leonard's and Harriet's parents, however, did a *complete* job; they felt such intense guilt about sex that it was inconceivable to them to be any other way. As you might guess, it is much easier to help someone like Don to change than someone like Leonard or Harriet. Don's guilt is strong enough to interfere with his sexuality, but not so strong as to inhibit his sexual drive or interest. Leonard's and Harriet's attitudes are so deeply entrenched that they do not feel much need to have sex and have no interest in expanding their sexual repertoire.

Questions about how specific sexual preferences develop are much more difficult to answer. Experts cannot agree about issues as general as why some people prefer homosexual to heterosexual activity, so anything psychologists have to say about more specific preferences is little more than educated guesswork. Often, there is something in the background of individuals that seems to explain their preferences, but many times all that we can do is speculate. For instance, no one really knows why some people have a strong preference to have sex in the morning, while many others believe that sex, like drinking, should only be done after the sun goes down.

The one thing we do know is that early experiences can have a profound effect on one's later sexual patterns. Perhaps this can be seen most clearly in men who have a fetish centering on women's clothing. Peter, for example, remembers that his first sexual experiences involved his older sister's underwear. "I was fourteen when I first started to masturbate. After the first few times, I found that it would be more exciting for me if I held some of my sister's underwear while I was doing it. I would think about other girls, but my fantasies seemed more real when I had something concrete to focus on. After a while, I would get excited just by seeing women's underwear. Also, I never really liked pictures of women when they were completely nude; I thought the women in the underwear ads in the Sears catalog were much more exciting than the photos in men's magazines. I never thought much about it until I started to have sex with women. Then I discovered that I just couldn't get excited if they took all of their clothes off. Several women told me to get lost because they thought I was a weirdo, but I was lucky to find someone who understands me and is willing to go along with it."

Men are much more likely than women to develop patterns and preferences such as this, which can be thought of as mild forms of a sexual deviation. The most likely explanation is that these patterns are developed in association with masturbation—as was the case with Jim. If adolescent boys begin to masturbate using unusual fantasies or objects, then sexual excitement becomes conditioned to these thoughts or objects. And because boys are more likely than girls to masturbate, and because they tend to be more aggressive in using props—such as pictures or objects—they are more likely to develop unusual sexual scripts.

Women may like to do things that are out of the ordinary on occasion, but it is rare for them to feel that they *have* to follow a particular script. Peter simply was not able to respond sexually unless his partner wore underwear that he found exciting. He was not being stubborn, and it was more than a simple preference; in fact, he tried many times to have sex without asking his partners to wear clothes that turned him on. He felt trapped by his sexual script. Fortunately, Peter was lucky enough to find a woman who liked dressing up for sex. She thought it was fun to wear different kinds of sexy underwear, but for her, it was just a little something extra, and if Peter were to suddenly change and want her to stop wearing the underwear, it would not bother her. Unlike Peter, she could take it or leave it.

It is important to remember that people do not choose their sexual scripts. Don did not choose to feel guilty every time he felt sexually attracted to a woman. Leonard and Harriet did not choose to feel that activities such as oral sex were disgusting and perverted, and Peter did not choose to feel aroused only when his partner was wearing sexy underwear. So the people who live with them should not feel rejected or inadequate because their partner does have such patterns.

Living with the Imperfect Lover

Defining what is normal and what is abnormal is largely a matter of consensus. For most of the patterns described in this book, this does not present much of a problem; for instance, almost everyone agrees that the person who feels compelled to scrub the kitchen floor twice a day is little strange. As we mentioned earlier, sex is different because there is not a clear-cut consensus about what is normal and what is not, and so it is not always easy to tell who has the "problem" when a couple has sexual differences. In fact, many experts have argued that within a relationship, it is not possible for just one person to have a problem, and that it is the relationship that has the problem. This view seems a little extreme, since there are many cases where it is pretty clear who has the problem. But you should be careful not to assume that it is your partner that is the strange one simply because you do not like the way that your sexual relationship is going; you could very well be a little strange yourself. The problems discussed in this chapter, perhaps more than in any other, are likely to require some changes on the part of both people if they are to be solved.

Q: My husband is the wham-bam-thank-you-ma'am type. We have very little foreplay before he starts, and then when he has his orgasm, he gives me a smile and a pat, and rolls over and goes to sleep. I've tried to talk to him about it, but it doesn't seem to have any effect. I don't enjoy it when it's over in two minutes, but I've run out of ideas. Is there any way to get him to change?

A: Yes, but it is going to take a lot of persistence on your part. Of all the complaints that women have about sex, number one is that men do not take enough time for foreplay, so don't feel that you're alone. (The most common complaint for men is that their partners are too passive.) I would guess that your husband takes your complaints seriously and probably has even promised himself that he would do better, but it is hard for him to stick with his good intentions because his view of sex is different from yours. Of course, there are lots of exceptions, but generally men view foreplay as a means to an end—the end being to get an erection. Once they have reached that end, they are eager to get started and do not see any point in waiting any longer. Even if their partners tell them a thousand times that it would better if they waited a little longer the next time, when the next time comes, they will fall back into their old pattern.

The only way that you will get him to change is to refuse to begin until you feel that you are ready. Keep on talking to him about your feelings; be gentle about it, but let him know that you do not enjoy intercourse unless you feel aroused first and that you are not going to do it unless you do feel aroused. Let him know that it is best for both of you that you keep this resolution. If you were to continue to have sex when you did not enjoy it, it would only be a matter of time before it became very distasteful to you. Once people, both men and women, begin to worry about whether they will have an orgasm, it becomes very difficult, and often impossible, for them to have one, so if he wants to have a willing partner, he owes it to himself to make sure that you enjoy your encounters, too.

Don't expect your husband to be happy about your new resolution. It will be hard for him to adjust, and the chances are that you will have a few difficult weeks or even months. There is a good chance that he may develop a problem having erections. When you tell him that you're not ready once he lets you know that he is ready to start, he may loose his erection, and this is sure to worry him to the point where he may find it difficult to become erect subsequently. Let him know that his reaction is typical for men when they try to change their patterns and that it will only be a short time before things are back to normal for him. But it is something that both of you will have to go through if your sexual relationship is to make it over the long run.

In the meantime, don't be shy about providing him with pleasure during foreplay, too. Sometimes couples fall into the habit of viewing foreplay as something that is necessary to get the woman ready for the "real thing"; in these cases, it is not surprising that the men tend to view it as a necessary bother to be gotten over with as quickly as possible. Educate your husband. Show him that foreplay can be as arousing to him as it can be for you. If you stick with your resolution, and if you are a good teacher, the chances are excellent that your husband can become a tender, caring, and proficient lover.

Q: One night, after we had been to a party and were feeling no pain, my wife and I told each other about our sexual fantasies. I admit that it was pretty exciting to talk about them, but I've started to worry that she may carry out her fantasies sooner or later.

Her fantasies center on having sex with strangers. She said that when she sees an attractive man when she's out—like at the grocery store—she imagines that they are both aware of their attraction toward each other and they go somewhere and have sex without even telling each other their names. Even worse, she has fantasies about being gang-raped; she imagines that two or three men take her somewhere and force her to satisfy them for hours on end—at the same time! Worst of all, she admitted that she has these fantasies while she's having sex with me. That makes me feel bad enough, but what I'm really worried about is that she may get the urge to do something about her fantasies of having sex with strangers. Because she is so attractive, lots of men do flirt with her, so she wouldn't have any trouble if she decided to go ahead with it.

A: There is virtually no chance that your wife will act out her fantasies. Most women, and men, have sexual fantasies and for a very large percentage of them, they are just that—fantasies. They have no desire to carry them out in real life. Thoughts and images that may be very sexually exciting usually translate into very harsh realities—and most women know that.

Your wife's fantasy of being raped is the most common fantasy for women. But in fantasies, the appearance of the rapist, his technique, the setting, and her response can all be controlled; this is considerably different from real-life rape where the woman has no control whatsoever and is usually afraid for her own life. Many men have taken the fact that lots of women have fantasies of being raped as evidence that deep down they really want to be raped, but nothing could be further from the truth. Women know that it is the fantasy that is exciting, and that they would be horrified by the reality of rape.

It is equally unlikely that your wife will act out her fantasy of having sex with strange men whom she meets in grocery stores. Once again, virtually all women who have fantasies of any kind can distinguish clearly between fantasy and reality. I would guess that she doesn't even have these fantasies right at the moment; if she is like most people, she will probably have them during times when her mind is not occupied with real-life issues. While she is shopping, she may notice attractive men, but she probably won't have any fantasies about them until later—when she is driving home, or taking a bath, or doing anything else that doesn't require any concentration.

A majority of women have fantasies of other men or other settings while they are making love with a regular partner, so you should not take this as a sign that she does not find you exciting or that she does not love you. In fact, it could be evidence that you are a great lover; if sex were not exciting for her, she wouldn't have fantasies about it in the first place. Also, her telling you that she has these fantasies while you are having sex suggests that she feels very close to you and trusts you. While most women do have such fantasies, most of them do not share them with their partners.

Q: I've reached the point where I am thoroughly disgusted with my husband. I've always known that he liked pornography, but until lately, he was at least discreet about it. Now that our children have left home and he doesn't have to fear they will see his filth, he has started quite a collection of magazines and movies. What bothers me most of all is that after he spends an evening looking at that stuff, then he wants sex with me. I hate the thought that he needs that kind of stimulation before he is interested in me. I've told him how I feel, but all he says is that it's perfectly normal to enjoy sexy pictures and movies and that I'm the sick one because I refuse to look at them with him. Who do you think is the sick one?

A: I don't think either of you is "sick." The differences between you and your husband are a matter of taste and preference—not a matter of normal or abnormal. Most men *and* women do find sexy pictures and movies exciting. The biggest differences among people are in what they consider to be sexy; some people find that tender, romantic scenes of a couple doing nothing more than kissing are the sexiest, while others like movies with explicit sex scenes. I don't think that there is anything more "normal" about preferring one over the other. So your husband's enjoyment of sexually explicit magazines and movies should not be taken as a sign that he is some kind of pervert.

His reaction of being interested in taking you to bed after watching his home movies is very typical. Anyone becomes more interested in having sex when sexually aroused, regardless of the source of the arousal. Think about your own reactions. I bet that you can recall times when you saw a movie or a television show that made you a little more interested in your husband's body. The fact that you might feel aroused when you see Clark Gable kissing Vivien Leigh means that you have basically the same reactions as your husband. You are just different from him in what you find exciting.

If your husband could not have sex with you unless he looked at his magazines or his movies first, then I think you would be justified in feeling hurt. It still would not mean that he was a "pervert," but it would be a pattern that would be hard for any woman to live with. But it is common for men to develop patterns like this, and once they are established it is very hard for them to change. If this is the case, you might try talking to him about your feelings. Let him know that at least sometimes, you would like to have the feeling that he wants to make love to you just because you are you.

Women's sense of sexuality is much more stable than men's. If a woman has healthy attitudes toward sex and thoroughly enjoys it, it takes a lot before she will develop a problem in responding sexually. Not so for men; sometimes a single insensitive comment from a partner can cause a man to have problems developing an erection. So if it is the case that your husband has to watch a sexy movie before he can have sex with you, it probably does not say anything about his feelings for you. He simply has established a pattern that is difficult for him to break out of, and he probably fears that he would fail if he tried to have sex without going through his ritual.

These patterns can be broken, but it does require a lot of patience on the part of both people. Your husband will have to be willing to try, knowing and fearing that he might fail. Most men view the possibility of such failure as extremely humiliating, so you will have to be patient with him, because he will probably have some resentment toward you for coercing him into trying to change. Try not to take it personally. Remember that it is only natural to blame anyone who happens to be around when one feels threatened.

If he agrees to try to change his pattern, the chances of success are high. Just tell him that you want to lie next to him and for the two of you to caress each other, and if he doesn't feel like having intercourse, that's fine. Once the fear of failure is removed, he will find that he is in the mood and ready physically. If he has not had problems in having erections before, it should take only a few days to a week or two before he feels comfortable with the change. Once this happens, he will probably feel pleased that he is no longer a prisoner of his old pattern, and his sense of his own sexuality is likely to be stronger than ever.

Q: My sexual relationship with my wife is great except for one sore point. She refuses to give me oral sex. I can't understand it, because she doesn't seem inhibited in any other way, but she won't even try it. She says that she doesn't understand it either, but the idea just doesn't appeal to her and she can't force herself to do it. I think she must have some hangups about sex to feel so strongly about it. Do you think therapy would help? It is really important to me for her to do it.

A: I don't think that a therapist could convince her to try it if you have not been able to. A therapist could help if she were generally inhibited about sex, but your wife doesn't sound as if she fits into this category. I would say that her refusal to have oral sex falls into the category of tastes and preferences. And everyone is entitled to have a few of these.

The only thing that you might try, if you haven't already, is to make sure that concerns about cleanliness cannot be one of her objections. Some people tend to be unreasonably fastidious, and obviously, oral sex is one activity that is likely to be affected by such feelings. Make a point of taking a shower before you plan to make love; make sure that she knows that you are getting yourself squeaky clean. I doubt whether this will be enough to change her mind, but it is worth a try.

The real barrier to her trying may be reflected by your statement that it is very important to you that she do it. If you have been pushing her hard, oral sex may have become the battleground on which the two of you are going to test your wills. The harder you push, the more rigid and defensive she may become. You are probably thinking, "If she really loved me, she would do it for me," and she is probably thinking, "If he really loved me, he wouldn't try to pressure me into doing it."

Why don't you try backing off on your demands? I would guess that as long as your wife feels pressured, she is going to remain adamant in her refusal to give it a try. She already knows that you would like her to do it, so you are not telling her anything new by bringing it up continually. Once she feels that you are no longer demanding it of her, perhaps she can adjust to the idea of trying it at her own pace. Sometimes it is easier to give a gift than to make a payment on demand, and even if she never tries it, remember that, as you said, you do have a great sexual relationship.

Some Final Thoughts

Differences in sexual tastes and preferences can be resolved without too much trouble if people can accept them as just that—differences. All too often, though, the differences are thought to be evidence of something more. So Jane thinks that Dick doesn't really love her because he doesn't make love to her every night of the week. And Dick thinks that Jane doesn't really love him because she won't have sex with him on his lunch hour. Neither of them would come to the same conclusion if they had differences about which movie to see or whether they should spend the weekend at the beach or the mountains, but sex is different.

Even though most people want to believe that sex and love go together, the fact is that things don't always work that way. Lots of men are able to have great sex with women they barely know, but are impotent with a woman whom they really love. Women often continue to enjoy their sexual relationship with their husband even though their love for him may be only a distant memory. The point is that a partner's sexual behavior should not be taken as evidence of his or her feelings. Of course, a man or a woman may lose interest in having sex with a partner as a result of fading love, but there are more people who have problems with their sexual relationship even though their overall relationship is as sound as ever.

It would be nice if sex were as it is in the movies; the man and the woman are filled with passion and it doesn't seem to matter exactly what they do—they are excited regardless of what their partner does for them. But real life is different, and everyday sexual relationships require compromises. The compromises can be successful if people can talk about them as openly as they talk about other kinds of compromises. It may not seem very romantic, but the "I'll go to the ballgame tonight if you'll go to the ballet with me next week" attitude can be used to make sexual relationships work. You may not get exactly what you want, but if you are willing to talk, compromise, and work at it, you could end up feeling pretty satisfied nonetheless.

Conclusion

"You Charge *How* Much an Hour?"
WHEN PROFESSIONAL HELP IS NECESSARY

Why Is It So Hard to Get Along?

Joan and Bill had been married for only three years, but already they couldn't be around each other for more than fifteen minutes without having an argument. Their strategy for dealing with their differences was simply to stop talking to each other. This did help them get through the day without exchanging any harsh words, but the resentment and anger were slowly but surely building in both of them. Unless they could find a way to break out of their deadly routine, it wouldn't take too much longer before their chances of being happy together would be gone forever.

Neither of them could understand what had happened. As Bill tells it, "Joan is not the same woman I married. The first year I knew her was the happiest time of my life. She made me feel so important; she would do anything for me. My family used to kid me because she was always asking if she could get me anything; they said I must have abducted her from a harem. Now I can't ask her for anything or she accuses me of being helpless. I don't want a servant for a wife, but I do want to have that old feeling back of being someone important in her life. I still love her, but she's becoming impossible to live with."

Joan has plenty to say about the changes in Bill as well. "I knew the honeymoon wouldn't last forever, but I never thought Bill would turn out to be such a self-centered, lazy, unromantic blob. While we were dating, he always was thinking of unusual, fun things for us to do. Now, all he wants to do on the weekends is read and watch television—he claims he can do both at the same time—and maybe go to a movie once in a while. If we don't go out, he won't shower or shave all weekend, so by Sunday night, he's as gamy as he is prickly. Then he wonders why I'm not enthusiastic about making love. Well, we don't 'make love' anymore. All we do is 'have sex.' "

They agree, however, that they would lose a lot if they went their separate ways. Joan values Bill's gentleness and his ability to really care about the kids, and Bill admires and respects Joan's quiet strength; she knows what she wants out of life and she can go after it without alienating anyone. They know they are both worthwhile people. So, they wonder, why is it so hard to get along?

Joan's and Bill's problems may sound trivial. After all, think of all the relationships in which there is physical abuse, alcoholism, and sadistic cruelty, to name just a few problems. I would agree that these problems are more serious than the ones Joan and Bill face, but I think they are of a different nature. If one of the partners in a relationship had a long-standing problem with alcohol, for example, I would see it as two individual problems—not a relationship problem. First, there is the drinking problem of one of the partners, and second, there is the problem of why the other partner would tolerate such behavior over a long period of time. Both of these people need help, but they are not the kind of people I am talking about here.

I am talking about people like Joan and Bill: people who are basically good, decent, reasonably well-adjusted people who just can't seem to get along with each other. Individually, they seem like perfectly normal people; while they have personality styles that may be keeping them from enjoying life to the fullest—don't we all?—neither of them has quirks so noticeable that they would be interested in seeking psychotherapy if it were not for the problems in their relationship. I am talking about relationship problems.

My belief is that the trivial things eat away and eventually destroy more relationships than the big, meaningful issues ever do. In fact, what is trivial and what is meaningful depends on whether you are on the inside looking out or the outside looking in. Anyone could look at Joan and Bill's situation and in thirty seconds come up with compromises that would solve their problems. But, although Joan and Bill are intelligent, logical, and reasonable people, they are not able to put these simple, straightforward compromises into practice. In other words, the problems are not so trivial to Joan and Bill. They are locked into an unsatisfactory style of interacting with each other.

I have known very few couples who have split up over a "big issue." I don't think there has ever been a couple who have visited their attorney and said, "We love and care for each other very much and enjoy almost every minute we spend together, but we just can't agree on whether we should save for our retirement or take expensive vacations, so we are getting a divorce." When the relationship is solid, the big issues have a way of working themselves out.

The one exception might be the issue of whether or not to have children. I have seen couples with solid relationships part ways, even though it was painful for both of them, because one wanted children and the other did not.

People feel a willingness, and even an obligation, to talk about the big issues while they are willing to sweep the little issues under the rug. We can understand other people's having different ideas about religion or about discipline of children, but we can't understand why someone can't remember to put the cap back on the toothpaste—or why someone else makes such a big deal about it. So we try hard to work out our differences on the big issues, but we ignore the little ones and hope they will go away. After all, they are so trivial—or are they?

The problem is that just because they are under the rug doesn't mean they aren't there. They are there, and the anger and resentment slowly builds around them. Then, when we have had all we can take, we turn the trivial issues into big issues. We don't run to our divorce lawyer because our spouse won't put the cap back on the toothpaste, but we do have to get out of the relationship because our spouse is a thoughtless, selfish slob. Nor would we ever admit that we are tired of being asked to put the cap on the toothpaste; we tell the world that we are married to a domineering, controlling shrew.

When the relationship is new and romantic love is in bloom, it doesn't seem so hard to work out these little differences. We may not even notice them because our attention is focused on the positive characteristics of our partner. But time takes its toll. We begin to take the positive for granted, and what were once the little quirks of our partner become like sandpaper that rubs us raw. The first twelve chapters were intended to give you some ideas about how you might go about changing the sandpaper back into the category of little quirks that you can live with, if not overlook. If you are willing to make the effort, and if you have not let your grievances accumulate for too long, there is a lot that you can do on your own. But there are times, such as in Joan's and Bill's case, when professional help is necessary.

Joan and Bill were both convinced that they were living with an imperfect person, but their own imperfections made it impossible for either of them to take the first step toward breaking out of their cycle of recriminations and hostility. They had lost their ability to talk to each other. Sure, they exchanged words, but they were not communicating; they were doing nothing more than trading accusations by the time they reached therapy. Talking, or real communicating, means listening to the other person; it means making an effort to understand not only what the other person is saying, but also what the other person is feeling. This is difficult to do at any time, but it is especially hard when we are angry. Anger fortifies our defenses, and when our defenses are up, we are mostly interested in proving how right we are and how wrong the other person is.

When people stop talking to each other, they stop trying to understand the other person's perspective. We all have a tendency to believe that other people view the world in exactly the same way we do, and when there is smooth sailing, we can make allowances for differences that crop up. But, the shy partner who feels uncomfortable about new people turns into the "antisocial jerk who tries to embarrass me around my friends" when communication breaks down. I have tried to explain these different perspectives in the first part of each chapter. It may take a good therapist some time to do this if a person is too angry to even consider the possibility that the partner is not acting out of plain malice or vindictiveness.

This narrowing of perspective, or rigidity, often makes it difficult to see possible compromises that are obvious to anyone else. Janet and Wes used to have terrible fights about in-laws. Janet's parents lived across the country, while Wes's lived across town, and Wes felt obligated to have the family visit his parents every Sunday afternoon. Janet did not dislike her in-laws, but she hated the routine of the Sunday-afternoon visits. She woke up every Sunday itching for a fight, and the trips to and from the Sunday ritual were usually spent in stony silence. Incredible as it seems, neither Wes nor Janet had ever considered the possibility of doing things any differently. Both had grown up in families where Sunday afternoons were spent visiting grandparents, so they just assumed it was something they had to do regardless of how miserable it made them.

When I suggested to them that there was no reason why Janet had to go along on every visit, they were obviously uncomfortable with the idea, but they agreed to try it. Wes felt very uncomfortable the first Sunday he showed up at his parents' house without Janet, but it did not take him long to realize that his break with tradition was more than repaid. He found it was much better to have Janet go along on the visits every now and then than to make her miserable by insisting that she go every week. And Janet found that the visits could even be pleasant after she no longer felt that her Sundays were scheduled for her for the rest of her life. Few solutions will be as obvious as this one, but most couples, even those who are not angry with each other, have a few blind spots, and a good therapist can help you pinpoint where yours may be.

So how do you know when it's time to throw in the towel on your attempts to turn things around on your own and find a good therapist? The first thing to look at is your anger level. If you find yourself feeling mad at your partner most of the time, you will have a very hard time taking the necessary step back in order to have an objective perspective. Ask yourself if you have stopped trying to understand your partner when he or she does something you don't like. Do you find yourself explaining away the nice things your partner does because they don't make up for the bad? Do you almost enjoy it when your partner "screws up" so you have a good excuse for being mad? If the answer to these questions is yes, then it's time to find a therapist.

Next, take stock of your own capacity to enjoy life. Do you feel as if all your energy is being sapped by trying to accommodate your partner's quirks? Do you feel that your routine has become more like a prison sentence from which you see no escape? Do you find that you virtually never look forward to spending time alone with your partner? Do you simply not have enough energy to try to change things? Once again, if you find yourself answering yes to these questions, it's time to get help.

Finally, if you have been trying to understand your partner and help him or her to change, keep track of the progress you are making. It is impossible to be specific about how fast progress should occur, but some rough guidelines might be of help. No one can change much in a matter of weeks, but if you have been giving it your best shot, and after a year you do not feel that you are any closer to the kind of relationship you would like to have, then it's time to make an appointment. The changes may be so gradual that you will not notice them as they occur, but you should be able to look back and say to yourself, "Things are better than they were a year ago." Keep in mind that progress is not always even; you might have several good months and then everything may seem to fall apart. But if you don't give up, if you try to begin anew, you will be starting from a higher plateau. Setbacks can be an opportunity for consolidating the gains you have made.

How to Find a Therapist

Psychotherapy is not cheap. Depending on the qualifications and the reputation of the therapist, the going rates are from sixty to a hundred dollars per session. If you are rich or if you have a good insurance plan, these fees won't be much of a problem; the better insurance plans pay 80 percent of the cost. Whatever it costs, it is a bargain if it helps preserve your relationship. Be sure to check your insurance policy before you make any commitments. Many policies do not cover mental health services at all, and some pay as little as $10 per session.

If you are not rich or if you do not have a good insurance plan, you can still have professional help in most areas of the country. The first place to look is local universities or medical schools that train psychologists and psychiatrists. Most of these will have clinics that offer services to the public on a sliding-scale basis; depending on your income, you may pay as little as a dollar or two for each session. You may see a therapist who is just beginning training, but he or she will be supervised by a seasoned professional. The next place to look is city or state agencies. Sometimes they offer services at no cost; other agencies might use a sliding-scale.

If you cannot find any of these agencies in your phone book, the best thing to do is start asking questions. Call your physician; most doctors make quite a few referrals for psychotherapy, so they are usually familiar with what is available in your area. If your physician can't help you, call someone who is in private practice and tell him or her about your situation. All ethical professionals will feel an obligation to help you find someone even if they cannot see you.

If you can afford to pay something, but not the full rate, you can bargain with therapists who are in private practice. It is not uncommon for therapists to waive the deductible, or some portion of it, for their clients who have insurance, and even if they don't, they may be willing to work out a payment plan you can live with. Established therapists who have a full case load are not likely to make these concessions, but if you look around, the chances are excellent that you could find a therapist who would rather get half the usual rate for an unscheduled hour than nothing.

I think anyone who lives anywhere near a medium-size city can find professional help at an affordable cost. But if you have tried everything with no luck, then talk to a friend. Pick one who is not opinionated and who is willing to listen to your story. Research has shown that some people are natural therapists; they can be very helpful to those who are in distress even though they have no formal training. A friend who can be sympathetic and objective about your situation may very well be able to help you to see some of the blind spots in your relationship.

Separating the Wheat from the Chaff

Although professional degrees are not much of an indication of quality, let's go over the major categories of mental health professionals. The first category, and my favorite (I never claimed to be impartial), is clinical psychologists. These people have received a doctorate in clinical psychology, and they have received four to five years of specialized training in the assessment and treatment of psychological problems. Because their training is in psychology and not in medicine, they are not allowed to prescribe medication, but they are trained to recognize the need for it and make referrals to physicians when they suspect that medication would be helpful.

Psychiatrists are the next category. Psychiatrists have completed medical school and a regular medical internship before taking a three-year residency to specialize in the treatment of psychological disorders. Because they are physicians, they are able to prescribe medication.

Clinical social workers make up the third major category. Most social workers have a master's degree in social work, although some do have a doctorate. The master's degree usually entails a year of formal classroom training and a second year of practical experience, while social workers with the doctorate have four to five years of training.

Regulations vary from state to state, but most states do have some legal restrictions as to who can use the titles of clinical psychologist, psychiatrist, and clinical social workers. Although certification is no guarantee of reliability, it never hurts to check if your therapist is certified by the state to practice psychotherapy. In most states, there are no legal restrictions about the use of all labels related to the practice of psychotherapy. For instance, in Virginia, in order to identify oneself as a clinical psychologist, it is necessary to meet the educational requirements and to pass a written and an oral examination; but there are no restrictions on the use of the title of psychotherapist, so there would be nothing to stop anyone from opening an office and offering services as a psychotherapist. It never hurts to make sure that you are getting what you are paying for.

Along with those in these three mental health professions, there are lots of other people who can be very effective in helping you resolve a relationship problem. Clergymen are a good example. Many seminaries now offer training in counseling, so ministers and priests can be helpful for many problems, and they can also make a referral to a professional when that is available. Some charitable organizations offer the services of volunteer counselors. These people receive some training from a professional, so they too can offer a supportive shoulder and recommend professional help when it is appropriate. The quality of these nonprofessionals, or paraprofessionals, can be uneven, but it is not unusual to find a highly sensitive and skilled therapist in their ranks. If money is a problem for you, it is certainly worth a try to find one of these people.

Okay. Suppose you have found a therapist. You have checked out his or her credentials and everything looks fine. You've worked out a fee that you can live with and you have made your first appointment. How do you know this person is really any good? We all know there are incompetents in every field, and the mental health profession is certainly no exception. How can you be sure that you are not getting a lemon? Or suppose your therapist *is* competent. How do you know that he is the right person for you? Even if your best friend saw this therapist and recommended him without reservation, because your situation and your personality are unique, he still may not be able to meet your needs.

It is not very hard to identify someone who is blatantly incompetent. I have heard stories from clients about previous therapists that would horrify anyone. There are therapists who drink during their sessions and occasionally fall asleep. There are therapists (almost always male) who tell their clients (either male or female) that the best way the therapist can be of help is to provide them with his sexual services. There are therapists who offer their clients nothing but medication until they become addicted. There are therapists who spend much of each session talking about their *own* problems.

These incompetents stay in business because they can find enough naive people who believe shrinks are so strange anyway that nothing they do should come as a surprise. Don't be afraid to trust your instincts. If your therapist does something, or suggests that you do something, that seems bizarre, then the chances are pretty good that it *is* bizarre. At any rate, a sensitive therapist would not ask you to do something that was completely unacceptable to you even if it was in the realm of accepted practice.

Even if your therapist is not blatantly incompetent—and the chances are excellent that he or she will not be—you still have to remember that there are varying levels of skill. You want the best, so you have to evaluate the services you are receiving. This can be tricky to do. If your therapist is skilled, there will be times when you hear things you won't like, when you feel uncomfortable, or when you believe that your therapist does not really understand you. But you are not looking for an ally in your battle with your spouse; you are looking for someone who can give you a new perspective on the situation, someone who can help you make some changes so you can be more effective in helping your partner to change. This will mean you cringe a little bit, but growth is rarely a painless process. So not liking what your therapist has to say is not necessarily a sign that he or she is not the right person for you. In fact, it could very well be a sign that things are going well.

If your therapy is going well, you will experience a range of emotions. There will be times when you feel scared, sad, discouraged, and uncomfortable, but there will also be times when you feel exhilarated by a new insight and grateful for the sympathetic and understanding ear. You need to be sensitive to this balance. If you never feel challenged by your therapist's comments or instructions, then the chances are you are not learning anything; on the other hand, if you consistently have the feeling that your therapist does not understand what you are saying, there is a good chance you are right. Even the most skillful therapists cannot be effective with everyone; they are human too, and there are some people they simply cannot relate to. If you have this feeling, talk to your therapist about it. If he becomes defensive, or if his answer does not make any sense to you, then perhaps you would be better off going elsewhere. There is always the chance that the problem is yours, so don't give up too soon; but don't let your therapist convince you to stick with it month after month if you continue to have the feeling that you are not communicating.

Another thing to look for in your therapist is flexibility. I would avoid anyone who said, "This is the way I do things and it's the only way." At last count, there were over a hundred different types of therapy, and you can be sure that not one of them is the only or the best method to treat *all* problems. So, for example, if you would like joint therapy with your partner but your therapist reports that he only sees individuals, find another therapist. Sometimes it is most effective to see the partners separately, but there are also times when it is better to see them together, or a combination of individual and joint sessions might be the best approach. I would want a therapist who could decide what was right for *my* situation, and not one who rigidly followed a particular procedure regardless of what my needs might be.

I don't mean to make it seem like an impossible task to find a competent therapist who is right for you. If you were to select a name randomly from the phone book, the odds are you would get good, professional help, since a majority of mental health professionals are competent. But I also know of a few therapists whom I would advise people to stay away from, and because there are people like this, you have to be an informed consumer. You would do some investigating before you decided where to have your car serviced and repaired. Take the time to do the same when looking for a therapist. After all, a good partner is much more valuable than any car could ever be.

Some Final Thoughts

Not every relationship is worth saving. Some people have problems so severe that the odds of their ever changing to a significant degree are slim. And even if they do change, you may not want to wait as long as it takes before your efforts begin to pay dividends.

More often, some partners are simply not right for each other. While neither may have any significant psychological problems, their styles may be too different for them ever to be able to achieve anything more than a peaceful, but empty, coexistence.

I do believe, however, that there is a trend toward giving up too soon. With the divorce rate in the neighborhood of 50 percent, we enter relationships with the expectation that if it doesn't work out we can always move on to something better. And with the sometimes nagging feeling that we must enjoy constant happiness and peak experiences twenty-four hours a day, it is no wonder that we feel the grass may be greener on the other side of the fence.

There is a "prayer" written by a well-known psychiatrist that says, in effect, "I'll do my thing and you do yours and if we come together, that's beautiful." Anyone who has been in a successful long-term relationship can recognize this for what it is—idealistic nonsense. A partnership means doing the other person's "thing" when you would rather be doing your own thing, on occasion. A relationship means caring as much about another person as you do about yourself. Self-centered people who care only about doing their thing make terrible partners, and they end up alone in the world.

So my point is: Give it a try. If you can still find a lot that is good about your partner, you probably have something worth saving. If, after giving it a try, you still find that the relationship brings you more unhappiness than happiness, you can do something about it then. But do consider what you would like to see when you reach the point where you are looking back at your life. The view can be very pleasant and gratifying if you share it with someone with whom you have been through good times as well as bad. Imperfect people *can* live happily ever after.